Skinny Feasts

DECEPTIVELY
RICH COOKING
THE LOW-FAT WAY

Skinny Feasts

dee HOBSBAWN-SMITH

Whitecap Books

Vancouver/Toronto

The information in this book is true and complete to the best of our
knowledge. All recommendations are made without guarantee on the
part of the author or Whitecap Books Ltd. The author and publisher
disclaim any liability in connection with the use of this information. For
additional information please contact Whitecap Books Ltd.,
351 Lynn Avenue, North Vancouver, BC, V7J 2C4.

Edited by Elaine Jones
Proofread by Elizabeth McLean
Cover design by Designgeist
Cover illustration by Elizabeth Simpson
Interior design by Warren Clark
Typeset by Warren Clark

Printed and bound in Canada.

Canadian Cataloguing in Publication Data

Hobsbawn-Smith, Dee.
  Skinny feasts

  Includes index.
  ISBN 1-55110-531-4
  1. Low-fat diet—Recipes. I. Title.
RM237.7.H62 1997   641.5'638   C96-910731-5

The publisher acknowledges the support of the Canada Council
and the Cultural Services Branch of the Government of British Columbia
in making this publication possible.

This book is for my sons Darl and Dailyn.
None of my life's lessons are as loving as the lessons
I keep learning from you two.

Acknowledgments

This work didn't spring into being overnight, and it didn't arrive unannounced. There have been many people who have contributed, and they all deserve to be publicly draped with laurels and plied with wine for their generosity and faith.

Special thanks to the women who early on were strong and independent role models, both as women and as cooks—my mother and grandmothers, Floreen Hofer Smith, Sarah Hofer and the late Doris Smith.

Thanks to Madeleine Kamman, my mentor since 1985, for being her stern, uncompromising genius self.

My wine-drinking friends at J. Webb Wine Merchant in Calgary, especially Janet Webb, Daylin Breen and Richard Harvey, have been instrumental in my gaining an appreciation of food and wine together. Janet and Daylin also provided the wine suggestions in *Skinny Feasts*. Thanks, sweeties! The next bottle's on me.

Heartfelt thanks to all my friends who have supported and encouraged my dreams and projects. Particular thanks to those who willingly tested and tasted, then fed me, especially my dear pals, Phyllis McCord, Susan Hopkins, Elaine Codling, Jane McConachie, Sarah Muller, Gail Norton.

The writers who held my hand as I learned the craft are my buddies Don Braid and Sydney Sharpe. Without their encouragement I would never have dared to believe in possibilities.

Special thanks to my editor, Elaine Jones, for her skill and patience while teaching brevity in the active voice.

The huge number of cooks across Canada and the United States who have worked with me, sharing their interest and enjoyment of cooking, have helped me coalesce my ideas. You are too many to name, but you know who you are, and I thank you all. In addition, thanks are due the cooking schools who trusted me and allowed me to voice my opinions and thoughts on food in years of teaching.

Thanks and love to all my family—my parents, sons and grandparents, my sister and my brothers and their spouses, my aunts and my cousins, my generous in-laws.

The biggest thanks are due my husband, Don.

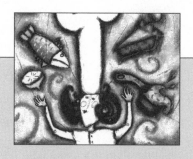

Table of Contents

Introduction

Many talented chefs have written, or contributed to, glossy books that bring restaurant food into the home kitchen. They are enticing books, often loaded with photographs of chefs in action above a hot gas range, or assembling layers of gleaming vegetables into picture-perfect dishes. It is great stuff—entertaining, at times theatrical, sometimes informative, but usually a reflection of the restaurant culture. It is food cooked in restaurant kitchens on restaurant stoves by professionals using specialized restaurant equipment.

These are great books to read or to cook from when you have a lot of time to putter in the kitchen. But what about the day in and day out, when the phone rings too often, when soccer practice intrudes four times a week, when school meetings, laundry and deadlines take precedence over cooking?

Those days—most days—are when cooks reach for the tried and true everyday cookbook. It sounds drab and boring, though, the everyday cookbook. Reach for *Skinny Feasts* instead.

Today many of us are engulfed by a sea of guilt about how and what we eat. Most cooks, eager to cut fat, reduce cholesterol counts and drop pounds, buy books that feature recipes with low-fat ingredients, reworked recipes, and above all, hope.

Skinny Feasts is a hopeful book. It is based on the premise that methods of cooking are just as important as the foods we choose to cook. And it does away with the notion of "good food, bad food." Instead of discarding all those foods currently in disfavor, it offers recipes that judiciously implement small amounts of these foods. As a result, there is whipping cream in this book. And sausage, and even bacon. But they are all used wisely, in small amounts, where their flavorful attributes overshadow their negative qualities.

You will find no dietitian's or nutritionist's analysis here. Neither is there a calorie count or tally of fat grams. Food is meant to be enjoyed—enjoyed responsibly, but enjoyed above all.

The ideas and recipes in this book revolve about the idea of choosing what one is willing to compromise on. I am unwilling to use ersatz ingredients and inferior foods, and I won't relinquish fat entirely because I acknowledge its role in food. In the kitchen, fat is a lubricant that also aids in heat transferral from pan to food. It is indispensable in creating crisp textures and intense flavors, such as are achieved with caramelization and browning. Fat can also be used to define entire cuisines, as well as contribute strong characteristic tastes. In addition, it is fat that can smooth textures and moisten foods, tenderize gluten, aid leavening and create emulsions.

That is a lot to ignore or overlook. So for me, compromise involves accepting different textures, using different cooking methods, using less oil rather than using none, and very carefully choosing the type of fat and where I apply it.

To best use this book, familiarize yourself with the following pages, which outline some basics of the Skinny Feast kitchen—cooking techniques and the principles of balancing the flavor of foods you prepare.

Kitchen Basics

Cooking Techniques

The importance of learning and understanding cooking techniques and processes is one of the integral steps in becoming a cook with faith in your own taste and judgment. Knowing how to cook frees you from slavish devotion to any recipe—which is simply a written record of how one dish was made on one day by one individual. A recipe functions best as a starting point for variation and experimenting.

The following methods of cooking are easily adapted to low-fat cooking and ingredients.

Poaching

Poaching is a moist-heat method of cooking. The raw food is immersed in hot, near-boiling liquid, which is usually seasoned and flavored. (The exception is when cooking large, whole fish, when cold liquid is called for to ensure even cooking throughout.) The temperature can be raised after the addition of the food, but it should not boil. Poaching is ideal for tender foods. A small amount of acid is usually added to help the coagulation of the protein. (The classic Huevos Rancheros, or eggs poached in tomato sauce, is a natural pairing to accomplish the setting of the protein in the eggs.)

The poaching liquid can vary. It could be water, "court bouillon" (water infused with herbs, wine, citrus and other aromatics), stock or wine. (Wine alone will taste rawly alcoholic; reduce it, simmer it with aromatics or add stock to mellow the taste.)

A lid or parchment paper is helpful to keep the steam in and to keep top surfaces from drying out. Pieces of food must be of uniform thickness to ensure even cooking.

Steaming

Steaming is another moist-heat cooking method, best used with food that is fine-textured and lean. The steaming liquid ranges from water to apple juice to ale, depending on the food and how it will be steamed. Food can be sealed in parchment paper and steamed or placed in a pot with a snug lid, as in the bistro classic of mussels in wine or ale with garlic, leeks and herbs. The idea is to keep the food above the boiling liquid, cover it and quickly cook it.

Sautéing

Sautéing is a dry-heat type of cooking, favored by an increasingly fat-conscious population. High heat and a small amount of oil or butter are the keys to developing the crisp, golden crust that is the main characteristic of fried food. It's easy to speed cooking time and reduce the threat of sticking and burning by adding small amounts of liquid. This means that the food is actually steaming in part, but it serves to reduce the fat, as well as ease the cooking itself.

The French verb *sauter*, "to jump," intimates that the pan and its fat should be hot enough for the food to jump out of the pan. The only differences between today's low-fat sautéing and that of yesteryear are the amount of fat used, the finish of the pan, and the absence of dredging or coating.

When sautéing, use tender products cut thinly for quick and even cooking. Make sure you have the right size of pan, and then just fill it. Too small a pan and the food will be overcrowded, resulting in a "boiled" mess without color or a crisp exterior. Too large and the juices will burn in the empty areas of the pan. The pan should have shallow sides and a wide diameter to encourage quick cooking. Nonstick pans will minimize the fat required, but will not result in a really browned piece of food.

Preheat the pan. Preheat the fat. Use high heat. Ensure the food is dry to produce a crisp finish on the outside. Cook until the meat's juices rise to

Whether you are grilling or sautéing, do not fiddle with the food; constant turning interferes with the formation of a crust. The meat will be rare when juices run again to the surface after turning. For red meats, the degree of doneness is also reflected in the color of the juices—red indicates still-red (rare) interior. For white meats, check by internal color (snip open the thickest part for a peek), or by texture. Soft and flaccid indicates rare; firm and springy indicates well-done.

the surface, then turn (once only) to the other side.

Let the food rest after cooking. This allows the protein strands to relax, so that the juices, forced into the middle by high heat, can redistribute throughout the meat. A few minutes is sufficient.

Stir-frying

Stir-frying is a hybrid moist-dry method of cooking with its roots in Asia, where woks are used over small fires for brief cooking periods. A wok has a small cooking area with high sloping sides. A small amount of food is cooked rapidly in the bottom of the pan, then pushed aside to make room for the next batch. This method of cooking uses a small amount of oil, high heat, additional liquid and constant stirring.

All food needs to be tender and cut to bite size. Add food in the order of cooking time required. Denser foods, like carrots, take considerably longer than soft foods, like mushrooms, so the carrots go into the pan before the mushrooms.

Pan-steaming

Pan-steaming is another hybrid of moist-dry cooking. Nonstick pans enhance this method of cooking by minimizing fat. The pan need not be preheated, and the temperature is kept low to ensure juiciness. The food is covered closely with a lid that sits right on top of the food to retain juices and tenderness. The food is turned several times and browning is not allowed to occur. This makes the most succulent breast of chicken I've ever eaten.

Use tender cuts of meat, poultry and fish, or vegetables, as you would in sautéing. The difference lies in the degree of heat, the frequency of turning, and the use of a snug, close-fitting lid to generate steam.

Turn the food frequently, keeping the heat low, and listen to the pan; sizzling noises indicate too high a heat. The lid must be smaller in diameter than the pan, so that the lid sits right down inside the pan on top of the food. This gives the steam less room to dissipate, thereby forcing the juices back into the food. For meats, the end result is a juicy, tender piece of food without added color or crispness.

Braising

This method works best for less tender cuts of meat and poultry thighs and drumsticks; it may be used for whole fish if care is exercised to avoid overcooking.

Use a heavy pot with high sides and a snug-fitting lid.

Vegetables are cut to a size appropriate for the cooking time, browned in a sauté pan, then removed to the bottom of the heavy pot. The meat is (optionally) dredged in flour, then browned and placed on top of the vegetables. The browning sediment in the sauté pan is deglazed, brought to a boil and poured over the foods. Cover tightly and put into the oven or cook on low heat on the stovetop. The juices may or may not be thickened at the end of cooking.

Roasting

This is the time-honored approach to cooking meat. The best results are achieved on a spit, as this precludes the development of steam, always present in oven roasting. (Steam interferes with sealing the surface of the meat, which ensures the concentration of juices within the caramelized outer surface.)

The degree of tenderness achieved through roasting is dependent on several factors. These include the age of the animal, its diet and the amounts of fat and collagen present. (Collagen turns into liquid gelatin as it cooks.) Another major contributor to tenderness is degree of doneness; a well-done roast has a very coagulated texture.

Always roast on a rack placed above a pan. This will prevent the bottom from pan-frying and will also collect the juices and drippings for gravy or sauce. Liquid may be added to the juices in the pan after the meat's surface has sealed; this will forestall burning the drippings.

Marinades and dry rubs will contribute much in the way of flavor. Marinate poultry no longer than overnight, fish for 30 minutes, and red meat from 12 hours to several days.

Meat with the bone in will roast more rapidly than boneless cuts pound for pound, as the bones act as heat conductors. Any food cooked on the bone will have more flavor than boneless food.

Roasting at medium-high (400°F/200°C) requires no presalting of the meat. It ensures a quicker seal, as does lightly brushing any nonfat surfaces with oil or melted butter. At high temperatures, the cut of meat will shrink noticeably, but the contrast of the caramelized exterior with the juicy center will compensate for the lost volume. Meats roasted at high heat will lose very little in the way of drippings, which may preclude making a gravy. (Lamb is best roasted at high heat.) At this cooking temperature, count on a roasting time of 15–20 minutes per pound (450 g) for rare to medium-rare.

Roasting at medium heat (325°F/165°C) will provide ample drippings for gravy as the meat will not seal as quickly. The amount of shrinkage is minimal when roasting at lower temperatures, and the outer surface will take longer to brown. The roasting time will be longer. (Pork is best roasted at medium heat.) At this temperature, plan on 25–30 minutes per pound (450 g) to reach rare or medium-rare.

Remember to deglaze the roasting pan with liquid to capture all the drippings, juices and crispy bits for sauce or gravy.

Grilling

Grilling and barbecuing are NOT one and the same. Grilling employs high heat, takes a brief period of time and is applicable to tender cuts of meats, poultry, seafood and vegetables that cook quickly. Food intended for the grill should be allowed to warm up instead of being put directly onto the grill from the fridge. Otherwise, the food may not cook evenly.

Barbecuing is traditionally used to turn inexpensive, less tender cuts of meat into smoky, messy and very tender, flavorful foods. As this uses a firepit and live fire, it is usually adapted to be done slowly in a large covered grill with smouldering chips of hardwood, briquets or low-running propane or gas; it is the smoke that does the cooking, not direct heat. If your gas barbecue has a rotisserie or two heat controls, you can compromise, unless you are inviting a Southerner to the festivities.

As heat sources, propane and natural gas seem to be interchangeable in terms of byproducts, although natural gas burns at a higher temperature. Both produce carbon dioxide and water when burned, so next to no flavor is imparted to the food. Natural gas is less expensive, and because it comes from a gas line there is no danger of running out, as with propane tanks. Both are easy, inexpensive, readily available and very clean. Allow a start-up time of about 10 minutes.

Charcoal briquets are made from wood scraps and sawdust. The wood is burned in a vacuum until it reduces to carbon, then it is compressed, along with starches and coal, into those dirty black cubes. Most brands have chemicals added to emit oxygen when ignited: this is intended to start the briquets burning more readily. But these chemicals and the coal do let off fumes that adversely flavor food. Presoaked charcoal briquets continue to release lighter fluid fumes throughout the entire cooking time; lighter fluid itself, added at the time of ignition, will burn off within a few minutes, and any residue on the grill will be incinerated. The start-up time is a minimum of 45 minutes to produce a bed of coals.

Hardwood briquets are formed from hardwood chunks burned in a vacuum. Again, they turn into carbon, but they also retain their original shape and have no additives or chemicals. They ignite readily and take about an hour to reach the ash-covered coal state that is ideal. Hardwood briquets do burn cleanly, and much hotter than charcoal briquets for a longer-lasting fire. They are hard to locate in some parts of the country.

Hardwood is a challenge to grill over. It will burn irregularly due to size, moisture content, age and consistency. This means it is harder and slower to arrive at a uniform bed of coals. Again, ensure the wood is unsprayed so there are no chemicals and pesticides to contaminate your food. Types include: fruitwood such as apple, cherry or crabapple, mesquite, hickory, oak, ash or nut trees, as well as alder, maple and diamond willow.

When grilling, it is possible to add additional flavor and atmosphere by generating smoke. This can come from a variety of sources. All smoke-generating sources need to be well soaked before being placed over a very low temperature to encourage smoke, not fire. Grapevine cuttings, only convenient in grape-growing areas, add a fruity, rich, smoky taste. Herbs (stems and stalks) and whole spices generate aromatic, perfumed or herbaceous smoke. Seaweed, washed and dried, adds an unmistakable salt tang that is ideal in the proper context, such as a clambake at the beach. Hardwood, nutwood and fruitwood all contribute their own unique flavors.

Preserving Food

I come from a long line of women who put food by, put food up and put food away, filling cold rooms, pantries, cellars and freezers. My mother confesses that not being able to set a full table at the drop of a hat involved embarrassment and a loss of face in the farming community. Preserving the flavors of summer is a habit that never leaves, and I admit to feeling a little panicky if my cupboard is bare of shimmering jellies, gleaming relishes, crisp pickles, suave chutneys and incandescent jams.

Pickling is an exact and unforgiving science. It requires attention to detail and an almost neurotic awareness of cleanliness. Any slips or carelessness can potentially cause illness in those you love best. Pay attention.

Use only jars designated for canning.

Recycling is admirable, but some glass jars are of a lighter weight than others, and are not designed for the stresses of canners. You can recycle canning jars and their rings, but not the lids that snap under the rings. Use them once, then toss them out.

All the recipes for preserves indicate processing: immersing hot, full, covered jars in a boiling water bath. Use a large pot with a rack so the jars do not sit right on the bottom of the pot. It needs a snug lid, which can be rigged from another pot or pan as long as it entirely covers the top of the canner. The water must cover the tops of the jars by at least 1" (2.5 cm) to ensure sufficient pressure to drive all the air out of the jars.

Headroom refers to the distance at the top of the jar that is left unfilled. The air contained in that space must all be driven out and a vacuum created, sealing the jar and creating a sterile environment. If the jar is overfilled, the contents boil out and over, impeding the seal. If the jars are underfilled, it takes too long to force out all the air left inside, and a vacuum is never created, spoiling the food. Rule of thumb for headroom is as follows: 1/4" (.5 cm) for 8-ounce (250 ml) jars, 1/2" (1 cm) for everything larger.

Sterilize everything. Be scrupulously tidy. Let two-part jar tops simmer in boiling water for 5 minutes to soften the sealing compound on the inner edge. Use a clean dry cloth to wipe the top surface of the jar after you fill it. Center the lids, place on the outer rings, tighten as snugly as you can, then loosen the ring a 1/8 turn to allow air to escape during processing.

Processing times depend on the jar size and altitude. Start timing when the water returns to a boil after all the full jars are immersed in the boiling water bath. Keep the pot on simmer while you fill the jars so that the water is as close as possible to boiling. Times for processing run an average of 15 minutes for half-pint (250-ml) jars, 20 minutes for pint (500-ml) jars, and 30 minutes for quart (1-litre) jars, with the lid on. Add 2 additional minutes per 1,000 feet (300 meters) above sea level.

The jars are heavy and the water bath is boiling, so minimize risk by using the best tools. Use a pair of canning tongs,

---

Most pectins require the presence of acid and sugar in specific proportions for jelling, but low-methoxyl pectin incorporates calcium salts (or bone meal) and lemon juice to set its natural source citrus pectin. This product was first developed by Euell Gibbons to help his diabetic brother. The most readily available low-methoxyl pectin is Pomona's Universal Pectin. Some years ago, an article in The Herb Companion magazine sent me looking for this natural citrus pectin, which allows canners to put up their own preserves with less sugar than most recipes require for setting and preservation. The main thing to remember when using Pomona's is the necessity of using small jars. Less sugar means less preservative, so it's important to refrigerate and promptly eat opened jars. Pomona's Universal Pectin is found at health-food stores. The package includes powdered pectin and a separate package of calcium, which is added at the end of cooking. If you can't find it, ask to have it brought in.

Use your senses. Listen to the jars as they cool, out of the draft; eventually each jar should PING, which indicates a seal. Some take longer than others, but sooner or later, sometimes late in the evening when you've given up, the last stubborn jar will PING. If it doesn't, place the suspect jar in the fridge, and use it as a test sample. The alternative is to empty the filling back into the pot, reboil it, resterilize the jars, get new lids, refill and reprocess the full jars, and wait for the PING. Look at the processed jars: no evidence of overboiling, no drips or leaks, no eroding brine eating away your labels? Is each lid concave, sucked down by the pressure of departing air? All's well. When you open each jar, look for bubbles, mold or other signs of fermenting. The brine or food should not be darkened or cloudy. Take the first bite with a discriminating palate. Any unexpected fizziness or softness will announce spoilage. Sniff well. Each food should smell of itself, with no musty or off odor. Any suspect jar is best discarded; better safe than sick.

which have a wide curving mouth designed for lifting jars, to lift the jars in and out of the pot. Use a wide-mouth canning funnel for filling the jars. Use spring-loaded tongs for lifting lids and rings. Don't can in bare feet no matter how hot the day. Make sure your feet are covered.

The Balancing Act— Adjusting and Balancing Flavors

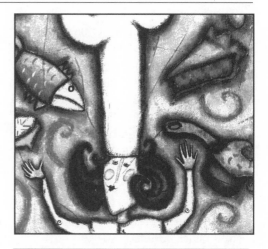

Condiments, contributors of a characteristic smell or taste, are frequently, but not always, added at the end of the cooking period or at the table. This is the moment the novice, watching a veteran cook fine-tune the flavor of a dish, exclaims in frustration, "How did you know that? How do you know what to add?"

Education of the palate to recognize flavors and nuances is usually an acquired skill rather than an inborn sense, although research is being done on what I call "taste-ability." (This is mostly research into the number of taste receptors located

When tasting a dish for balance, the trick is not just to think about what is present, but what is missing. Easily said. It takes practice and perseverance, with the best results when you taste a dish repeatedly through its seasoning stages. If a dish is flat or boring, keep tasting as you continue to add one component at a time.

within the mouth, where responses to sweet, sour, hot, salty and bitter are generated.) It is true that some people have more of a knack than others for judging balance of flavor, but this comes mostly from education gained through cooking, so get in there and dare yourself; each person must learn what he or she likes, and eventually understand why. Find an empty notebook if you're inclined to analysis, and keep track of your responses to dishes and flavor combinations. Look it over now and then, trying to pick out trends you like as well as patterns of what you don't enjoy.

The five types of condiments that are of utter importance in balancing flavors are:

- **Salty.** There are many forms of salt itself, including kosher salt, which is unadulterated and chemical free. In addition, there are anchovies, Worcestershire sauce, soy sauce, olives, capers, salty cheeses, fish sauce, fish paste and salted black fermented beans. Salt—if you don't use too much—enhances other flavors. It is the first thing to reach for when food tastes flat. Add it in small increments, stirring well and tasting after each addition.

- **Sweet.** This can be honey, sugars of  all types, syrups, jams and preserves, fruits and berries both fresh and dried, molasses, long-cooked onions, some Asian sauces. Honey is Mother Nature's blessing. Many foods we eat are no longer what She intended them to be. Tomatoes are a case in point, so a little sweetening will frequently

restore foods to where they ought to be. I will unabashedly use a sweetener to create that sweet-hot or sweet-tart finish that I love.

- **Acid.** Examples are wine, vinegar,  citrus juices, tomatoes, some fruits. A squeeze of lemon, vinegar or wine is an absolute must when seasoning a bean or grain dish. Like sugar, acid will help to create a peak of flavor and it can even out the edges of a too-sweet or too-hot dish. (It is important to remember that citrus zest adds more flavor than acid. The juice provides acid, and some degree of flavor, depending on variety.) If a sauce is too acidic, it can be softened by whisking in a knob of butter or a splash of a well-flavored oil. If a vinaigrette is too sharp but the other flavors balance, more oil (slowly added, with tastings along the way)

Herbs and spices are the aromatics. Aromatics, contributing character without losing their own identity, are usually cooked with the food. Herbs come from the leaves of perennial or annual plants and shrubs. Spices are sharp, tart, sour, bitter, pungent or caustic flavorings from the root, berries, bark or fruit of perennials. Whole herbs are best; ground herbs lose their character and flavor quickly, and instead add dusty, acrid flavors. These elements serve to heighten and intensify flavor, throw the dish's character into relief, and give each dish a characteristic stamp.

The majority of dishes in *Skinny Feasts* call for fresh herbs. This helps to create lightness on the palate that still carries intensity of flavor. Many fresh herbs are easily grown in pots or flower beds as perennials or annuals. Grow your herbs if you can, even if you start with a chive plant and a bit of thyme tucked in a corner of a sunny bed or in a pot. Add one or two plants each spring, and use those you grow; the more you snip, the more they'll produce. If gardening on any scale isn't at all appealing, buy fresh herbs as you need them. You can usually find them at farmers' markets, co-ops, good greengrocers and Asian markets. If you live in a small town and your grocer looks at you oddly if you ask about lovage or tarragon, by all means use dried herbs. Remember, though, that dried herbs are twice as potent at least as fresh herbs. As a rule of thumb, wherever you'd add 1 tablespoon (15 ml) of fresh, add 1/2 to 1 teaspoon (2.5–5 ml) of dried. Err on the side of caution; it's easy to add more, but once you've dumped it into the pot, it's exceedingly hard to get it out.

will aid the problem. A high-fat cheese or a splash of whipping cream will alter the balance of a sauce or gratin in the same way.

- **Hot.** All forms of peppers, tabasco, hot 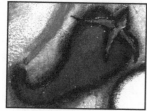 chilies both dried and fresh, chili pastes. The hot stuff is, to some people's way of thinking, one of the best things about food. I don't care for screamingly hot food, but a dash of hot chili flakes or a generous twist from the pepper mill can provide the lift for a cloying or smooth-textured dish. Any form of pepper should be added in small amounts; once it's in, it's there to stay, and excess heat is the hardest thing to rebalance, so be frugal and taste as you add. Take care with hot peppers.

The blistering capsaicin concentrated in the membranes of hot peppers can be very painful. This pungent alkaloid is used in dog and mugger sprays; tender skin will react just like that would-be assailant! Some people advocate wearing rubber gloves while handling hot peppers; if you decide to wear gloves, invest a few quarters for several pairs of dermatology-style gloves from your pharmacy.

- **Bitter.** Includes angostura bitters, Seville oranges, the onion family, bitter melon, coffee, grapefruit, bittersweet chocolate. A bottle of bitters can be a real asset in the kitchen. If a dish is too acidic, too sweet, too hot . . . a dash of bitters can help. The onion family can be either acrid and bitter, or they can be cooked long and slowly enough that they convert back to sugar. Use them both ways.

Pantry

In that most immovable and implacable of matriarchies, the French classification of sauces, any addition or alteration of an ingredient changes the name of the sauce, the dish and perhaps the world as we know it. That may be overstating the case, but today's cooks are influenced and inspired by cuisines from around the world, and that strict delineation of mother sauces and their derivatives is mostly left behind in cooking school. Unless one is blessed enough to live in the heart of France, of course!

The sauces and condiments presented here owe their heritage and origins to many cultures, including French.

Cherry Berry Compote

Makes 1 1/4 cups (310 ml)

I like cherries, more than any other fruit. Discovering varieties of dried cherries was a revelation to me, and I began to match different types of cherries with different foods. Like any other food match, the only absolute rule is whether or not you like it. Try tart dried sour cherries with lamb, or sweeter dried Bing cherries with baked Brie.

This compote freezes well, although I leave out the herbs and alcohol if I can, and stir it in upon thawing.

1 cup	boiling water	250 ml
1/2 cup	dried cherries	125 ml
1/2 cup	dried cranberries	125 ml
1 Tbsp.	puréed ginger root	15 ml
2 Tbsp.	black currant jam	30 ml
1	lime, juice and zest	1
2 Tbsp.	bourbon or single malt Scotch (optional)	30 ml
1 Tbsp.	minced fresh thyme	15 ml
	salt and hot chili flakes to taste	

Pour the boiling water over the dried cherries, cranberries and ginger. Cover and let stand for about 30 minutes or simmer briefly, covered, for 4 minutes in the microwave. Add the jam, the lime juice and zest, the bourbon or Scotch and the thyme, salt and chili flakes. Let stand to absorb all the liquid.

Dried cranberries and dried cherries are getting easier to find, thank goodness. Look for them in the bulk baking section or even on the packaged baking shelf of your health food store or market. Store them in well-sealed jars or containers to keep them supple. If the fruit has become too dry, simmer it in a little water briefly, covered, until it softens slightly.

Cranberry Compote

Makes 2 1/2 cups (625 ml)

This sauce would be lovely alongside a roasted turkey, but don't limit it to just the one bird; the wonderful astringency of this fruit makes it ideal for duck, goose, game, lamb or any grain dish, including fritters or pancakes. I also love to partner cranberries with pears; the contrast in flavor and texture is exciting.

If this is destined to become a dessert tart filling or compote, leave out the mustard seeds, celery seed, red onion and hot sauce, then increase the sweetness to taste.

I	red onion, minced	I
I Tbsp.	puréed ginger root	15 ml
1/2 cup	water	125 ml
2 cups	cranberries, fresh or frozen	500 ml
2/3 cup	honey	160 ml
I tsp.	mustard seed	5 ml
1/2 tsp.	celery seed	2.5 ml
I	orange, juice and zest	I
I	lemon, zest only	I
	salt and hot sauce to taste	
2 Tbsp.	minced fresh mint or lemon thyme	30 ml

Simmer the onion and ginger in the water until tender and transparent, then add the cranberries and honey. If required, splash in a little more water to prevent the berries from sticking. Stir in the mustard and celery seeds, orange and lemon zest. Simmer, stirring frequently, over medium heat until the berries split open, about 30 minutes. You may need to add additional juice or water if the compote gets too thick. Aim for a slightly loose texture that will spread a little on the plate.

Add the salt and hot sauce, add more honey if the compote is still too puckery, then stir in the mint or lemon thyme. Cool and store in the fridge, covered, for several weeks.

When I was growing up, we emptied a gelatinous tin of cranberry sauce into a cut-glass bowl that made its appearance every festive season with the roasted turkey. As a result, I grew up hating cranberries. Then I found fresh cranberries, frozen ones and eventually the tart and chewy dried cranberries that have become a staple in my cupboard. Such a relief; now I don't have to hate one of the best berries to come out of the Prairies.

Red Onion and Kielbasa Marmalade

Makes about 4 cups (1 litre)

This stuff has a mind of its own! It jumps onto pizza and into sauces, sandwiches, bread dough, beanpots and stews . . . you can never make too much. This is another dish that takes full advantage of a minute amount of smoky sausage for great bursts of flavor. If sausage doesn't appeal to you, simply leave it out; the dish will be different, but no damage will be done.

1 lb.	red onions, thinly sliced	450 g
1 Tbsp.	oil or butter	15 ml
1 link	kielbasa or other smoky sausage	1 link
2–4 Tbsp.	red wine vinegar or balsamic vinegar	30–60 ml
1/4 cup	brown sugar	60 ml
1 sprig	fresh rosemary	1 sprig
2 Tbsp.	minced fresh thyme	30 ml
	salt and pepper to taste	

Simmer the onion slices in the oil or butter over moderate heat, adding small amounts of water as needed to prevent browning. When the onions are becoming tender to the bite, at least 10 minutes, add the sausage, vinegar, brown sugar, rosemary and thyme. Stir well and cook slowly until the onions are tender and beginning to caramelize. Adjust the seasoning; this should be slightly sweet, with a hint of smoke, heat and acid, and an underlying herbal note.

Pickled Red Onions

Makes 8 cups (2 litres)

I first met pickled onions through Deborah Madison, the gifted author of The Greens Cookbook and The Savory Way. My heartfelt thanks for her generosity in letting me use this recipe from The Savory Way.

Choose dark red onions for the most intense color. Store the pickled onions in the fridge for up to a week for optimal crunch. They are great on sandwiches, pizza, salads, risottos, or anything that calls for crunchy onion.

4	red onions, thinly sliced	4
4 cups	boiling water	1 litre
4 cups	mild white wine vinegar or rice vinegar	1 litre
1 Tbsp.	sugar	15 ml
1 tsp.	salt	5 ml
1/2 tsp.	dried thyme	2.5 ml
	hot chili flakes to taste	

Place the onion slices in a colander in the sink. Pour the boiling water over them, discarding the water. While the onions are hot, transfer them to a glass or nonreactive bowl and add the remaining ingredients. Mix well, cover and chill.

Mango Sauce

Makes 1 1/2 cups (375 ml)

Use this wonderful sauce as a base for gorgeous plates of steamed and grilled vegetables and fish. Think of steamed asparagus pinwheeled over a pool of iridescent yellow, with half an avocado fanned out, and a clutch of grilled scallops tumbling over the avocado slices. Now consider bright broccoli and gleaming red bell pepper alongside steamed halibut. It's easy to paint pictures when one of the colors on the palette is mango!

This sauce can be frozen if you leave out the fresh herbs, adding them after thawing.

2–3	ripe mangoes, depending on size	2–3
2 Tbsp.	puréed ginger root	30 ml
2	oranges, juice and zest	2
1/4 cup	white wine	60 ml
2 Tbsp.	minced red bell pepper (optional)	30 ml
1–2 Tbsp.	honey to taste	15–30 ml
2 Tbsp.	minced fresh thyme	30 ml
1 Tbsp.	minced flatleaf parsley	15 ml
	salt and hot chili flakes to taste	

Peel and purée the mangoes, then add all remaining ingredients, thinning the sauce with additional orange juice if needed. Taste the finished sauce and balance the flavors with salt and hot chili flakes.

The best place to eat whole mangoes is in the bathtub, with no sleeves to catch the drips. A wide variety of mangoes are available, but Hadon and Kent are the best, with less fibrous strings and more luscious pulp. Ripe mangoes have an exotic sweet perfume that is as heady and intoxicating as any haute couturier's.

Pickled Ginger

Makes about 2 cups (500 ml)

Any sushi lover knows the joy of thin shavings of gari that cleanse the palate between bites. Gari, or pickled ginger, adds life and sparkle to any dish. It is best with young ginger, blooming with a translucent pink skin. Use it in vinaigrettes, sauces, soups, stews, gratins, bean dishes and anywhere else a dash of mild acid is desired.

1/2 lb.	ginger root	225 g
2 cups	Japanese rice vinegar	500 ml
1–4 Tbsp.	sugar or honey	15–60 ml
	salt and hot chili flakes to taste	

Peel the ginger and shave it thinner than thin with the grain. Place it in a glass or ceramic bowl, then add the vinegar to cover. Stir in the sugar or honey, a sprinkle of salt and the hot chili flakes. Cover, refrigerate and taste in a week's time. It will keep indefinitely in the fridge unless the pickle addicts discover it.

Black Bean Sauce

Makes 3–4 cups (750 ml–1 litre)

black bean sauce is a classic, a staple of southern Chinese cuisine, and it deserves to be eaten in every household in the world. I use this basted on ribs; steamed with mussels and clams; brushed onto grilled fish, especially salmon; with whole crab; and as a sauce on pizza and pasta, particularly with barbecued duck or pork.

It keeps well, so make extra and store it in the fridge for up to a week. If you are tempted to make vast vats, leave out the fresh herbs and add them when you use the sauce.

1	onion, minced	1
1	leek, minced	1
1	red bell pepper, minced	1
1 Tbsp.	canola oil	15 ml
2 Tbsp.	puréed ginger root	30 ml
2 Tbsp.	puréed garlic	30 ml
1	orange, juice and zest	1
1/2 cup	dry white wine or sake	125 ml
3/4 cup	hoisin sauce	185 ml
2 Tbsp.	lemon juice	30 ml
1–2 cups	water	250–500 ml
2 Tbsp.	soy sauce	30 ml
	hot chili flakes to taste	
2 Tbsp.	dried fermented black beans	30 ml
2	green onions, minced	2
2 Tbsp.	minced cilantro	30 ml
1 Tbsp.	sesame oil	15 ml

Sauté the vegetables in the oil, cooking them until tender. Add the remaining ingredients except the green onions, cilantro and sesame oil. Simmer for several minutes, until the flavors are friendly and it is reduced and thickened to the desired texture—slightly thicker for pizza, thinner for a steaming medium or sauce. Remove from the heat and add the remaining ingredients.

Fresh Fruit Salsa

Makes about 2 cups (500 ml)

This winter recipe calls for pears with dried cranberries, for a tangy counterpoint. In summer, I chop mangoes and peaches, then stir in a chopped MacIntosh apple for its snap—particularly fine with fish. A different texture can be achieved by grilling the fruit, then puréeing it and adding fresh chopped fruit to the purée.

2	ripe pears, cut in 1/2" (1-cm) dice	2
1	orange, lime or lemon, zest only	1
1/2	apple, sliced into matchsticks	1/2
2 Tbsp.	minced dried cranberries or cherries	30 ml
2 Tbsp.	puréed or minced ginger root	30 ml
1–2 Tbsp.	honey or maple syrup to taste	15–30 ml
2	green onions, minced	2
2 Tbsp.	fresh herbs (thyme, basil, mint, oregano, tarragon, cilantro, chives, chervil)	30 ml
	salt and hot chili flakes to taste	
1–2 Tbsp.	vinegar or citrus juice	15–30 ml

Combine all ingredients and serve alongside rice, curries, grilled dishes, and any other bare spot on the plate.

Sambal Oelek

Makes about 1 1/2 cups (375 ml)

This Javanese version of a fresh salsa uses ripe, succulent tomatoes in season. I like to heap it onto soft, squishy bread for a very juicy tomato sandwich, or onto toasted garlic-rubbed croutons for a snappy finger food to enjoy with a glass of wine and a saucer of olives while dinner finishes cooking. It also works well as a steaming medium for clams and mussels.

2–3	tomatoes	2–3
2	jalapeño peppers	2
1 tsp.	sugar	5 ml
1 tsp.	light soy sauce	5 ml
1–2 cloves	garlic	1–2 cloves
	salt and hot chili flakes to taste	
	lemon juice to taste	

Seed the tomatoes by slicing them in half horizontally, then squeezing each half over a sieve set on a bowl to catch the liquid. Discard the seeds, chop the tomatoes into tidy 1/2" (1-cm) dice, and add to the tomato liquid. Split the hot peppers, remove and discard the seeds and membranes, and dice very finely. Add the remaining ingredients and balance with the salt, hot chili flakes and lemon juice. Let stand for half an hour if possible to let the flavors mingle. It's best eaten the same day.

Bean Salsa

Makes about 3 cups (750 ml)

Seasoning is the key to serving bean dishes. I treat beans as a salad or salsa, flavor them with lots of acid and citrus, and serve them in small amounts beside other foods. As a result, I've fed more beans to more people than I'd ever hoped to. For a smoky, hotter flavor, add a rehydrated seeded ancho or morita chili pepper, finely chopped or puréed. Also try black turtle beans with sherry vinegar, or lots of citrus juice with Great Northern white beans.

2 cups	cooked beans, any type(s)	500 ml
3	green onions, minced	3
1/4 cup	minced fresh herbs, your choice	60 ml
2 Tbsp.	puréed ginger root	30 ml
1/2 cup	minced sweet bell pepper	125 ml
1/2	tart, firm apple, diced	1/2
2 Tbsp.	honey	30 ml
2–4 Tbsp.	red or white wine vinegar	30–60 ml
2	lemons, limes or oranges, zest only	2
	salt and hot chili flakes to taste	

Combine all ingredients, mix well and allow to mellow for several hours before serving.

Pear Coulis

Makes about 3 cups (750 ml)

This delicate purée is good with savory filo cups stuffed with chèvre, or with any mild cheese dishes. It is light enough to pair with Seared Scallops (page 96) or Pork Medallions (page 117). It has nothing in common with canned applesauce except for its color, its slightly grainy texture, and the time it takes to make it—almost as quick as opening a can.

2	pears, ripe	2
2 Tbsp.	puréed ginger root	30 ml
1 12-oz.	bottle pear cider, hard or soft	1 350-ml
2 Tbsp.	minced fresh thyme	30 ml
1	lime, juice and zest	1
	salt and hot chili flakes to taste	

Peel, core and dice the pears. Combine them with the ginger and cider in a pot and simmer until the coulis thickens. Purée.

Add the thyme and lime. Season with the salt and hot chili flakes.

Fresh Mint Chutney

Makes about 1 1/2 cups (375 ml)

This doesn't keep, nor does it freeze particularly well, but it is so exquisitely fresh that you'll want to make it all summer, as long as your mint patch flourishes. Make it as hot as you enjoy to serve alongside curries and grain dishes, and remember it when you serve lamb off the grill.

1 cup	fresh mint leaves, firmly packed	250 ml
1 cup	parsley, firmly packed	250 ml
2	green onions	2
2	jalapeño peppers	2
4–6 cloves	garlic	4–6 cloves
1	orange, juice and zest	1
1/4 cup	lemon juice	60 ml
1 tsp.	garam masala	5 ml
1 Tbsp.	sugar	15 ml
1 tsp.	fennel seeds, cracked	5 ml
	salt to taste	
1/4–1/2 cup	water	60–125 ml

Pack the mint and parsley into the bowl of a food processor. Cut the onions into 2" (5-cm) lengths and add them. Trim the jalapeños, discarding the seeds and membranes, and add them to the food processor's bowl. Remember not to rub your eyes or touch any sensitive parts of your body after you slice the hot peppers! Add the remaining ingredients except the water and process to a fine purée. Blend in the water, adding more if needed to make a loose, fluid paste.

Store, covered, in the fridge for no more than 3 days. The ingredients will darken and the flavor balance will alter with age; this is really best eaten within 3 days.

Sorrel-Spinach Sauce

Makes about 3 cups (750 ml)

This makes a refreshing cold summer soup as well as a perfect partner to salmon. Or use it as a dip for crudités, a pasta sauce, especially when partnered with poached shrimp on linguini, or as a tart, lean sauce to layer with sweet potatoes and Yukon Golds for an end-of-summer gratin.

I bunch	spinach	I bunch
I bunch	sorrel	I bunch
2	shallots	2
I tsp.	unsalted butter	5 ml
1/2 cup	dry white wine	125 ml
I	lemon, zest only	I
1/2 tsp.	cracked fennel seeds	2.5 ml
2 Tbsp.	minced fresh thyme, tarragon or lemon thyme	30 ml
2	green onions, minced	2
2 cups	buttermilk	500 ml
	salt and hot chili flakes to taste	

Wash the spinach and sorrel, discarding the stems. Do not spin dry. In a sauté pan, sauté the shallots in the butter, cooking until tender without browning. Add the wine, bring to a boil and add the spinach, turning the leaves with tongs until they just wilt.

Remove to a food processor and purée finely, along with the sorrel leaves. Add remaining ingredients, thinning to the desired consistency with buttermilk. Adjust the flavors and serve cold.

Hazelnut Crouton Topping

Makes I cup (250 ml)

One way to use nuts is as a butter, spread on crusty bread and broiled; the warm croutons add textural interest to salads while keeping calories to a manageable level. (See page 48 for tips on skinning hazelnuts.)

1/2 cup	hazelnuts, toasted, skinned and chopped	125 ml
I tsp.	ginger root	5 ml
I tsp.	lemon thyme	5 ml
I	lime, juice and zest	I
	salt and hot chili flakes to taste	
I	baguette, sliced into rounds	I

Purée all ingredients except the baguette in a food processor. Adjust the seasoning, thin with water if needed, then spread it on crusty slices of bread. Pop them under a broiler just before it is time to eat.

Roasted Tomato Sauce

Makes about 6 cups (1.5 litres)

This is my personal favorite when it comes to tomato sauces. It has all the right stuff—speed, tidiness, great flavor and a freshness that tells you immediately that this came right out of the garden. In addition, it needs next to no babysitting, and can mind itself without splashing while you enjoy a glass of wine. Make extra and use it in layered vegetable dishes, pasta or risotto and then save the tail end for a seasonal vinaigrette.

3 lbs.	ripe Roma tomatoes	1.3 kg
2	onions, sliced	2
6 cloves	garlic, whole or sliced	6 cloves
2 Tbsp.	olive oil	30 ml
2 Tbsp.	honey	30 ml
4	green onions, minced	4
4 Tbsp.	fresh basil	60 ml
1 Tbsp.	lemon juice	15 ml
	salt and hot chili flakes to taste	

Place the tomatoes in one layer in a nonstick ovenproof pan, spread the onions and garlic over top, drizzle with the olive oil and roast in a hot oven (about 450°F/230°C) until the tops are charred and the vegetables are tender, about 45 minutes to an hour. Remove from the oven, coarsely purée, add the remaining ingredients and balance the flavors with the salt and chili flakes.

Red Curry Paste

Makes 1 1/2 cups (375 ml)

This is fiercely hot and works well as a base for any red curry. My favorite chili combination is ancho and morita chilies. To use, gently reheat a small amount of paste in water, then steam or poach vegetables, meats or fish in the liquid. To make sauce, thicken liquid with cornstarch dissolved in cold water at the end of the cooking process.

6	dried red chilies	6
1	onion, finely minced	1
6 cloves	garlic, minced	6 cloves
2 Tbsp.	minced fresh cilantro	30 ml
2 tsp.	ground cumin	10 ml
1 Tbsp.	ground coriander	15 ml
1 tsp.	turmeric	5 ml
1 tsp.	ground pepper	5 ml
2 tsp.	paprika	10 ml
1	lemon, zest only	1
1 tsp.	salt	5 ml
1 Tbsp.	canola oil	15 ml

Place all ingredients in a food processor or blender and purée to a smooth paste. Cover and store in the fridge. It will keep for a week, although the garlic will become more pronounced as it ages. Don't try to freeze it; the raw onion juices leach out and alter the flavor.

Caramelized Pecans

Makes about 4 cups (1 litre)

I first saw these being made by master chef Jacques Pépin. He simmered the nuts briefly in boiling water, then seasoned them simply with salt, sugar and cayenne, and passed them about to be eaten by the handful as students sat rapt before his sleight of hand. I have dared to fiddle with the master's idea, changing the technique to ensure crisper nuts, and adding the haunting flavor of star anise. Serve these high-voltage treats on salads, as an aperitif, on fruit compotes, on flatbreads, on pasta and risotto, and out of hand as a quick pick-up when energy is waning in the middle of the afternoon.

Store any uneaten nuts, caramelized or raw, in the freezer.

4 cups	pecan halves	1 litre
4 cups	boiling water	1 litre
2 Tbsp.	unsalted butter	30 ml
4 Tbsp.	white sugar	60 ml
1/2 tsp.	salt	2.5 ml
1 tsp.	cayenne	5 ml
1 tsp.	ground star anise	5 ml

Place the nuts in a colander or strainer, and holding them carefully over the sink, pour the boiling water over the nuts. The water helps minimize the tannins in the skins without making the nuts soggy.

Combine the nuts and remaining ingredients in a nonstick sauté pan. Cook over medium-high heat until the pecans are dark and glossy, about 5 to 10 minutes. Shake and stir constantly to prevent burning. Once the nuts are crisp and brown, spread them in a thin layer on a baking sheet lined with parchment. Let them cool entirely. Store, well wrapped, in the freezer, and exercise restraint—these nuts are addictive.

Star anise is a beautiful, star-shaped spice with the pungent scent of licorice. Buy it whole in Asian markets and grind it as needed in an electric spice mill. (Hand-powered mortar and pestle may not be able to crack this tough nut.) This is a strong and assertive flavor, so use it sparingly to create a haunting sweet-sharp undertone.

North African Berber Spice Blend

Makes 1/3 cup (80 ml)

This complex paste shows the influence of the spice trade routes of a bygone era. It makes a good dry rub or marinade base for meats and vegetables destined for the grill, and is an integral part of North African Lamb (page 114). To use it as a baste for grilling or roasting, add water, wine or orange juice to thin the spices to spreading consistency. You can sprinkle this sparingly on squash slices before you bake them, or rub it on chicken breasts before you marinate them for Chicken in Yoghurt (page 106).

For a flavorful compound butter, blend a little (or a lot) of this mix into softened butter, form it into a small log of 1" (2.5 cm) diameter, wrap it well and freeze it. Shave off slices of the butter as you need it, dropping the slices onto grilled food for a flavor boost.

1 tsp.	powdered ginger	5 ml
1 tsp.	red pepper flakes	5 ml
1 tsp.	ground cardamom	5 ml
2 tsp.	ground coriander	10 ml
1 tsp.	ground star anise	5 ml
1 tsp.	ground anise seed	5 ml
1 tsp.	turmeric	5 ml
1 tsp.	dry mustard	5 ml
1 tsp.	ground fenugreek	5 ml
1 tsp.	ground nutmeg	5 ml
1 tsp.	ground cinnamon	5 ml
1 tsp.	ground allspice	5 ml
2 tsp.	cayenne powder	10 ml
1 tsp.	ground black pepper	5 ml

Combine all ingredients in a small sauté pan and cook over medium-high heat for a minute or two, until it smells toasty and aromatic. Cool and store, covered, until needed.

Making this entirely from whole spices that you painstakingly grind yourself is not too realistic in today's busy kitchen. It is possible with a good electric spice mill and/or a heavy mortar and pestle, and the flavor is vastly superior to that of preground spices. If you can, grind some of the spices, but don't worry if your kitchen doesn't contain cardamom or coriander in any form but ground. Use what you have, and if you are missing one or two components, make it anyway—no one is likely to know but you. Don't omit the dry-roasting stage, though; it lends a depth of flavor that is impossible to achieve otherwise.

Preserves

For tips and important information on preserving,
please refer to the "Preserving Food" section of Kitchen Basics.

Pear, Orange and Cranberry Conserve

Makes 4–5 half-pint (250-ml) jars

I like to have tart relishes on hand for when I get tired of dill pickles, which I never do. That isn't to say this sits forever in my cold room; I take it out for turkey and pork dishes, when the entire jar disappears in one sitting.

2 cups	cranberries, fresh or frozen	500 ml
4	pears, peeled, cored and chopped	4
1	orange, zest only	1
2 cups	orange juice	500 ml
1–2 cups	sugar	250–500 ml
2 Tbsp.	lemon juice	30 ml
1/2 tsp.	fresh nutmeg	2.5 ml

Combine and simmer until thick. Ladle into sterile half-pint jars and process for 15 minutes.

Blueberries with Ginger and Lemon

Makes 4–6 half-pint (250-ml) jars

This can be simmered to thicken for a jammy finish, or left on the loose side as a sauce or condiment. Try it on pancakes, waffles, ice cream, sorbet or yoghurt, chocolate cake or angel food cake. You can downplay the sweetness to give it a sharp edge as a condiment for savories. Use small jars because of the low sugar content.

3 cups	fresh blueberries	750 ml
1	lemon, juice and zest	1
1/2–1 cup	sugar	125–250 ml
1/4 cup	puréed ginger root	60 ml

Combine all ingredients in a heavy-bottomed pot and simmer until the compote is as thick as you like. Ladle into sterile half-pint jars and process for 15 minutes.

Basil and Lemon Wine Jelly

Makes 6 4-oz. (125-ml) jars

Using wine is an easy way to achieve clear jellies without resorting to a slow-dripping, messy jelly bag. This makes a wonderful gift, but it's not inexpensive, so track down the smallest jars you can find. You can substitute any other full-flavored white wine for the Chardonnay.

1 bottle	Chardonnay	1 bottle
2 cups	fresh basil leaves	500 ml
1	lemon, juice and zest	1
1	orange, zest only	1
1/2 tsp.	fennel seeds	2.5 ml
3 1/2 cups	sugar	875 ml
	Pomona's pectin as needed (see page 8)	
	Pomona's calcium solution as needed	

Bring the wine to a boil. Add the basil leaves, lemon juice and zest, orange zest and fennel seeds and infuse over very low heat for 15 minutes. Strain and discard solids. Add sugar to taste. The final volume will be dictated by the amount of evaporation during cooking, so measure the total liquid at the end and add pectin and calcium as required. Ladle into sterile 4-oz. (125-ml) jars and process for 10 minutes.

Zinfandel and Thyme Jelly

Makes 6 4-oz. (125-ml) jars

This is darkly potent, and whenever I brew it, I am certain that this is how the cauldrons of powerful warlocks and witches smell. Plan to serve this with lamb, duck, beef or rabbit, and give it to avid wine-drinking friends. They'll never forget it.

1 bottle	Zinfandel	750 ml
6 sprigs	fresh thyme	6 sprigs
6 sprigs	fresh rosemary	6 sprigs
1	lemon, juice and zest	1
1/4–3/4 cup	sugar	60–185 ml
	Pomona's pectin as needed (see page 8)	
	Pomona's calcium solution as needed	

Make an infusion of the wine, thyme and rosemary. Gently simmer without boiling for 15 minutes. Strain and discard solids. Bring to a boil, and add the lemon and sugar. Taste, adding more sugar if you prefer. Measure the liquid, which will be dictated by the amount of evaporation during cooking, and add Pomona's pectin and calcium as required. Put up in 4-oz. (125-ml) jars and process for 10 minutes.

Plum Butter

Makes 6–8 half-pint (250-ml) jars

There is no butter at all in this simple spread, just fruit and sugar. If your market has damson plums, buy them. They make absolutely the best plum butter. The amount of sugar you add will vary according to the plum you choose, so add and taste, add and taste, then rebalance with extra lemon juice to keep it from being too sweet. Because of the relatively low sugar content, put the butter up in half-pint jars, refrigerate after opening and enjoy promptly.

2 lbs.	plums, pitted and quartered	900 g
1–2 cups	sugar	250–500 ml
1/2 cup	lemon juice	125 ml
1	cinnamon stick	1

Pit and quarter the plums, then simmer in a heavy-bottomed pot over medium heat. You may need to add a little water until the juices start to flow from the plums. Stir in sugar and lemon juice to taste, add cinnamon stick, then simmer the plums until they thicken, about 20 minutes, stirring regularly to keep the juices from burning. Ladle into sterile jars and process for 15 minutes.

My buddy Roy, the produce genius, came over on a Sunday morning for a canning marathon. Roy is about the size of a Mack truck, and he arrived with dozens of cases of fruits and vegetables under his arms, looking to get set up for Christmas gift-giving. We worked nonstop, just the two of us, for about 12 hours, with little bits of help from my youngest child as his interest came and went. The end result of our day was over 100 jars of relishes, pickles, chutneys and jams, including a few jars of plum butter. The kitchen was so humid we could've wrung out the air and canned it too by the time we called it a late night, but Roy and I filled our shelves with rows and rows of jars, some of which made it to the gift-giving season, some of which Roy is still hoarding.

Red Bell Pepper Rhumba

Makes 12–14 pint (500-ml) jars

This sparkling savory jelly has been a staple in our fridge for years, each season seeing a slight alteration or addition. Not that it requires fixing, but some cooks can't stop tinkering. As its name suggests, this jelly commemorates the year of the dance fixation, when everything was rechristened with a dance label. Don't limit yourself to just red bell peppers—sweet yellow and orange peppers give this jelly an unearthly luminescence. I like to use this with roasted and grilled meats and fish, curries, and egg and bean dishes.

8 cups	bell pepper pieces, mostly red	2 litres
1 cup	hot red pepper pieces	250 ml
3 cups	white sugar	750 ml
4 cups	apple cider vinegar	1 litre
1 tsp.	pickling salt	5 ml
1 Tbsp.	Pomona's pectin (see page 8)	15 ml
1 Tbsp.	Pomona's calcium solution	15 ml

Purée or finely chop the peppers, then bring to a boil in a large heavy pot along with the sugar, vinegar and salt. Simmer for 5 minutes, then stir in the pectin and mix very well. Boil hard for 1 minute, remove from the heat and add the calcium. Ladle into sterile jars and process for 15 minutes. Allow a month or so to age. (Mine never lasts that long before being sampled.)

Variation

Smokin' Joe is Red Bell Pepper Rhumba with one or two ancho and morita chili peppers rehydrated, ground up and stirred in. The resulting jelly is a smoky, smoldering blast furnace that ages well and gets hotter. Drop a whole tiny hot chili on the very top of each full jar before you seal and process them; even if you mislabel them, the sight of that pepper will remind you of the latent heat contained within.

One canning season, for some unremembered reason I decided to give every type of preserve a name derived from one dance or another. As a result, my cold room was littered with foxtrots, rhumbas, cha-chas, tangos, mambos and every other dance under the sun. There was no room for a pirouette, never mind a high kick. Not all of them have survived; I tend to try one or two new preserves every season, some of which don't make next season's repertoire, but a few dances have twirled their way into my permanent collection.

Chili Cha-Cha

Makes 8 pint (500-ml) jars

This chili sauce is at least four generations old, handed down from my dad's family to my mom and then on to me. I use it as baksheesh when I need a favor, and it makes the best Christmas present, needing nothing other than a ribbon.

My version is subtly different from my mother's jars, and my grandmother is no longer around to compare notes. I put my pickling spice directly into the mix rather than tying it up in cheesecloth; I think you get more concentrated, clearer flavors, but you do have to warn people to beware of peppercorns and cloves between their teeth. I used yellow tomatoes one year for a chili sauce that was a warm orange rather than the normal red; regardless of the color, choose meaty tomatoes with more flesh than juice.

24 cups	Roma tomatoes, quartered	6 litres
6 cups	finely sliced celery	1.5 litres
6 cups	finely diced onions	1.5 litres
1/2 cup	pickling salt	125 ml
4 cups	white sugar	1 litre
2 cups	white vinegar	500 ml
2 oz.	pickling spice (by weight—see p. 32)	60 g
3	bell peppers, finely diced	3
	hot chilies to taste (optional)	

Combine the tomatoes with the celery, onions and pickling salt in a very large stainless, glass or other nonreactive bowl. Let the mixture stand at room temperature all day. In the evening, transfer the vegetables into a large colander or strainer with a bowl beneath it to catch the drips. Let it drain overnight. The next morning, discard the water and put the vegetables in a shallow heavy-bottomed pot. Add the sugar, white vinegar, pickling spice, bell peppers and hot whole chilies, if desired.

Bring the mixture to a boil, stirring well to mix. Reduce the heat and simmer until the mixture is saucelike in consistency; it will depend on the design of the pot as well as on the type of tomatoes you are using, but expect somewhere around 20 to 35 minutes. Stir regularly to prevent sticking.

Ladle into sterile jars and process. Cool, label and allow to mature for several weeks before you give them to your friends.

My mother freezes her tomatoes whole, and when she has time in the middle of winter, she chops them coarsely in her blender or food processor before starting the recipe. That eliminates the problem of tomato skins collecting on the surface.

Traditional Dills

Makes 6–8 quart (1-litre) jars

This is another family recipe that I've taken liberties with; I season these dills more liberally than my mom and grandmother ever did. You'll never buy dill pickles again once you've had these. Feel free to add more or less garlic, and if you don't fancy dill pickles with a snap of heat, omit the hot chilies. If you live in an area with very hard water, preboil the water for the brine. Let it stand overnight, then gently pour it off to leave the mineral sediment behind. Or buy distilled or spring water.

3 lbs.	pickling cucumbers	1.3 kg
8 cups	water	2 litres
3 cups	white vinegar	750 ml
1/2 cup	pickling salt	125 ml
1 head	garlic cloves, peeled	1 head
8	hot red chilies	8
1 Tbsp.	whole peppercorns	15 ml
24	allspice berries	24
1 Tbsp.	whole coriander	15 ml
8	bay leaves	8
16 sprigs	fresh dill in 2" (5-cm) lengths	16 sprigs

Wash the cucumbers and trim off blossom ends. If they are small, leave them whole; if longer than 3" (7.5 cm), slice into even pieces crosswise or lengthwise.

Bring the water, vinegar and salt to a boil, then reduce the heat to a simmer. Drop 2 garlic cloves, a hot red chili, a few peppercorns, allspice berries, and coriander seeds, a bay leaf, and a piece of fresh dill into each jar. Pack the cucumbers into the jars, using a chopstick to help snugly position them. (Packing tip: use square-shouldered jars, buy small cucumbers, and lay the sliced or whole cukes in horizontal rows rather than trying to pack them vertically. The end result is tidy and space-effective.)

Lay a second piece of dill over the cukes. Return the brine to a boil, ladle it over the cukes and seal the jars. Process for 20 minutes. Store for 4 to 6 weeks before sampling.

I've been fortunate to be the pickle judge for several years at our region's fall fair. Every September, I taste pickles amid a huge collection of arts and crafts, and it takes me back 30 years to when my folks trundled me and my pony to fall fairs. My pony was a lot like me, short, stubborn, and determined to do things his own way. Together we won jumping ribbons and trophies for clearing fences no shortlegged pony had any business trying. Fall fairs were pretty special to me then, too.

Thousand Island Relish

Makes about 14 pint (500-ml) jars

*T*his is hugely addictive. I eat it on or with everything. The recipe originally came to me from my Grandma Sarah, but my jars and hers don't look too similar. I tend to make a chunkier, sharper-flavored relish, and I have omitted the turmeric that gives Grandma Sarah's relish a yellowish tint.

12	large cucumbers	12
8	large onions	8
3	green bell peppers	3
2	red bell peppers	2
1/2 cup	pickling salt	125 ml
4 cups	cold water	1 litre
8 cups	white vinegar	2 litres
4 cups	white sugar	1 litre
1 1/2 Tbsp.	mustard seed	22.5 ml
1 Tbsp.	celery seed	15 ml
2 Tbsp.	pickling spice (below)	30 ml
6 Tbsp.	dry mustard	90 ml
3/4 cup	all-purpose flour	185 ml

Grind or chop the vegetables coarsely in a meat grinder or food processor. Sprinkle with the salt and add the water. Let stand for one hour, then drain thoroughly, discarding the liquid. Combine the remaining ingredients, pour over the vegetables and stir well. Bring to a boil and ladle into sterile jars. Process for 15 minutes and put away for a month to mellow.

Pickling Spice

*O*f course you can buy this already mixed and packaged, but I believe you get a better blend if you mix it yourself. Most well-stocked kitchens will have most of these spices. This keeps well in your cupboard, but aim for making as much as you will use in one season.

Use whole spices, in equal amounts by weight.

allspice berries	cinnamon stick, broken
bay leaf, crumbled	whole cloves
black peppercorns	coriander seeds
cardamom seeds	mustard seeds
celery seeds	hot red chilies

Mix together in whatever volume you are likely to use over the canning season. Store in a covered jar until needed.

The Nine-Day Waltz

Makes 4 quarts (4 litres)

My mother's classic sweet pickle is guaranteed to transport you to another time, and type, of life. She tells me that it takes very little time, but the time is stretched out over a week and a half. These are great pickles, so don't be dissuaded by the number of days involved in their making.

4 quarts	2–3" (5–7.5 cm) pickling cukes	4 litres
4 quarts	boiling water	4 litres
2 cups	pickling salt	500 ml
4 quarts	cold water	4 litres
2 quarts	white vinegar	2 litres
6 cups	white sugar	1.5 litres
1/2 cup	pickling spice (see opposite page)	125 ml

Wash the cukes very well, trim off the blossom end and cut into 3/4" (2-cm) slices. Place in a crock or a ceramic or stainless bowl. Combine the boiling water and salt, then pour the brine over the cukes. Cover with a cloth and let stand for 3 days at room temperature.

On the third day, drain the brine, boil it and pour back over the cukes. Repeat on the sixth day. On the ninth day, drain and discard the brine. Return the cukes to the crock or bowl.

Bring the cold water to a boil, then pour over the cukes. Let stand 6 hours. Drain, then rinse the sliced cucumbers with additional cold water. Pack into hot, sterile jars. Combine the vinegar, sugar and pickling spice. Boil for 5 minutes, then pour the syrup over the cukes. Seal the jars and process for 20 minutes. Wait at least 10 days before allowing the locusts to descend.

Autumn Mincemeat

Makes 4 quarts (4 litres)

No meat, but definitely minced. You could really make this at any time of the year, but the fall is best. It gives the flavors a chance to mellow before late fall and winter tart-making. If you wanted to, this could serve as a very fruity sweet chutney alongside a hot curry, but it is best in tarts and galettes as well as on ice cream or yoghurt, pancakes and waffles.

5 cups	tart apples, peeled and chopped	1.25 litres
5 cups	ripe pears, peeled and chopped	1.25 litres
2	oranges, juice and zest	2
1	lemon, juice and zest	1
2 cups	honey or brown sugar	500 ml
1 lb.	Thompson seedless raisins	450 g
1 lb.	currants	450 g
1 cup	apple cider	250 ml
1/4 cup	apple cider vinegar	60 ml
2 tsp.	ground cinnamon	10 ml
1 tsp.	ground ginger	5 ml
1 tsp.	mace	5 ml
1 tsp.	allspice	5 ml
1 tsp.	ground cloves	5 ml
1 tsp.	salt	5 ml
1 cup	Calvados or brandy (optional)	250 ml

Combine all ingredients except the Calvados or brandy in a large, heavy-bottomed pot. Bring to a boil, then reduce the heat and simmer, stirring often, until the fruit is soft and thickened, about 20 to 30 minutes. Sterilize the jars and lids, then stir in the alcohol at the last minute. Put up in jars, process for 30 minutes, cool and label. Store in a cool dark cupboard for a month before you start to use it.

Variation

Use up prolific amounts of green tomatoes in late summer by substituting chopped green tomatoes for pears to make a slightly less sweet **Green Tomato Mincemeat**. The tomato version tends to be a little sturdier in texture, but only you and your garden will recognize those tomatoes.

Salad Dressings

Salad dressing has evolved far beyond a splash of oil and vinegar in predetermined, rigid ratios. Changing tastes and expanding culinary influences have encouraged a broad range of attitudes and ingredients. One of the most influential trends is the continuing preoccupation of North Americans with purging their diets of fat. Salad dressings, once made mostly of oil, have been under constant renovation and adjustment.

Use highly flavored oils rather than neutral oils in dressings; it takes less to make an impact. A little goes a long way with roasted sesame oil or extra-virgin olive oil.

Sweet acids like balsamic vinegar, sweet Japanese rice vinegar or orange juice will require less oil than a more astringent red wine or sherry vinegar. Add acids cautiously and experiment with differing types and brands of vinegars and acids. Fresh citrus juice makes a lovely dressing, but it is prone to fermenting after a few days, so make it in smaller amounts.

You can also temper your vinaigrette with honey, adding it cautiously as well. This will make your salad dressings more accessible to wine pairings, minimizing the head-on power struggle of acid in wine against acid in vinaigrette.

Mustards, valued for their ability to stabilize emulsions, add piquancy and sometimes a biting edge. Select mustards you enjoy for both their flavor and texture. In dressings that are rustic and chunky, I like grainy mustard, saving smooth mustard for where it will match the finished texture of the dressing.

Cooked, puréed fruit and vegetable pulp is one way to add intense flavor to a dressing that is reduced in fat content. Dressings bound with puréed fruit use less oil and have more interest and texture than the old oil and vinegar standby. Vegetable and fruit purées do make dressings thicker and sometimes grainy, but thin them with water or juice until they are manageable. Or opt to use them as dips and spreads in their thicker state.

A small amount of intensely flavored, rich ingredients, like blue cheese or nuts, in a salad dressing allows us to continue to enjoy these foods, albeit in a different format and in smaller quantities.

Roasted Pepper–Lime Vinaigrette with Lovage and Miso

Makes about 1 cup (250 ml)

*T*his vinaigrette uses vegetable purée for volume and flavor. How you season it will vary with the seasons and your inclination. Try the suggestions here, but don't be afraid to experiment with your own variations. I like this dressing on potato salad, pasta salad, grain salad, and sturdy greens, as well as with grilled fish or chicken.

1	roasted pepper, sweet or hot	1
3	garlic cloves	3
1 Tbsp.	miso	15 ml
2	limes, juice and zest	2
1 Tbsp.	grainy mustard	15 ml
3 Tbsp.	honey	45 ml
1/2 cup	rice vinegar or sherry vinegar	125 ml
1/3 cup	canola oil	80 ml
2 Tbsp.	lovage leaves	30 ml
	salt and hot chili flakes to taste	

Purée the pepper and garlic, then add the miso, limes, mustard, honey and vinegar. Add the oil and lovage slowly, with the machine running. Balance the flavors with salt and hot chili flakes.

Variations
For **Roasted Pepper and Rosemary Vinaigrette,** omit the miso and lovage, and add 1 Tbsp. (15 ml) minced fresh rosemary and/or fresh thyme.

For **Roasted Pepper and Cilantro Vinaigrette,** omit the lovage, and add 1 tsp. (5 ml) roasted sesame oil and 1 Tbsp. (15 ml) fresh cilantro.

For **Roasted Pepper and Olive or Caper Vinaigrette,** omit the lovage and miso, and add 2 Tbsp. (30 ml) chopped olives or capers and 2 Tbsp. (30 ml) minced parsley or chives.

For **Roasted Pepper and Balsamic Vinaigrette,** omit the lovage, limes and miso, add 1 Tbsp. (15 ml) minced fresh rosemary and substitute 2 Tbsp. (30 ml) balsamic vinegar for the sherry or rice vinegar.

For **Roasted Pepper and Dried Chili Vinaigrette,** rehydrate 1 ancho, morita or other dried chili in hot water to cover. Let steep, or simmer if time is a factor, then remove the seeds and membranes. Purée with the soaking water, then stir into the vinaigrette.

Roasting peppers is a matter of a few moments' work. At the height of the pepper season, I find myself roasting case after case of peppers, from sweet squat Hungarian peppers to long, tapered, thin-skinned Shepards. Hot peppers can be roasted as well, with resulting smoky undertones of flavors.

To roast peppers, place them directly on the flame of a gas stove and turn the heat wide open. Blister the cellulose, or outer skin, until it is blackened past the point of looking like food. This will require a few minutes and several turns with spring-loaded tongs; many people lose their nerve and remove the pepper before it is sufficiently charred. As Lady Macbeth admonishes, screw your courage to the sticking point, and your roasting will not fail!

Once the peppers are blackened all over, remove them to a plastic bag. Tie the bag and toss it into the sink—it will always leak. Wait ten minutes for the steam to loosen the skins, then open the bag and gently peel off the loose skins under running water. Pop the pepper open and discard the seeds and membranes, cautiously or with gloved hands if doing hot varieties.

If it is fall, with winter looming, freeze the peeled peppers in very small bags to revive into soup, cassoulet or sauce when the only fresh peppers at the market are commanding a queen's ransom.

If you do not have a gas stove, use your outdoor grill or the oven broiler with the rack as close to the heat as possible. Slice and seed the peppers, then place them with their skin sides closest to the heat.

Puréed Peasant Vegetable Vinaigrette

Makes about 1 1/2 cups (375 ml)

*T*his collection of vegetable-based dressings is among my favorites. I particularly enjoy them on sturdy, bitter winter greens, grilled fish, grilled or roasted vegetables and pasta and grain salads.

The variations on this theme are endless: garlic, shallots and rosemary; roasted parsnip and sage; caramelized onion and tarragon; roasted carrot, shallots and rosemary. If you are really watching your fat intake, steam any of the suggested vegetables, then purée.

2	onions, peeled and quartered	2
1 head	garlic, paper on	1 head
2 sprigs	fresh rosemary	2 sprigs
1–2 Tbsp.	extra-virgin olive oil	15–30 ml
2–3 Tbsp.	honey	30–45 ml
1 Tbsp.	grainy mustard	15 ml
2–4 Tbsp.	balsamic or red wine vinegar	30–60 ml
2	green onions, minced	2
	water or stock for thinning	
	salt and freshly ground pepper to taste	

Set the oven at 450°F (230°C) and put the onions into a small roasting pan or ovenproof baking dish in a single layer. (Too deep a layer, and they will steam and take much longer.) Add the garlic, intact and in its paper, then add one sprig of rosemary and drizzle the olive oil over all.

Slide the pan into a hot oven, and roast the onions until brown on top and tender inside, about 45 to 60 minutes, depending on the size.

Once they are tender, remove them to a food processor, adding the roasted garlic by squeezing the pulp out of each separate wrapper. Process into a smooth purée, then add the remaining rosemary leaves and all the remaining ingredients. Process to the texture you like—smooth or chunky. Thin to taste with water or stock, adding salt and pepper at the end to balance the flavors.

Variations

These variations all assume that you have roasted, baked or steamed vegetables on hand. The time to make this style of dressing is when you have leftovers, or when you are about to roast vegetables for another purpose. In either case, the substitutions replace one type of cooked vegetable with another type of cooked vegetable.

For **Roasted Tomato and Basil Vinaigrette**, substitute 2 to 3 roasted Roma tomatoes for the onions and 1/4 cup (60 ml) minced fresh basil for the rosemary.

To hasten the process of roasting vegetables, it is possible to cheat constructively. (Whoever said that cheaters never prosper obviously never put dinner on the table every evening!) Add about 1/2" (1 cm) water or stock to the bottom of the roasting pan, add the items to be roasted, cover securely and pop into a hot oven. When the food is three-quarters cooked, remove the lid and turn the heat up to brown the tops and reduce any remaining liquid to a glaze. Then be sure to add that liquid to your sauce or dressing or soup.

For **Roasted Parsnip and Sage Dressing**, substitute 1 medium roasted parsnip for the onions and 1/4 cup (60 ml) minced fresh sage for the rosemary.

For **Roasted Carrot and Dill Dressing**, substitute 1 to 2 roasted carrots for the onions and 2 Tbsp. (30 ml) minced fresh dill for the rosemary. Add 1/2 tsp. (2.5 ml) cracked caraway seed if desired.

For **Roasted Sweet Potato and Tarragon Dressing**, replace the onions with half a roasted yam or sweet potato. Replace the rosemary with 2 Tbsp. (30 ml) minced fresh tarragon.

For **Roasted Beet and Dill Dressing**, use 1 to 2 roasted golden or purple beets with 2 Tbsp. (30 ml) minced fresh dill in place of the onions and rosemary. Roast the beets whole and in their skins, wrapping them in aluminum foil. Slip the skins off like an old jacket when the beets are cooked.

Miso-Gari Vinaigrette

Makes about 2 cups (500 ml)

I love this Asian-inspired dressing with fish and on winter greens (page 129). If your miso supply has suddenly dried up, leave it out or substitute salted dried black beans in very small amounts.

1–2 Tbsp.	white miso	15–30 ml
1/4 cup	soy sauce	60 ml
1/4 cup	melted honey	60 ml
2 Tbsp.	sesame oil	30 ml
2 Tbsp.	minced cilantro	30 ml
3	green onions, finely minced	3
2 Tbsp.	minced pickled ginger (see page 17)	30 ml
1 cup	Japanese rice vinegar	250 ml
1	lemon, juice and zest	1
	salt and hot chili flakes to taste	

Combine all ingredients and refrigerate until needed. Best within 3 days of being made.

Miso is one of those amazing ingredients that can insinuate itself into any number of dishes. It is a high-protein fermented paste made from soy beans that may be flavored with rice or barley. Flavors and colors vary, so the best bet is to buy several varieties and taste them to see which you prefer. Generally, the lighter the color, the lighter the flavor. Miso is found in good Asian supermarkets and in health food stores, and is always stored in the fridge. A spoonful of miso dissolved in hot water makes miso soup, one of the world's most restorative instant soups.

Ponzu Vinaigrette

Makes 1 1/4 cups (310 ml)

*O*ne method of making dressings with big flavor but little oil is to choose highly flavored oil where very little is needed to make an impact; Japanese sesame oil is an example. Ponzu is a traditional dip served with cooked foods in Japan. I have used the basic ingredients to make a satisfying dressing or baste that works equally well on noodles, greens or grilled foods.

1/2 cup	rice vinegar	125 ml
1/2 cup	fresh lemon juice	125 ml
1/4 cup	dark soy	60 ml
	hot chili paste to taste	
1 Tbsp.	minced ginger root	15 ml
2 Tbsp.	minced cilantro	30 ml
2 Tbsp.	minced chives or green onions	30 ml
2 tsp.	sesame oil	10 ml

Whisk together all ingredients.

Among Asian ingredients, there are huge variations in quality and style. Japanese vinegar, for example, is mellow and sweet while Chinese vinegar is similar to our white vinegar, more acidic and harsher on the palate. Having decided on Japanese vinegar, you will have to sample several styles, choosing among sushi vinegar, brown rice vinegar, and so on. Buy several and experiment to decide which you prefer.

For hot chili paste, I choose "Delicious Hot Chili Garlic Sauce," with the red rooster on the label. For sesame oil, I buy Kadoya brand from Japan; once you taste it, you may never buy the unroasted sesame oil in health food stores. This Japanese style is rich and deep, and a little goes a very long way! Be sure to store it and other oils in your fridge to prevent them from going rancid.

Soy sauce is available in two distinct styles: dark and light. This refers to its viscosity, not its salt content (although there are salt-reduced soy sauces on the market). Dark soy does a slow-moving slide back down the inside of the bottle when shaken, leaving a trail behind it, while light soy is less thick. Sample and decide what ones you enjoy. In addition, try mushroom soy, another dark and mysterious variation on the theme.

Citrus Vinaigrette

Makes about 1 cup (250 ml)

When you use as much citrus zest as I like to, the fruit basket is inevitably littered with the stripped remains of oranges, lemons, limes and grapefruit. Once the colored zest is removed, the fruits begin to harden and dry out. The secret is to juice them as soon as you zest them, then refrigerate or freeze the strained juice.

The blended juices make a very appealing salad dressing that works well on tender greens and mesclun, as well as on salads with fruit and/or nut garnishes. It's perfect on Roasted Beets in Citrus (page 145), any grain salad, Darl's Honey Lemon Chicken (page 103), and on Fennel Apple Slaw (page 146).

3/4 cup	citrus juice	185 ml
1 Tbsp.	smooth Dijon mustard	15 ml
2–4 Tbsp.	honey, melted	30–60 ml
3 Tbsp.	olive oil	45 ml
1 Tbsp.	minced chives	15 ml
1 tsp.	minced fresh thyme	5 ml
	salt and hot chili flakes to taste	

Whisk together the citrus juice, mustard and honey. Slowly add the olive oil, whisking, shaking or stirring vigorously to emulsify. Stir in the herbs, and add salt and hot chili flakes. Refrigerate until needed, shaking or stirring well to reblend if it separates.

Variation

For **Kumquat Tahini Vinaigrette**, make Citrus Vinaigrette, adding 2 to 4 kumquats, puréed or minced, and 1 Tbsp. (15 ml) tahini. Blend well. This makes a richer, sharper dressing.

The amount of honey you add to this dressing will be decided by the type of juice you use. Lime juice needs about double the sweetener of orange juice, excepting so-tart blood oranges. If using orange juice, remember that it is more likely to ferment than either lime or lemon juice, so don't make more than you can use in several days. Otherwise, expect to keep this safely in the fridge for up to a week. Leave out the herbs if you make extra to use over the course of several days—the herbs will soften and discolor as they age in the acid.

Berry Vinaigrette

Makes about 1 1/2 cups (375 ml)

This fresh and fruity dressing works well for fruit and vegetable salads, grain salads, poultry and even tuna or swordfish. I have used frozen berries, but this is best in the summer, when fruits and berries are fresh.

2 cups	fresh berries, sliced or whole	500 ml
2–8 Tbsp.	honey (will vary with the fruit used)	30–120 ml
1/4 cup	rice or fruit-infused vinegar	60 ml
2 Tbsp.	minced fresh thyme or lemon thyme	30 ml
1 Tbsp.	puréed ginger root	15 ml
1/2 cup	canola oil	125 ml
1	lemon/lime/orange, zest only	1
	salt and hot chili flakes to taste	

Wash and purée berries. Melt the honey and stir in along with remaining ingredients. Adjust the sweetness with extra vinegar or use citrus juice to ensure the dressing has a little bite to it.

Variations

For **Cherry Ginger Vinaigrette**, substitute pitted fresh tart cherries, like Queen Anne or Montmorency, for the berries.

For **Peach, Plum or Apricot Vinaigrette**, substitute peeled and pitted ripe fresh peaches, plums or apricots for the berries.

For **Cranberry Vinaigrette**, use 1/2 cup (125 ml) raw or cooked cranberries in place of the berries. Because cranberries are high in pectin, this vinaigrette will be thicker and may require thinning with orange or lime juice.

For **Dried Fruit Vinaigrette**, rehydrate and chop or purée dried cherries, dried cranberries or dried apricots, and use in place of the berries.

White Zinfandel Vinaigrette

Makes about 1 1/2 cups (375 ml)

Rather than launch into another ode to pink food, I'll merely suggest that you serve this surprising dressing with chicken salad, pan-steamed salmon, tender greens and crunchy apple or nut salads.

1 bottle	white Zinfandel	1 bottle
1/4–1/2 cup	honey	60–125 ml
1/4 cup	lime juice and zest	60 ml
2 Tbsp.	Dijon mustard	30 ml
	salt and hot chili flakes to taste	
1/2 cup	canola oil	125 ml
2 Tbsp.	minced fresh thyme	30 ml

In a nonreactive pot, reduce the wine to about 1/2 cup (125 ml). After it is reduced, transfer the wine to a bowl and mix it with the honey, lime juice and zest, mustard and the salt and chili flakes. Whisk in the oil slowly, mixing continually to form an emulsification. Stir in the fresh thyme.

Variation
For **Ginger Zin Vin**, add 2 Tbsp. (30 ml) puréed ginger root or finely slivered pickled ginger.

This pink vinaigrette evolved out of a class I co-taught on food and wine pairings. One of the classic struggles for wine-drinkers is the clash between wine and salad dressings; the acids go head-to-head, and inevitably there is no clear winner, only wine that appears flabby and salad that doesn't clear the palate. My attempts to pacify things led me around the garden several times before I hit on this solution. The honey is the key: its sugar content tempers the acid of the dressing, allowing the accompanying wine to retain its true character. Using a white Zinfandel rather than the normally red version of this quintessential American grape is the best bet; red wine reduced by three-quarters of its volume would be so tannic and high-acid that a cook could spend hours of time rebalancing it.

Caramelized Apple Vinaigrette

Makes about 2 1/4 cups (560 ml)

I prefer to use apples with pink or red on their skins because they color the dressing. The variety will affect the tartness of the dressing, so please yourself, but do choose organically raised apples if possible. I like Gala, Jonagold, Northern Spy and Gravenstein. This is good on soba noodles, bitter or Asian greens, and Appley-Dappley Salad (page 147). Made on the sharp side, it is great with pork and grilled chicken.

2	organic apples	2
2 Tbsp.	puréed ginger root	30 ml
2 Tbsp.	grainy Dijon mustard	30 ml
1/2 cup	honey, melted	125 ml
1/2 cup	apple cider vinegar	125 ml
1/4 cup	fresh herbs, your choice of thyme, basil, marjoram, oregano, parsley, tarragon	60 ml
1/4 cup	canola oil salt and hot chili flakes to taste	60 ml

Wash the apples well but do not peel them. Slice each into about 8 pieces, removing the core. Cook the apple slices in a nonstick pan without any oil until they are well colored. Slice, chop or purée them in a food processor, then add the remaining ingredients to form an emulsified vinaigrette.

Rhubarb Lime Vinaigrette

Makes about 1 cup (250 ml)

More pink food! This sweet-tart dressing is lovely, especially on grilled salmon with tender spring greens and asparagus. It arose from a need to use up a prolific producer. You can only eat so much stewed rhubarb for breakfast, and then it's time to find other ways to use up the stuff.

1/2 cup	rhubarb	125 ml
1/4 cup	water	60 ml
1 tsp.	puréed ginger root	5 ml
2 Tbsp.	honey	30 ml
1	lime, juice and zest	1
1/2 cup	canola oil	125 ml
1 Tbsp.	minced chives	15 ml
1 Tbsp.	minced fresh thyme salt and hot chili flakes to taste	15 ml

Chop the rhubarb into 1" (2.5-cm) lengths and simmer with the water in a small covered pot until the rhubarb is tender. Stir in the ginger and honey while the fruit is still warm to allow the honey to melt. Add the remaining ingredients and whisk together, then taste. If necessary, add more honey or lime juice, depending on the tartness of the rhubarb.

Pear and Chive Vinaigrette

Makes about 1 cup (250 ml)

This vinaigrette is the Jekyll and Hyde of the salad world; it can be mild and delicate, or it can be pungent with wasabi, the brash horseradish paste so dear to sushi fans. The strength of the dressing will dictate where it is used. In its most pungent form, serve with grilled swordfish or tuna. In its kinder, gentler incarnation, serve with tender greens, grilled white fish, asparagus or rice salads.

1	pear, peeled and sliced	1
1/4 cup	canola oil	60 ml
1 Tbsp.	puréed ginger root	15 ml
2 Tbsp.	honey	30 ml
1–6 tsp.	wasabi	5–30 ml
1/3 cup	sherry vinegar or Japanese rice vinegar	80 ml
2 Tbsp.	minced chives	30 ml
	salt and hot chili flakes to taste	

In a nonstick pan, cook the pear slices over high heat in a small amount of the canola oil. Allow the slices to brown, turning as needed. Put through a food mill or purée in a food processor. Add remaining ingredients and whisk well.

Wasabi, or Japanese horseradish, comes in a powdered green form or a paste in groceries that carry Japanese goods. I prefer the powder; its delicate green tint is a wonderfully ironic counterpoint to its fierce character. Reconstitute by adding water to the powder and stirring until smooth. Make and use small amounts: this is a culinary powderkeg! In a pinch, substitute regular horseradish.

Prairie Sage Vinaigrette

Makes about 1 1/4 cups (310 ml)

This is a straightforward herb-infused vinaigrette. To vary it, change the herbs you add, use a different type of mustard, or change the type and flavor of the acid component.

3 Tbsp.	grainy mustard	45 ml
1/4 cup	honey	60 ml
1/2 cup	sage-infused vinegar (see opposite page)	125 ml
4 Tbsp.	minced fresh sage	60 ml
2 Tbsp.	minced chives or green onions	30 ml
1/2 cup	canola oil	125 ml
	salt and hot chili flakes to taste	

Combine all ingredients except for the oil. Mix well, then slowly whisk in the oil to form an emulsification.

Maple Thyme Vinaigrette

Makes 1 1/2 cups (375 ml)

*T*his vinaigrette resulted
from an experiment with
lemon and maple in a dessert;
my palate immediately made a
lateral leap to a savory dish.
The precise amounts of acid to
syrup may vary, but remember
to keep the dressing on the
tart side. Too sweet or too oily,
and the effect is lost. This is
especially fine in salads with
fruit elements.

Maple syrup is less expensive
when bought in bulk from a
drum at a health food store. The
maple syrup available this way
is often a darker grade, but I
find it more intensely flavored
as well.

1/3 cup	maple syrup, preferably dark	80 ml
1/3 cup	thyme-infused white wine vinegar	80 ml
2 tsp.	Dijon mustard	10 ml
1	lemon, juice and zest	1
1/2 cup	canola oil	125 ml
1/2 cup	minced fresh lemon thyme or thyme	125 ml
	salt and freshly ground pepper to taste	

Whisk together all the ingredients. Taste and balance
the flavors. Set aside until needed.

Herb-infused vinegars are a quick, easy way to add flavor to food.
Start with good, flavorful vinegar, and pick or buy fresh herbs at
the height of the season when they are cheap and plentiful. Stuff
clean herbs and spices into jars, cover them with vinegar and
steep for a month before using. Softer herbs like basil and sage
need to be strained out and discarded after the steeping time has
elapsed. Add fresh sprigs to gift bottles to identify their flavors.

Amazing things happen when you add the blossoms of edible
flowers to herb-infused vinegars. I made a beautiful orange thyme
vinegar one summer with handfuls of orange calendula blossoms
and thyme sprigs in white wine vinegar. Chive blossoms yield a
pungent purple vinegar, and bachelor buttons make a light violet
vinegar. Check a good gardening book for listings of edible flowers.
Many of them are perennials, and easily grown. Some colors
imparted by edible flowers will fade in direct light; setting out
bottles of flower-tinted vinegar to glow on a window ledge may
result in fading.

Hazelnut Vinaigrette

Makes about 1 1/4 cups (310 ml)

Peanut butter was a staple of my childhood, and now I loathe the smell of it. It is one of those things I had too much of, but because I enjoy nuts I decided to make nut butters and nut dressings. The moral of the story is to use other nuts if you feel as strongly about hazelnuts as I do about peanuts.

1/4 cup	hazelnuts, toasted, skinned and chopped	60 ml
1 Tbsp.	puréed ginger root	15 ml
2 Tbsp.	minced lemon thyme	30 ml
1 Tbsp.	smooth Dijon mustard	15 ml
1	lime, juice and zest	1
4 Tbsp.	honey	60 ml
1/4 cup	sherry vinegar	60 ml
1/3 cup	canola oil	80 ml
	salt and hot chili flakes to taste	

Whisk together all ingredients. Store in the refrigerator until needed. If you plan on keeping this dressing more than one day, omit the chopped nuts and add them just before you are going to use the dressing to keep them from going soft.

Variation

For **Pistachio Mint Vinaigrette**, omit the hazelnuts and thyme, replacing them with equal amounts of undyed pistachios and fresh mint.

Hazelnuts are one of the finest nuts in the world for cooking and eating but their skins defeat many people. To convince hazelnuts to shed their skins, spread them in a single layer on a baking sheet and pop into a medium-hot oven, about 375°F (190°C). Check them every 5 to 7 minutes, and when the skins slip off easily when rubbed between your fingers, it's time to remove them from the oven. Transfer the hot nuts to a kitchen towel and roll them up for 5 minutes. The steam generated will loosen any stubborn skins. Roll the nuts in the towel to remove the skins, popping any recalcitrant nuts that won't shed back into the oven for a second toasting.

Quark Tarragon Dressing

Makes 3 cups (750 ml)

Quark is a European fresh cheese, very tart and delightful, that has found a new home with North American cheesemakers. It is lean and soft, and purées willingly in this mild dressing. It is available in a low-fat version as well, which may be more likely to curdle, so use less lemon juice, and add it slowly, stirring. If the dressing does curdle, toss it into a blender and whirl it around for a few seconds. This is particularly good on grilled or roasted potatoes and vegetables.

2 cups	quark	500 ml
1/4 cup	minced fresh tarragon	60 ml
2	shallots, minced	2
4 cloves	garlic, puréed	4 cloves
2 Tbsp.	minced chives	30 ml
1/4 tsp.	fennel seeds, cracked	1.2 ml
1	lemon, juice and zest	1
1/4 cup	canola oil	60 ml
1/4 cup	tarragon-infused vinegar (see page 47)	60 ml
	salt and hot chili flakes to taste	

Combine all ingredients and whisk well, adding cool water or buttermilk to thin if desired.

Tarragon, the "little dragon" so beloved of French cuisine, is a cousin of the daisy. The mild licorice flavor of tarragon, and its tough, never-say-die presence in the garden make it a favorite of gardening cooks. Its generous production makes it easy to put away copious amounts of infused vinegar before frost nips it, and it happily marries with most vegetables for harmonious summer salads.

Savory Yoghurt Cheese

Makes about 1 1/2 cups (375 ml)

This has the unctuous, rich feel of something much more sinful. It's almost a letdown when I tell people that it's good old healthy yoghurt. As a savory topping, use on fritters, corncakes, new potatoes and other vegetables, and as a base for Chicken in Yoghurt (see page 106).

3 cups	yoghurt	750 ml
1	lemon, zest only	1
2 Tbsp.	minced chives	30 ml
	salt and pepper to taste	

Drain the yoghurt through a fine mesh sieve or a double layer of damp cheesecloth for about 1 hour. (Use the discarded whey for baking some great bread.) Stir in the remaining ingredients and serve.

Variation

For **Sweet Yoghurt Cheese**, add honey to taste to the drained and unseasoned yoghurt, as well as 1/2 tsp. (2.5 ml) each of freshly grated nutmeg, ground star anise and cinnamon. Use orange zest instead of lemon if you prefer. This sweet dressing makes a wonderful topping for fresh fruit, pancakes, waffles, cereal or any dessert where you might be tempted to spoon on ice cream or whipped cream.

Choose a yoghurt that is not stabilized with gelatin for this dressing. If gelatin is listed in the contents, or if a puddle of whey does not collect on the surface, odds are that the yoghurt has stabilizers in it to hold everything solid. If, after 40 minutes sitting in a sieve or colander, your yoghurt is still a big puddle with nothing drained out, it has lots of gelatin in it. Try a different brand next time, but this time just stir everything together for a looser texture than a drained yoghurt would yield.

Blue Cheese Dressing

Makes about 2 cups (500 ml)

The fat content of this dressing derives from the blue cheese. I tend to choose a crumbly variety like Stilton, Danish, American Maytag or Canadian Ermite rather than a double-cream style like Cambozola. Don't be shy with the hot chili; this dressing will take a lot of heat! I like to serve it with any grilled vegetables, but especially eggplant and peppers. Gently warmed, it's dynamite with roasted or grilled potatoes.

2–4 oz.	blue cheese, crumbled	60–115 ml
2–3	anchovies, chopped, oil discarded	2–3
2 Tbsp.	capers	30 ml
1/4 cup	Kalamata olives, pitted and chopped	60 ml
4 cloves	garlic, puréed	4 cloves
2	green onions, minced	2
3 Tbsp.	minced fresh thyme	45 ml
2–4 Tbsp.	red wine vinegar	30–60 ml
1 cup	sour cream, yoghurt or buttermilk	250 ml
	hot chili flakes to taste	

Combine all ingredients, whisking by hand to prevent the olives turning the dressing a grim shade of purple. Cover and allow to mellow in the fridge for several hours.

Buttermilk Dressing

Makes 2 cups (500 ml)

This mild, creamy dressing can double as a dip or even treble as a topping for baked or mashed potatoes. A cooking contest featuring buttermilk interested me in using buttermilk in savories as well as in sweet baking; reading the recipes submitted by the contestants was like a brief spin around the globe with a side jaunt to outer space. Most imaginative. And then I try to sell you on a simple little salad dressing!

1 cup	yoghurt, drained, or low-fat sour cream	250 ml
1 cup	buttermilk	250 ml
1	lemon, juice and zest	1
1/2 cup	mixed fresh herbs, your choice of thyme, oregano, basil, parsley, rosemary, tarragon	125 ml
3 cloves	garlic, minced	3 cloves
	salt and hot chili flakes to taste	

Choose a yoghurt without gelatin and drain it through a fine mesh sieve or damp cheesecloth for at least 30 minutes. Discard the liquid whey (or save for bread baking), then stir together all the ingredients. This dressing will become increasingly garlicky as the days go by. To minimize the garlic, you may wish to use roasted garlic (see page 69) or none at all. This is my favorite dressing for new potatoes, either steamed or grilled.

Greenhouse Dip

Makes about 5 cups (1.25 litres)

This is my take on that classic of the '50s: Green Goddess Dressing (which forever brings to mind Jayne Mansfield with herbs, vines and leaves entwined in her hair and cascading down her shoulders like Demeter). It's hard to make this addictive dressing in small amounts; I make a large quantity and share it with my friends, who are always thrilled to help me out. It is great with asparagus, carrots, peppers, salmon, rice, grilled flank steak, earthy greens, and anything else you want to experiment with.

It is not especially low in fat, but generally dips are eaten in small quantities. If you prefer, replace the mayo with yoghurt, but the resulting dressing will be a little edgier.

2 bunches	green onions, green part only	2 bunches
1 bunch	cilantro, stems discarded	1 bunch
1 bunch	parsley, stems discarded	1 bunch
6 cloves	garlic	6 cloves
2 Tbsp.	puréed ginger root	30 ml
2 cups	mayonnaise	500 ml
2 cups	sour cream	500 ml
1 Tbsp.	cumin	15 ml
1 Tbsp.	coriander	15 ml
1 Tbsp.	Worcestershire sauce	15 ml
2 Tbsp.	lemon juice	30 ml
2 Tbsp.	light soy sauce	30 ml
1–2 tsp.	hot chili paste	5–10 ml
1 tsp.	sesame oil	5 ml

Cut the green onions into 2" (5-cm) lengths, reserving the white part for use in another dish. In a food processor, finely purée the onions, cilantro, parsley, garlic and ginger. Add the remaining ingredients and process until well blended. Taste and balance with additional lemon juice, soy sauce or hot chili paste as your palate dictates.

Soups and Stocks

Soup is one of the great comfort foods. A bowl of good soup has the power to thaw frost-bitten fingers, mend broken hearts, soothe hurt feelings, restore damaged egos, and strengthen waning bodies. It isn't a food to be taken lightly.

There are a few stringent rules to be observed when making a pot of soup. The first is to include only ingredients you like. This is no place to be burying those overcooked or burnt remnants of a less-successful meal. Toss those ruins out, not into the stockpot or the soup pot. Next, it generally becomes confusing to the palate if every pot of soup includes the entire contents of your refrigerator. Be selective about the number of ingredients you include. The next rule is to make more than you need for one meal. Soup is almost always better for standing a day in the fridge, and very few of us are so organized that we consciously cook one or two days in advance. So make some for tonight, some for tomorrow and some for the freezer.

Not every pot of soup needs stock as its underpinning. For those that do, have frozen tubs of stock on hand, but many soups are fine with water as a liquid, or need only a spoonful of miso added at the last to lift the flavor. Soups with legumes as their primary ingredient are best made with water—the stock flavor usually disappears behind the flavor of lentils, split peas or beans. Beware of the salt content in some commercial broths; hidden salt can change the balance of any dish.

Stocks

The primary role of stock is as a supporting player in the soup pot. Stock can also be used in sauces, gratins and gravies, but soup is usually in my thoughts when I put the stockpot on the stove.

There are many sources for flavorful stocks. Poultry is the most common and easily the most versatile, sliding into fish soups without missing a beat, and holding its own in meat or vegetable-based soups as well. Veal, beef, lamb and other meats all make fine, rich stocks, although it takes a serious amount of rebalancing to use any of them in dishes that carry other strong or conflicting flavors. Fish stock, or fumet, is best used exclusively for fish-based dishes. Vegetable-based stocks are as neutral as chicken stock, and contribute a lighter flavor and texture, although they cannot be reduced and used as thickening like meat-based stocks.

Poultry and Meat Stock

- Start with clean, sound bones with no trace of "off" odor. The bones can be fresh or frozen.
- Wash fresh bones well with cold water. Drain well and place in a heavy-bottomed stockpot. Frozen bones can be placed directly into the pot without previous thawing.
- Cover bones with cold water. This leaches out blood, plasma and other impurities, which can be skimmed off the top surface, resulting in a clear stock. Hot water seals the bones' outer surface, resulting in a cloudy stock.
- Bring to a boil and skim off any scum and fat that accumulates on the surface. Skim the stock regularly during the cooking process.
- Reduce the heat to a simmer. Boiling emulsifies any remaining fat, resulting in a greasy and/or cloudy stock.
- Add coarsely chopped vegetables (called mirepoix in classical French cooking, and specifically limited to onion, celery, carrot, leek and garlic cloves). The cut size is dictated by the length of time the stock will be cooking. Generally, I split the garlic head, toss the carrots and celery stalks in whole, and chop the onions in halves or quarters.

- Do not add any cabbage or pepper family vegetables, which make a strongly flavored, sulfurous stock. Other acceptable additions include tomato trimmings, mushroom trimmings and stems, and herbs, both leaves and stalks. You can add parsley, thyme, bay, basil, oregano, rosemary and whole peppercorns (a collection called bouquet garni) after the stock has been boiled and skimmed.
- While stockmaking should be a frugal endeavor, it is not a repository for vegetable scraps that are better suited to the compost bucket. It is also not vegetable soup. For every 3 pounds (1.5 kg) of bones, use 1 pound (.5 kg) of vegetables. (You can store vegetable trimmings and herb stalks in the freezer for a truly frugal stock, as long as the vegetables are sound and clean.)

Most cooks tie their bouquet garni in a twist of cheesecloth before tossing it into the stockpot, with or without a string attached for easy recovery. I have long since stopped doing this, and I add my herbs and spices loose. I never mind the odd fleck of herbs that escape the strainer, and I believe that the flavors have a better chance to permeate the entire pot if loose.

Adding too many vegetables to the stockpot can result in a sweet stock that is difficult to rebalance. In particular, onions, carrots and celery carry large amounts of sugar. The solution is to use some but not a lot of these vegetables.

- Simmer for 4 hours if using chicken bones. Meat-based stocks require 6 to 12 hours of simmering, or even overnight, depending on the size of the bones. It's a good idea to have your butcher cut the bones into 2" (5-cm) pieces so you can make the stock in one day. Simmer it uncovered.
- No salt: if added now it will unbalance the finished stock should you choose to reduce it to a thicker, more concentrated state.
- Replenish the water level if the bones become exposed, but remember the idea is to build something strongly flavored; too much water will dilute the end result. I usually let the water diminish just to the top of the bones and vegetables to ensure the stock will have enough body and flavor.
- Strain the stock promptly, and cool to room temperature before refrigerating. To minimize splashing and the carcasses tumbling into your sieve, slide your largest wooden spoon into the stockpot and position it to hold the majority of the bones in place against the side of the pot. Have your receptacle in the sink or even on the floor for a large pot to lessen the effort of lifting and controlling a large potful of hot liquid. The stock would be easier to handle if you let it cool in the pot, but a small amount might reabsorb into the bones and it could become cloudy.
- When cool, refrigerate the stock uncovered. When the stock is cold,

remove any fat that has congealed on top. Then cover the stock and store in the refrigerator for up to 5 days. Beyond that, it is safest to freeze the unused stock in useful sizes until it is needed. I find 2-cup (500-ml) and 4-cup (1-litre) sizes the most useful for freezing stock.

Brown Stock

To get a rich brown stock instead of an amber or golden one, place clean bones in a roasting pan and roast at 450°F (230°C) until very brown, about 1 1/2 hours. You can use chicken or other poultry, veal, lamb or beef bones. Add the vegetables halfway through so they brown as well. (For additional color and depth of flavor, leave the peels on the

---

Any meat- or fish-based stock may be reduced after straining to achieve a more concentrated flavor and heavier, more viscous texture. Reducing the volume by up to half guarantees a strong, gelatinous, flavorful liquid, but the trade-off is lessened volume. For most soups, I don't reduce the stock, but for sauces and other more concentrated dishes, I do. Reduction to the consistency of a glaze results in *glace de viand*, or meat glaze. This is a flavor agent, used to enhance sauces rather than as the liquid basis and, as such, is used in very discreet amounts, added by the spoonful rather than by the cupful. If you reduce your stock to achieve this, remember to transfer the liquid into successively smaller pots to avoid burning your end result. Freeze in an ice cube tray, then tumble the little bricks into a plastic bag or tub after they are solidly frozen. Expect a total yield of less than a cupful of meat glaze from a pot that began as 8 quarts (8 litres), and treat it like gold.

onions, or brown onion halves in a sauté pan without any oil until deeply brown, nearly black.) Remove the bones to a stockpot, discard any fat from the roasting pan, then deglaze the roasting pan with water or white wine, scraping up the brown bits. Pour the deglazing liquid, along with 2 Tbsp. (30 ml) tomato paste, into the stockpot. Carry on as above.

Fish Fumet

This is a different kettle of fish from any other stock because fish and their bones cook so quickly.

- Use clean, sound, fresh bones without a whiff of ammonia or age. Match the type of bones to the ultimate use for the stock. (Using strong salmon stock for a delicate sole dish won't work.)
- Rinse fresh bones well under cold running water. Discard the gills. Chop or break large pieces into a size that will fit your stockpot.
- Put the bones into a stockpot and cover with cold water. Bring to a boil and skim off all scum.
- Add mirepoix (coarsely chopped vegetables) and bouquet garni and simmer 45 minutes, smashing the bones with a wooden spoon at intervals to extract maximum flavor.

Fish bones are so perishable that it's better to make your fish stock immediately, and freeze the finished stock, rather than trying to freeze the bones to use later.

- Strain through cheesecloth, discarding solids and keeping the liquids. Cool, then chill. Use within 5 days or freeze.

Vegetable Stock

Without fish or meat bones to contribute their flavor and gelatin, vegetable stocks tend to be lighter in both texture and flavor. Use copious amounts of vegetables in this stock to ensure that light doesn't translate into wishy-washy.

Start with a mirepoix (coarsely chopped vegetables including onions, leeks, celery and carrots), add a bouquet garni, and then potato peels or potatoes cut into 1" (2.5-cm) cubes. Add cold water to cover and any flavor agents you like, remembering not to muddy the pot with too much variety. Use ginger root slices and lemon grass stalks for a stock with Asian undertones, or several dried mushrooms for a pungent mushroom stock. Use root vegetables, like parsnips, beets or carrots, for a sweet, root-based stock, or one or two smoked dried chilies for an aromatic, slightly smoky vegetable stock. For a gently salty stock with a slight sea tang, add several pieces of kombu, sugar kelp or other mild seaweed.

Simmer 45 minutes or until all the ingredients are tender but not falling apart. Strain.

A good practice is to save the cooking water from beans and potatoes to use in soups.

Pumpkin, Pear and Parsnip Soup with Ginger

Serves 6 to 8

As a child, I thought pumpkins existed in two forms: a bulbous shape stuffed with a stubby candle and grinning garishly, and the smooth-textured pie on our Thanksgiving table. Not until I became a grownup did I realize that pumpkin has more to offer. You can purée this soup into a smooth and velvety texture, or serve it in the chunky state. Make it in advance and give it a day or several to mature.

Partner this soup with Alsatian and German wines. Choose from Gewurztraminer, Pinot Gris or Riesling.

2 tsp.	unsalted butter	10 ml
1	leek, sliced	1
4	medium carrots, sliced	4
4	medium parsnips, sliced	4
4 Tbsp.	minced ginger root	60 ml
1	ripe pear, peeled and sliced	1
1 tsp.	dried oregano	5 ml
1/2 cup	dry white wine	125 ml
1 14-oz. tin	pumpkin purée	1 398-ml tin
6 cups	chicken stock	1.5 litres
2	oranges, juice only	2
1 tsp.	lemon juice	5 ml
4 Tbsp.	honey	60 ml
	a dash of hot chili paste	
4 tsp.	salt, or to taste	20 ml
1 Tbsp.	whipping cream	15 ml
	orange zest and fresh oregano as garnish	

Melt the butter in a heavy-bottomed stockpot. Add the sliced vegetables, ginger and pear, and cook until tender. Do not allow to color. Add the oregano, wine and pumpkin and stir well. Stir in the chicken stock and simmer until all is tender. (If you desire a puréed soup, purée the ingredients now.) Add the remaining ingredients and cool. Cover and refrigerate until needed. Reheat gently, stirring often. Do not boil. Garnish with fresh orange zest and fresh oregano, or drizzle a teaspoon of heavy cream over each serving.

Parsnips are among the great unwashed in the vegetable kingdom, taking their lowly place with other peasant staples, such as turnips and carrots. They can develop a woody core and soft, thick skin as they age. Despite it all, parsnips are a delicious vegetable that roasts and caramelizes well because of their high sugar content. They contribute a lovely undertone in soups.

Sweet Potato and Spinach Soup

Serves 4

This works well with winter squash instead of sweet potato, although the soup may be looser in texture when made with squash. Use other sources of heat if you have no jalapeños on hand, but don't omit the hot stuff; it contrasts well with the soup's smooth texture and interesting, slightly sweet garnishes.

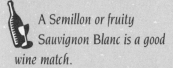 *A Semillon or fruity Sauvignon Blanc is a good wine match.*

1 lb.	sweet potatoes or yams	450 g
1 tsp.	canola oil	5 ml
1	jalapeño pepper, seeded and minced	1
4 cloves	garlic, minced	4 cloves
1 Tbsp.	minced ginger root	15 ml
1	bay leaf	1
1 tsp.	ground coriander	5 ml
1	onion, finely sliced	1
2 cups	chicken stock	500 ml
1 bunch	spinach leaves	1 bunch
1	lime, zest and juice	1
	salt and hot chili flakes to taste	

GARNISHES:
toasted cashews
fresh minced cilantro
Savory Yoghurt Cheese (page 50)
Sambal Oelek (page 19)

Peel and finely dice the sweet potatoes or yams, then immerse them in a bowl of cold water to prevent discoloration while the rest of the soup is prepared.

Heat the oil in a heavy-bottomed soup pot, and add the jalapeño, garlic, ginger, bay leaf, coriander and onion. Cook until it becomes hot and fragrant, add a small amount of water to prevent browning, and continue cooking until the onion is tender, about 5 minutes.

Drain the yams or sweet potatoes, then add them and the stock to the pot. Bring to a boil, reduce to a simmer, cover and cook until completely tender.

Meanwhile, tear off the stalks of the spinach by holding the leaves in one hand and twisting the stalks off with the other hand. Wash the spinach leaves thoroughly, then roughly chop. Set aside until the soup is finished.

When the vegetables are tender, purée the soup. Reheat the purée, add the lime zest and adjust the flavors with salt, hot chili flakes and lime juice.

Thin with additional hot stock if you like a thinner soup. Stir in the spinach and allow to wilt. Serve immediately, garnishing with Savory Yoghurt Cheese, Sambal Oelek, toasted cashews and fresh cilantro.

Variation
For a different texture and color, purée the soup after you add the spinach.

Puréeing can be as simple as smashing all ingredients with a potato masher right there in the pot. This yields a rustic, chunky texture that has its own charm. If you like a more velvety finish, invest in a good food mill, a hand-held wand, a blender or a food processor. Each results in different textures and effects on your pocketbook.

Techniques vary for each. With the wand, stick it into the pot below the surface of the soup, turn it on and make like Cinderella's fairy godmother. Wave it around! Not too vigorously, though, and be sure to keep the wand immersed to avoid splashing. When using a food mill or food processor, strain out all the solids and purée them first, then stir in the remaining liquid for the smoothest texture. With a blender, be sure to have both solids and liquids in the jar at the same time. Make sure the lid is on to avoid painting the ceiling a lovely shade of orange, and pulse off and on until the lumps are gone. Then blur everything together with several longer bursts of speed.

Sweet Potato and Lentil Soup

Serves 6

1	leek, sliced	1
1	carrot, sliced	1
2	celery stalks, sliced	2
1	onion, sliced	1
6 cloves	garlic, minced	6 cloves
2 Tbsp.	puréed ginger root	30 ml
1 Tbsp.	canola oil	15 ml
1 Tbsp.	ground cumin	15 ml
1 Tbsp.	ground coriander	15 ml
1 Tbsp.	garam masala	15 ml
1 tsp.	fenugreek	5 ml
1 tsp.	turmeric	5 ml
1/4 tsp.	cayenne	1.2 ml
1 tsp.	mustard seed	5 ml
1 Tbsp.	curry powder	15 ml
1 Tbsp.	Hungarian paprika	15 ml
1	sweet potato or yam, finely diced	1
1 cup	lentils	250 ml
4 cups	water or stock	1 litre
1	apple, diced	1
1/4 cup	raisins	60 ml
1/4 cup	honey	60 ml
1	lemon, juice and zest	1
	salt and hot chili flakes to taste	

GARNISHES:
minced green onions
toasted coconut
yoghurt
cilantro

Sauté the vegetables, garlic and ginger in the oil until tender. Add the spices, stirring constantly, and cook until they release their fragrance. Add the potato or yam, lentils, water or stock, apple and raisins. Simmer, stirring frequently, until tender. Adjust the flavors with honey, lemon, salt and hot chili flakes. Garnish with green onions, coconut, yoghurt and cilantro.

Curry blends and garam masala are herb and spice mixes of varying flavors and degrees of heat. Both can be bought commercially, but you get cleaner, truer tastes if you mix your own. Curry powder, mostly used in dishes originating in southern India, can include coriander, cumin, mustard and fenugreek seeds, as well as hot chilies, whole peppercorns and turmeric. Increase or decrease the heat by adjusting the amount of chilies. Cinnamon and cloves can be added for a Moghul style. Garam masala, used as seasoning for the foods of northern India, varies with the region, but its components can include cumin, coriander, hot chilies, cardamom, cinnamon, cloves, peppercorns, bay, mace, fennel, thyme and nutmeg.

Red Bell Pepper Vichyssoise

Serves 6 to 8

Autumn is the time to make this soup, when peppers of all sizes, shapes and colors are tumbling off the tables at farmers' markets across the country. This soup has a decidedly sweet finish to it, so if you wish to make it smokier or hotter, add a couple of dried smoked chilies, such as moritas or anchos. And, naturally, you can use orange or yellow peppers if you get a good deal on them.

Choose a crisp Sauvignon Blanc from Chile or California.

3 lbs.	red bell peppers	1.3 kg
1/2 lb.	potatoes, diced	225 g
1	onion, diced	1
6 cloves	garlic, minced	6 cloves
1 Tbsp.	unsalted butter	15 ml
3 sprigs	fresh rosemary	3 sprigs
4 cups	chicken stock	1 litre
1/4 cup	whipping cream	60 ml
1 Tbsp.	honey	15 ml
1	lemon, zest and juice	1
	salt and hot chili flakes to taste	

Roast and peel the peppers (see page 37). Dice the potatoes and set aside, covered with cold water to prevent discoloration. Sauté the onion and garlic until tender in the butter. Add the rosemary, potatoes, stock and roasted, peeled peppers. Simmer until tender, then purée if desired. Finish the soup with the cream, then adjust the balance with the honey, lemon, salt and hot chili flakes. Serve hot or cold.

Squash Soup with Saffron and Leeks

Serves 6

Squash season arrives each fall in splendid and colorful diversity, and this soup makes the most of their sweet, nutty flavor. I prefer winter squashes like butternut, hubbard, turban, kuri or kabocha because their flavor is more intense, but for a light, delicate, late summer soup with a looser texture, try zucchini, young crooknecks or other soft-skinned summer varieties.

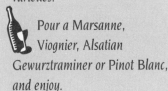

Pour a Marsanne, Viognier, Alsatian Gewurztraminer or Pinot Blanc, and enjoy.

2	leeks, cleaned and finely sliced	2
4 cloves	garlic, minced	4 cloves
1 Tbsp.	minced ginger root	15 ml
2 tsp.	canola oil	10 ml
1/2 cup	white wine	125 ml
pinch	Spanish saffron	pinch
1 lb.	squash, peeled and diced	450 g
4 cups	cold water or vegetable stock	1 litre
2 Tbsp.	minced fresh thyme	30 ml
	salt and hot chili flakes to taste	
1	lemon, juice and zest	1
	squash seeds roasted in soy, honey and cayenne for garnish	

In a heavy-bottomed pot, sauté the leeks, garlic, and ginger in the oil, adding small amounts of water to prevent burning and sticking. When the vegetables are tender, add the wine and saffron. Bring to a boil, then add the squash and water or stock. Return to a boil, cover and reduce heat. Cook until tender, 30 to 45 minutes. Purée if desired, thinning with additional water if needed. Add the thyme and balance the flavors with the salt, hot chili flakes and lemon. Top with toasted squash seeds.

To roast squash or pumpkin seeds, clean the seeds, discarding the strands and any pulp that clings to them. Mix a little cayenne with a tablespoon (15 ml) each of soy and melted honey, and coat the seeds. Spread them out on a pie plate or small cake pan and roast in a hot oven until the seeds are crusty and nicely toasted.

Red Onion Soup

Serves 8 generously

*M*y childhood memories of onion soup include TV trays and the eerie music of Doctor Who to counterpoint the thick, gooey layer of melted cheese on top of our weekly soup. This one is not quite that taste-memory, nor is it the classic version of Les Halles market in the heart of Paris, but it will warm you to your toes. If you can't find good red onions, use sweet onions, like Walla Walla, Maui, Vidalia or even Spanish.

Try a young, fruity Zinfandel or choose a Loire Cabernet Franc or Sauvignon Blanc.

3 lbs.	red onions, thinly sliced	1.3 kg
1 head	garlic, minced	1 head
2 Tbsp.	unsalted butter	30 ml
3–4 sprigs	fresh thyme	3–4 sprigs
1/4 cup	Demerara sugar	60 ml
1/4 cup	red wine vinegar	60 ml
6 cups	chicken, beef or vegetable stock	1.5 litres
1/4 cup	red wine, port or Madeira (optional)	60 ml
	salt and hot chili flakes to taste	
1/2 cup	soft chèvre	125 ml
8 slices	baguette	8 slices

Slowly cook the onions and garlic with the butter, thyme, sugar and vinegar until absolutely meltingly tender, about 45 minutes. Add small amounts of water intermittently to prevent the onions from sticking and burning. Add the stock and the alcohol. Heat to a simmer and adjust the flavors with the salt and hot chili flakes.

Spread the cheese on the baguette slices and slide under the broiler until bubbly and beginning to color. Float one slice on each bowl of soup.

Chèvre, that hugely variable cheese of goat's milk, can range in fat content as well as in texture and intensity of flavor. Poke around the local farmers' market to find a local producer, then experiment with as many varieties as you can.

Leek and Potato Soup

Serves 4 to 6

*K*nown as Potage Bonne Femme, this soup of the good wife is a simple dish that could simmer as a woman labored through the day. Truth to tell, it doesn't need all day to cook; 35 minutes is ample time. This soup is the hands-down favorite in our house. Although it is easy to substitute other vegetables for the leeks, my growing sons love leeks above all others.

This soup does well with a crisp, dry Chenin Blanc, a white Bordeaux, or a Sauvignon Blanc.

1 tsp.	butter or oil	5 ml
1	large onion, sliced	1
1	leek, white part mostly, sliced and washed	1
2 cloves	garlic	2 cloves
3	medium potatoes, sliced	3
4 cups	chicken stock	1 litre
1 Tbsp.	whipping cream	15 ml
1/2 tsp.	freshly grated nutmeg	2.5 ml
	salt and hot chili flakes to taste	
	minced chives or other fresh herb for garnish	

Heat the oil or butter in a heavy-bottomed saucepan, add the onion, leek and garlic and cook until tender. Add a little water to prevent browning.

Add the potatoes and stock. Cover and cook until tender.

Purée, adding additional stock to thin the consistency as needed. Purée finely for a smooth, refined texture or leave it chunky for a more robust soup. Stir in the cream and nutmeg. Adjust the seasoning with salt and hot chili flakes and serve with fresh herbs sprinkled on top for garnish. If you prefer, omit the whipping cream and top each serving with a spoonful of Savory Yoghurt Cheese (page 50).

Double Corn Soup

Serves 4

This is suave, uncomplicated and comforting, a perfect restorative after a tough day. I reached into my cupboard one particularly harried night, opened two cans, and had a pot of fresh soup on the table inside 20 minutes. If you cook potatoes specifically for this soup, use the potato-cooking water instead of water to thin the soup.

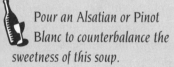 Pour an Alsatian or Pinot Blanc to counterbalance the sweetness of this soup.

1	onion, finely minced	1
2 Tbsp.	puréed ginger root	30 ml
2 tsp.	canola oil	10 ml
1/2 cup	white wine or sake	125 ml
2 14-oz. tins	canned creamed corn	2 398-ml tins
1 cup	finely diced, cooked potatoes	250 ml
2 cups	fresh or frozen corn kernels	500 ml
1–2 cups	water	250–500 ml
	salt and hot chili sauce to taste	
	minced fresh cilantro for garnish	

In a heavy-bottomed pot, cook the onion and ginger with the oil until the vegetables are tender. Stir in small amounts of water to prevent sticking or browning.

Add the wine or sake, bring to a boil, and stir in the canned corn, cooked potatoes, and fresh or frozen corn kernels. Stir well, then slowly add water to thin to the desired texture. Bring to a boil and simmer briefly until all ingredients are heated through. Add salt and hot chili sauce as needed, and garnish each serving with minced fresh cilantro.

Spring Asparagus Soup

Every spring, for a few glorious weeks, asparagus is on the market shelves. In my kitchen, i put fresh asparagus into every dish, pot and pan during this brief window of spring flavor. For a lighter dish, omit the beans and rice. No matter what else, serve this soup with crusty bread.

Grassy asparagus needs grassy Sauvignon Blanc.

2 tsp.	canola oil	10 ml
1	onion, minced	1
2 Tbsp.	puréed ginger root	30 ml
1 lb.	asparagus	450 g
1/2 cup	white wine	125 ml
1/2 cup	cooked white beans	125 ml
1/2 cup	cooked basmati or wild rice	125 ml
4 cups	water	1 litre
4 Tbsp.	white miso	60 ml
1	lemon, juice and zest	1
2 Tbsp.	minced fresh thyme	30 ml
	salt and hot chili flakes to taste	

In a heavy-bottomed pot, heat the oil and sauté the onion and ginger until tender, adding small amounts of water as needed to prevent browning. Wash the asparagus and snap off the woody ends at the point they naturally break. Discard the ends and chop the asparagus into 1" (2.5-cm) lengths on an angle.

Add the wine to the simmering onions and bring to a boil. Stir in the asparagus, beans, rice and water. Cover, bring to a boil and reduce heat to a simmer. Cook until the asparagus is bright green and the rice and beans are heated through. Remove from the heat, whisk in the miso, lemon and thyme. Check the salt level, adding hot chili flakes and more lemon juice if needed to balance the miso's salt content.

Winter Vegetable Soup

Serves 8 to 10 generously

This is my version of stone soup, made when it seems that the cupboard is bare of anything interesting to eat. It is hearty, unpretentious, full of flavor, and it improves with age. People could do worse than to adopt the nature of this soup!

Choose a southern French wine: a red, such as Grenache or Mouvèdre, or a white, such as Marsanne or Rousanne.

1–2 oz.	ham, minced	30–60 g
1 Tbsp.	olive oil	15 ml
1	onion or leek, sliced	1
6 cloves	garlic, minced	6 cloves
1 stalk	celery, diced	1 stalk
2	carrots, diced	2
1	bay leaf	1
1 tsp.	dried basil	5 ml
1 tsp.	dried oregano	5 ml
1/4 head	Savoy or nappa cabbage, finely sliced	1/4 head
2 cups	Yukon Gold potatoes, cubed	500 ml
1 cup	cooked beans	250 ml
1/4 cup	raw lentils or barley	60 ml
8 cups	beef stock	2 litres
1/4 cup	raw rice or raw pasta shells	60 ml
	salt and hot chili flakes to taste	

Sauté the ham in the oil, then add the onion or leek, garlic, celery and carrots and cook until tender, adding small amounts of water as needed to prevent browning. Add the herbs, cabbage, potatoes, beans, lentils or barley, stock, and rice or pasta. Bring to a boil, reduce heat, cover and simmer until tender. Adjust the flavors with the salt and hot chili flakes.

White Bean and Roasted Pepper Soup

Serves 6

Any bean dish needs the addition of a small amount of acid to help bring up the flavors. This soup offers a garnish of piquant roasted pepper tossed in herbs and vinegar as a foil to the mild flavor of the beans. Use any leftover roasted peppers as a topping for toasted crostini, add them to potato or pasta salad, or eat them right out of the bowl.

This can be as hearty or as light as you wish. If you leave out the chicken stock, you have a wonderful bean purée that makes a great dip for vegetables, a healthy thickener for soups, a spread for sandwiches, or a filler for fajitas, tortillas, quesadillas, and any other kind of folded flatbread.

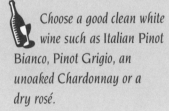

Choose a good clean white wine such as Italian Pinot Bianco, Pinot Grigio, an unoaked Chardonnay or a dry rosé.

2	leeks, cleaned and minced	2
1	onion, minced	1
4 cloves	garlic, sliced	4 cloves
1	celery stalk, minced	1
2	carrots, minced	2
1 tsp.	canola oil	5 ml
2 sprigs	fresh rosemary	2 sprigs
6 sprigs	fresh thyme	6 sprigs
1/2 cup	minced cooked lamb, ham or lean beef	125 ml
2 cups	cooked beans, such as Great Northern	500 ml
4 cups	chicken stock	1 litre
1	red bell pepper	1
1	yellow bell pepper	1
1	orange bell pepper	1
1 tsp.	minced fresh rosemary	5 ml
1 Tbsp.	minced fresh thyme	15 ml
1 Tbsp.	red wine vinegar	15 ml
1 tsp.	balsamic vinegar	5 ml
1	lemon, zest only	1
1 tsp.	extra-virgin olive oil	5 ml
1–2 tsp.	red wine vinegar	5–10 ml
	salt and freshly ground pepper to taste	

Sweat the leeks, onion, garlic, celery and carrots in the oil in a heavy-bottomed pot, adding small amounts of water as needed to prevent the vegetables from coloring or burning. When the vegetables are tender, add the rosemary, thyme, meat, beans and stock. Simmer for 20 to 30 minutes; roast and peel the peppers while you wait (see page 37).

Slice the roasted peppers into strips and toss with the rosemary, thyme, both vinegars, lemon zest, and olive oil. Season with salt and pepper. Set aside while the soup finishes cooking. Adjust the flavor of the soup, adding salt, pepper and small increments of vinegar if necessary. It should not be bland, nor should it be overly acidic. Serve with a dollop of roasted pepper strips atop each serving.

Heirloom Bean Soup

Serves 6 to 8

The type of bean you use in this soup is up to you— the choices now available are mind-boggling. I have used a combination of borletto (cranberry) and trout (Jacob's cattle) beans, but you could use Appaloosa, calypso, cannelini, soldier, fava, flageolet, Jackson Wonder, rattlesnake, Spanish Pardina, Spanish Tolosana, Swedish brown, tongue of fire, Great Northern white, or anything else you like.

For this hearty soup, choose a light Italian, Spanish or Portuguese white, a fruity red Beaujolais, or a Grenache.

6 heads	garlic, unpeeled	6 heads
4 sprigs	fresh thyme	4 sprigs
1 tsp.	olive oil	5 ml
	salt and pepper to taste	
3/4 cup	water or vegetable stock	185 ml
1	leek, finely diced	1
2	onions, finely diced	2
2 sprigs	fresh rosemary	2 sprigs
2 tsp.	olive oil	10 ml
1/2 cup	sundried tomatoes, rehydrated if aged	125 ml
1 lb.	Yukon Gold potatoes, finely diced	450 g
4 cups	cooked beans	1 litre
	salt and pepper to taste	
1/2	lemon, juice and zest	1/2
1 cup	Savory Yoghurt Cheese (page 50)	250 ml
4 Tbsp.	minced fresh chives	60 ml

Pack the garlic heads in a single layer into a small ovenproof pan. Add the thyme, olive oil, salt, pepper and water or stock. Cover with aluminum foil and roast in the oven at 450°F (230°C) until tender, about 1 hour. Remove and cool, reserving the water.

In a heavy-bottomed stockpot, cook the leek, onions and rosemary in the olive oil until the vegetables are tender. Add small amounts of water as needed to prevent browning.

Squeeze the pulp of the roasted garlic out and purée with the sundried tomatoes; add 3/4 of the purée to the stockpot. Stir in the potatoes, beans and garlic-roasting water. Simmer until tender. Season with salt, pepper and lemon juice, thinning with water or stock if needed. Put half the soup pulp through a food mill or purée in a food processor, then stir it back into the soup as thickener.

Stir the remaining garlic-sundried tomato pulp into the Savory Yoghurt Cheese along with the chives. Place a dollop on each bowl of soup before serving. If you prefer, spread the garlic-tomato paste on crusty bread slices and toast them under the broiler.

Clam Chowder

Serves 8

This light soup needs about 45 minutes to simmer and, like most soups, its flavors will intensify and mellow if at least some of the soup is eaten a day after it is made. If you do have leftovers, pick the clamshells out of the soup before refrigerating.

Muscadet or Chilean Sauvignon Blanc would be great with this soup.

2 slices	side bacon, diced	2 slices
1	bay leaf	1
1	onion, finely minced	1
2	carrots, finely diced	2
1	leek, thinly sliced	1
1	celery stalk, finely diced	1
1/2	red bell pepper, finely diced	1/2
6 cloves	garlic, minced	6 cloves
2 cups	water	500 ml
1 tsp.	dried thyme	5 ml
1/2 cup	dry white wine	125 ml
2 cups	finely diced Yukon Gold potatoes	500 ml
2 5-oz. cans	clams	2 150-ml cans
2 cups	chicken, fish or vegetable stock	500 ml
1/4 cup	heavy cream (optional)	60 ml
2–4 Tbsp.	cornstarch	30–60 ml
1	lemon, zest only	1
3	green onions, minced	3
	salt and hot chili flakes to taste	
2 1/4 lbs.	fresh clams in the shell	1 kg

Sweat the bacon in a heavy-bottomed stockpot until it is tender and cooked through. Discard all the fat after it renders out. Add the bay leaf, the diced and sliced vegetables, garlic and water. Cover and cook the vegetables without allowing them to brown.

When the vegetables are tender, stir in the thyme and wine. Bring to a boil and add the potatoes. Drain the juice from the canned clams into the pot, setting the clams aside to be added later. Add the stock and simmer, covered, until the potatoes are tender. Add the canned clams and cream if desired, then return to a boil. Dissolve the cornstarch in a small amount of cold water and stir half of it into the boiling soup. Allow the starch to thicken, adding more as needed. When the soup is the right consistency, add the lemon zest, green onions, salt and hot chili flakes.

Scrub the clamshells vigorously with a stiff brush to remove sand and grit. Add them to the finished soup while it is boiling. Cover and steam for several minutes, just until the clams open wide.

Taste the broth again, rebalancing it if necessary. Serve with a generous amount of crusty rye or sourdough bread, and give each person lots of napkins and a bowl for discarded shells.

Variation

For **Corn Chowder,** omit the clams and add 3 cups (750 ml) fresh, frozen or canned corn.

My family spent seven years on the east coast of Vancouver Island when I was a child. I never recognized it as Eden until I'd been away for years and years. We picked oysters, dug clams, fished for salmon, beachcombed for sea kelp and seashells. I remember a memorable weekend at the beach, doing nothing but eating in the rain. We roasted salmon over the fire and steamed oysters open, each of us eating dozens, flavored only with their own briny juices. It took me decades to willingly countenance another oyster peering up at me.

Black Mushroom and Miso Soup

Serves 4

The restorative power of miso soup is always most obvious to me when we all troop down to our favorite sushi bar for dinner. No matter how scrambled the day or curdled my brain, the first sip of miso soup invariably calms me down and restores my soul. Inky and mysterious, slivers of dried black or shiitake mushrooms float throughout this soup. Add cubes of tofu or slivers of meat and thin noodles for a heartier meal.

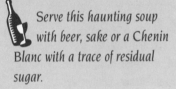 *Serve this haunting soup with beer, sake or a Chenin Blanc with a trace of residual sugar.*

8–10	dried black or shiitake mushrooms	8–10
4 cups	water	1 litre
1	leek, thinly sliced	1
4 cloves	garlic, minced	4 cloves
1	red bell pepper, julienned	1
2 tsp.	canola oil	10 ml
8–10	cultivated mushrooms, sliced	8–10
2 Tbsp.	cornstarch (optional)	30 ml
1/2 cup	sake	125 ml
2 Tbsp.	dark soy sauce	30 ml
4 Tbsp.	white miso	60 ml
1	orange, zest only	1
1–2 Tbsp.	Japanese rice vinegar	15–30 ml
	hot chili paste to taste	
	fresh cilantro or chives, minced	

Put the dried mushrooms into a small pot, cover with half the water, and cook for several minutes, until the mushrooms rehydrate and soften. Remove the mushrooms to a cutting board to cool. Strain the cooking liquid to remove any grit, reserving the liquid for the soup pot.

In a heavy-bottomed pot, sauté the leek, garlic and red bell pepper in the oil until tender, adding small amounts of water as needed to prevent browning. Wash and thinly slice the fresh mushrooms, then add them to the pot. Trim off and discard the woody stems of the rehydrated mushrooms. Thinly slice the caps and add them to the pot. Stir well, cooking until all is tender. Add the remaining 2 cups (500 ml) water and mushroom soaking liquid, and bring to a boil. Stir in the cornstarch dissolved in a little cold water. Boil briefly until clear. Remove from the heat. Stir in the sake, soy sauce, miso, orange zest, vinegar and hot chili paste. Garnish with minced cilantro or chives.

Variation
For **Clam and Miso Soup**, add several clams in the shell per person to the pot of boiling soup. Cover tightly and steam several minutes until the clams open wide.

Tomato-Ponzu Gazpacho with Sorrel Leaves

Serves 6

Gazpacho is a cold soup with two faces. One is vibrant, red and saturated with olive oil. The other is rich, smooth, white and enriched with ground almonds or bread. This version is splashy and red, but its flavors are Asian in origin. Ponzu, a Japanese dipping sauce based on soy, citrus and rice vinegar, replaces the red wine vinegar that tarts up many gazpacho recipes. Sorrel, the "green apple" perennial herb, adds a refreshing note to this nontraditional version. Choose impeccably fresh, juicy fruits and vegetables for this soup; because of its simplicity, its quality relies entirely on the produce you select.

Complete the cross-cultural game by pouring a Portuguese Vinho Verde.

1 1/2 lbs.	tomatoes	675 g
1	red bell pepper	1
1	green bell pepper	1
1/2	medium red or mild yellow onion	1/2
1/2	Long English cucumber	1/2
4 cloves	garlic, puréed	4 cloves
1/2 cup	finely shredded fresh sorrel leaves	125 ml
2	green onions, finely sliced on the angle	2
1	lemon, juice and zest	1
1/4 cup	Japanese rice vinegar	60 ml
2–3 Tbsp.	soy sauce	30–45 ml
1 tsp.	wasabi or horseradish (optional)	5 ml
1 Tbsp.	melted honey or sugar	15 ml
1 cup	tomato juice	250 ml
1 Tbsp.	sesame oil	15 ml

Slice the tomatoes in half horizontally, then gently squeeze each half over a sieve atop a nonreactive glass or stainless steel bowl. Discard the seeds that collect in the sieve. Dice the tomatoes into 1/4" (.6-cm) cubes, and add them to the reserved tomato juice in the bowl. Cut the peppers, onion and cucumber into 1/4" (.6-cm) dice. Add the diced vegetables, garlic, sorrel and green onions to the tomatoes.

Whisk together the lemon juice, vinegar, soy sauce, wasabi or horseradish, honey or sugar and tomato juice. Whisk in the sesame oil. Pour the dressing over the chopped tomatoes, herbs and vegetables. Chill and serve cold.

Roasted Tomato Soup

Serves 6 (with leftovers for other dishes)

This is my absolutely favorite fuss-less tomato soup/sauce. No splatters to chisel off the stovetop, no hours of simmering out all the freshness. Make extra and use it in layered vegetable dishes or on pasta, or serve the tail end with risotto. Save the last half-cup for a Roasted Tomato and Basil Vinaigrette (page 39).

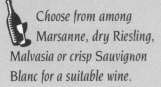

Choose from among Marsanne, dry Riesling, Malvasia or crisp Sauvignon Blanc for a suitable wine.

3 lbs.	ripe Roma tomatoes	1.3 kg
2	onions, thinly sliced	2
6 cloves	garlic	6 cloves
1 Tbsp.	olive oil	15 ml
4 cups	chicken stock, heated	1 litre
1 bunch	green onions, minced	1 bunch
1/2 cup	minced fresh basil	125 ml
1 Tbsp.	honey	15 ml
	salt and hot chili flakes to taste	

Lay the tomatoes in one layer in a nonstick ovenproof pan, spread the onions and garlic over top, drizzle with the olive oil and roast in a hot oven (450°F/230°C) until the tops are charred and the vegetables are tender, about an hour. Remove from heat, coarsely purée, and add the hot stock, green onions and basil. Balance the flavors with the honey, salt and hot chili flakes.

Fish and Shellfish

Although its price is rapidly escalating as stocks dwindle, fish is growing in popularity as more people look for ways to reduce their meat consumption. Fish makes a lean alternative, and even the fatter species have health benefits that offset their higher fat and calorie count. Smaller portions help it go farther, depending on the richness of the fish and the other dishes being served.

Appropriate cooking methods and inspired seasoning can convert even those who are confirmed non-fish-eaters. The important considerations when cooking fish are matching the texture to the cooking method and being careful to not overcook it. Aim a little short of your normal timing. I usually set a mental stopwatch for 5 minutes whenever I grill fish, then after the pieces are flipped, I add another 2 minutes for a total of about 7 minutes for a piece 1" (2.5 cm) thick over medium-high heat. Especially with fish, there are no absolute cooking times. Look at the sheen of the fish; it should change from its raw high gloss to dull and flat when done. If white juices coagulate on the top, it usually means too much time has passed, so next time reduce the cooking time and/or the temperature of the grill. The color should lighten as the fish turns opaque from cooking.

Shellfish, especially molluscs in their inedible shells, are easily overcooked. In general terms, quickly cook clams, mussels, scallops and oysters until their shells gape half open and their flesh is just firm. Crustaceans, like lobsters, shrimp, prawns, crayfish and crabs, exhibit an intense color change once they are cooked, usually going red or pink (although some varieties of shrimp and prawns go white when done).

Salmon with Bacon, Vermouth and Cabbage

Serves 4

Drinking a Cinzano one summer evening, I caught the scent of grilling salmon wafting its way through the neighborhood. A sip, a sniff, another sip, and an idea was born. Salmon is deceptively rich and it pairs rather unlikely ingredients with great success. The vermouth is sweet red Cinzano, which plays off well against the earthy flavors of smoky bacon and mild Savoy cabbage. Use trout if you prefer a slightly lighter dish.

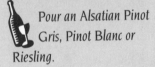

Pour an Alsatian Pinot Gris, Pinot Blanc or Riesling.

2 slices	side bacon, finely sliced	2 slices
1	medium onion, finely sliced	1
4 cloves	garlic, minced	4 cloves
1/4 head	Savoy or nappa cabbage, finely shredded	1/4 head
1	lemon, juice and zest	1
2 tsp.	minced fresh thyme	10 ml
1/2 cup	sweet red Cinzano	125 ml
4 5-oz.	salmon filets	4 150-g
	salt and pepper to taste	

In a nonstick sauté pan, cook the bacon until it releases its fat and begins to color. Discard the fat, then add the onion and garlic to the pan. Cook until tender and transparent, about 5 minutes, adding small amounts of water as needed to prevent burning or coloring.

Add the cabbage, lemon juice and zest, and cook the cabbage until it loses its bulk and softens, about 5 minutes. Add the thyme and Cinzano. Bring to a boil, reduce the liquid by half and then add the salmon filets, rearranging the vegetables in the pan to cover the fish. Cover and reduce the heat to low. Steam the fish about 7 minutes, or until just done. Taste the vegetables and add salt and pepper as needed.

This dish is wonderful served with plain linguini, Garlicky Mashed Potatoes (page 134) or Lentil Salad (page 121).

Using smoky or high-fat foods as flavor agents rather than main ingredients is a sensible way to use less for more. The bacon used in this dish adds its unmistakable flavor and aroma, but 2 slim slices add a minimal amount of fat. If you wish, substitute prosciutto or pancetta, but this dish is by its very essence a peasant dish.

Salmon with Mango Sauce

Serves 4

*T*his one doesn't heat up the house, doesn't take any time, and is awesome for its simplicity. The colors are summery, and to add a little green to the plates, steam some asparagus, broccoli or snow peas. If salmon doesn't appeal, choose another full-flavored fish that grills well, such as monkfish or halibut. Basmati rice, steamed green vegetables and grilled pineapple slices complete the meal. For a variation in texture try substituting Fresh Fruit Salsa (page 19) made with mangoes for the sauce.

 Serve a Viognier or a Marsanne.

1 Tbsp.	puréed ginger root	15 ml
1	orange, zest only	1
1 Tbsp.	minced fresh thyme	15 ml
1 Tbsp.	canola oil	15 ml
	freshly ground black pepper	
4 5-oz.	salmon filets	4 150-g
2 cups	Mango Sauce (page 17)	500 ml

Combine the ginger, orange zest, thyme, oil and pepper. Spread evenly over both sides of the salmon filets. Let stand for 10 minutes while the grill is heating. Grill on medium-high heat for about 8 minutes, or until the fish is just done and flaky at the center. Pool some mango sauce on each plate and place a piece of grilled salmon on top.

Every time I use fresh thyme, basil, rosemary or sage, I store the stripped twigs in a bag in my freezer to use in stockmaking or barbecuing. The little bags add up in quite a hurry if you use fresh herbs on a regular basis; then it's mostly a question of catching them all as they tumble out of the overstuffed freezer door.

Cedar-Planked Salmon with Honey and Mustard

Serves 6 to 8

This is what results when a person grows up in more than one region of North America. The cedar or alder plank is a West Coast native way of cooking salmon, and the mustard glaze is inspired by the acres of fresh mustard that add a yellow floral note to the patchwork of crops across the Prairies. Use an oven or your outdoor grill, and be sure the wood is unsprayed and pesticide-free. If you can't be sure, don't use it. I buy a bundle of cedar shingles, stash them in the garden shed, and haul them out one at a time for this dish. If you are grilling, treat the plank or shingle like wood chips, and soak it well to minimize flaming. Serve this salmon with a risotto or pilaf.

A bottle of fresh, bright Pinot Noir or a fruity Sauvignon Blanc would be a good wine choice.

3 Tbsp.	canola oil	45 ml
3-lb.	piece of salmon, skin on	1.3-kg
1/2 cup	honey	125 ml
4 Tbsp.	mustard	60 ml
1	lemon, zest only	1
4 Tbsp.	minced fresh thyme or sage	60 ml
	hot chili flakes and salt to taste	
	lemon, cut in wedges, for garnish	
	sprigs of thyme or sage for garnish	

Preheat oven to 450°F (230°C) or heat the grill to medium-high. Brush the wood with the oil and lay the fish skin-side down on the wood. Mix together the honey, mustard, lemon zest, minced herbs, hot chili flakes and salt.

Brush the exposed surfaces of the fish with half the glaze, then transfer to the oven or the grill. Do not overcook: allow about 7 minutes per inch (2.5 cm) of thickness. If you are uncertain, use a small sharp knife to separate several flakes at the thickest part—when done, it should no longer be transparent, but opaque.

Remove the fish from the heat and brush with the remaining glaze. Serve from the board. Garnish with lemon wedges and sprigs of fresh thyme or sage.

Experiment with mustard varieties and flavors in this dish. I tend to choose grainy mustard, but use whichever style and brand you prefer. If you opt for a honey mustard, though, remember to reduce or remove the honey in the glaze to compensate.

Grilled Salmon with Sorrel-Spinach Sauce

Serves 4

Sorrel and salmon is a traditional combination in the French culinary repertoire, and I often wonder if some classic sauces arose out of the sorrel bush's unfailing generosity of production. I know I sometimes go out and pick some just because it is so prolific! The wood chips should soak for an hour, which allows just enough time to make the sorrel-spinach sauce, apply the rub to the fish and let it cure.

 Ask your wine merchant to suggest a dry Vouvray, a Muscadet or a high-acid Riesling.

4 5-oz.	salmon filets	4 150-g
4 Tbsp.	fresh tarragon	60 ml
2 tsp.	cracked fennel seed	10 ml
	freshly cracked pepper to taste	
1	lime, zest only	1
1 tsp.	mustard seed	5 ml
1 Tbsp.	olive oil	15 ml
1 cup	Sorrel-Spinach Sauce (page 22)	250 ml
	chive blossoms for garnish	

Place the salmon filets in a shallow pan. Combine all ingredients except for the sorrel-spinach sauce and chive blossoms, and smear onto the flesh side of the salmon. Marinate at room temperature for 30 minutes. Preheat the grill to medium. Lightly oil the grill and cook until the fish is just done, between 7 and 10 minutes, depending on the thickness. Turn when two-thirds done if desired, or cook entirely skin-side down.

If you are using wood chips for smoke, drain them and place on one side only of the grill, on the lava rocks and under the bars, with the heat set at low on that side. Place the fish on the other side of the grill, over medium heat. Close the lid and do not peek. It will billow smoke—don't panic and don't call the fire department! Wait until 5 to 7 minutes elapse before looking.

Serve the grilled salmon on a pool of Sorrel-Spinach Sauce with a chive blossom or two for garnish.

Spring Asparagus, Salmon and Hazelnut Salad

Serves 6

A sparagus is the harbinger of spring and warm sunny days. I start buying it as soon as the first bunches show up in the market, ignoring the exorbitant price. If the nut vinaigrette is too rich for you, substitute the refreshingly tart Rhubarb Lime Vinaigrette (page 45).

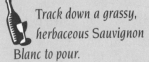 Track down a grassy, herbaceous Sauvignon Blanc to pour.

1 lb.	young fresh asparagus	450 g
1 bunch	fresh spinach or mesclun	1 bunch
6 5-oz.	salmon filets	6 150-g
4 Tbsp.	hazelnuts, toasted, skinned and coarsely chopped (see page 48)	60 ml
3/4 cup	Hazelnut Vinaigrette (page 48)	185 ml

Wash the asparagus, snapping off and discarding the brittle ends. Wash the greens, drying them well to allow the dressing to stick. Place the salmon on a baking sheet, skin-side down, and sprinkle the hazelnuts over the top surface. Roast the salmon in a preheated 450°F (230°C) oven until tender and flaky. To be sure you aren't overcooking the fish, check it after 7 minutes; cut a little nick in the fish at the thickest point, and see if the fish has become opaque and dull in color compared to its slick, translucent appearance when raw.

Steam the asparagus, toss it in a little of the dressing and arrange it on plates. Toss the greens in the vinaigrette, and arrange them next to the asparagus. Place a salmon filet on each plate and serve hot.

Although nuts are high in oil and calories, if they are used sparingly, as a garnish, they can make up part of a skinny feast. Remember to store your nuts in the freezer to prevent them from becoming rancid. Not much tastes as terrible as a bad nut, except maybe a burnt bean.

Braised Mushrooms with Slivered Barbecued Salmon

Serves 6

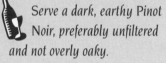

Just remember, looks don't count first with cooks, and it's a good thing . . . once, to my chagrin, this dish was seriously considered for The Ugliest Dish of the Year Award by a group of professional eaters. It didn't win, and they did enjoy eating it. This dish works equally well if you substitute barbecued duck for the salmon.

Serve a dark, earthy Pinot Noir, preferably unfiltered and not overly oaky.

16	Chinese black mushrooms, dried	16
1 Tbsp.	canola oil	15 ml
2 lbs.	Asian eggplant, cut into 1/2" (1-cm) dice	900 g
2 Tbsp.	puréed ginger root	30 ml
2 Tbsp.	puréed garlic	30 ml
2–4 cups	chicken stock, vegetable stock or water	.5–1 litre
1 bunch	green onions, cut into 3" (7-cm) lengths	1 bunch
4 Tbsp.	dark or mushroom soy sauce	60 ml
1 Tbsp.	honey	15 ml
1/2 lb.	hot-smoked salmon, broken into chunks	225 g
1 tsp.	sesame oil	5 ml
1/2 tsp.	hot chili flakes	2.5 ml

GARNISHES:
sesame seeds
cilantro sprigs

Soak the mushrooms in hot water until soft and pliable. Discard the stems and strain and reserve the soaking water. Heat the oil in a nonstick sauté pan, and stir in the eggplant, ginger and garlic. Start adding stock or water, including the mushroom-soaking water. (The eggplant, greedy little sponges, will soak up lots of liquid, so add enough that the dish always looks juicy.) Stir in the green onions and mushroom caps, then the dark or mushroom soy sauce and honey. Simmer 20 minutes, or until the eggplant and mushroom caps are tender.

Add the chunks of hot-smoked salmon, sesame oil and hot chili flakes and heat until warm through. Serve over rice or noodles. Sprinkle with sesame seeds and garnish with sprigs of cilantro.

Salmon and Cabbage Ballotine

Serves 10 to 12

In classical French cooking, ballotines are chicken legs which have been boned, stuffed and roasted. This dish contains no chicken, no legs, and isn't roasted, but it is a very fine dish featuring salmon that is rolled in cabbage leaves and then poached. The delicate flavor of the herbs and the mild cabbage pair well with the salmon.

This is fine served warm or cold, so make it in advance for a special occasion. It can be dressed up with a grain pilaf or salad, Chickpea and Mint Salad (page 120) or Fresh Mint Chutney (page 21).

Open a bottle of rosé, a light Pinot Noir, or a Sauvignon Blanc.

1	onion, finely sliced	1
1 head	garlic, split horizontally	1 head
1 stalk	celery, finely sliced	1 stalk
1	carrot, finely sliced	1
1	leek, chopped	1
1	bay leaf	1
1 tsp.	black peppercorns	5 ml
6 twigs	fresh thyme	6 twigs
1 Tbsp.	minced ginger root	15 ml
1	lemon, juice and zest	1
8 cups	water	2 litres
1	Savoy or nappa cabbage	1
1	onion, minced	1
1 stalk	celery, minced	1 stalk
1 tsp.	olive oil	5 ml
2 1/4 lbs.	salmon filet, skinless and boneless	1 kg
2 tsp.	minced fresh thyme	10 ml
1 tsp.	minced fresh dillweed	5 ml
2 tsp.	minced fresh lemon balm	10 ml
2	green onions, minced	2
1	egg (optional)	1
1	lemon, zest and juice	1
	salt and hot chili flakes to taste	
1 Tbsp.	whipping cream (optional)	15 ml

Make the poaching liquid first. Place the onion, garlic, celery, carrot and leek in a large, heavy ovenproof dish, then add the bay leaf, peppercorns, thyme, ginger, lemon and water. Bring to a boil and simmer for 30 minutes to extract the flavors and reduce it slightly.

While the poaching liquid is simmering, pull about 12 leaves from the outside of the head of cabbage. Immerse each leaf into the simmering liquid, cooking it just long enough to soften the fibers and make the leaf pliable. Cool the leaves under cold water. Trim out the thick stem from the center of each leaf.

Sauté the minced onion and celery in the olive oil, adding small amounts of water as needed to prevent browning. Place half the sautéed vegetables in a food processor with half the salmon, and purée. Add the fresh herbs, green onions, the egg if you are using one, the lemon juice and zest, salt and hot chili flakes. Add the cream if you wish at the very end, being careful not to overprocess the mixture.

Slice the remaining salmon into 1/2" (1-cm) strips up to 10" (25 cm) long, then assemble a bed of overlapping cabbage leaves on a clean teatowel, using all the blanched and trimmed leaves. The bed should be 2 layers deep and about 12" (30 cm) long and 8" (20 cm) wide. Starting and ending with the salmon strips, build layers of salmon strips, sautéed vegetables and purée on the middle of the cabbage leaves, leaving 3 to 4" (7.5 to10 cm) on all sides. Roll it up jellyroll fashion, encasing the whole in the teatowel. Tie the ends with butcher twine, then tie the cylinder at intervals.

Gently place the wrapped cylinder in the hot poaching liquid, cover and bring to a boil. Reduce the heat to a simmer and cook about an hour. On a cutting board, carefully unwrap the cylinder and check for doneness. If cooked through, allow to cool for 10 to 20 minutes before slicing into rounds about 1/2" (1 cm) thick.

Grilled Tuna Salad

Serves 6 as dinner

If you start with the traditional ingredients of Salade Nicoise—tuna and potatoes—and cook them on the grill, the result is a thing of splendor. A Puréed Peasant Vegetable Vinaigrette (page 38) adds to the delight, but a simple vinaigrette or a Buttermilk Dressing (page 51) is fine too.

If the propane tank is empty or the weather is too cold for even the most intrepid griller, use the broiler in your oven, and warm your house and heart with the scent of tuna cooking. It is the last minute or two of cooking tuna that counts most; don't overcook it, for fear of the canned tuna texture syndrome.

 Serve a fully dry French or Californian rosé or Malvasia.

6 5-oz.	tuna steaks	6 150-g	
2 Tbsp.	minced fresh thyme or rosemary	30 ml	
1	lemon, juice and zest	1	
2 cloves	garlic, minced	2 cloves	
1 Tbsp.	freshly cracked pepper	15 ml	
1 Tbsp.	olive oil	15 ml	
1 lb.	new potatoes, scrubbed	450 g	
2 lbs.	fresh green beans, trimmed	1 kg	
3	eggs	3	
6	Roma tomatoes	6	
6 cups	mixed greens	1.5 litres	
1 cup	Kalamata olives	250 ml	
1 2-oz. tin	anchovy filets, drained	1 60-g tin	
1 cup	vinaigrette or dressing	250 ml	

Put the tuna steaks on a shallow baking sheet. Mix together the thyme or rosemary, lemon, garlic, pepper and olive oil. Coat the surfaces of the steaks and let them stand 15 minutes while you finish preparing all the other ingredients.

Cut the potatoes into 1" (2.5-cm) cubes unless they are very small new potatoes. Steam until tender, drain and set aside. Steam the green beans until tender, then refresh under cold water to crisp and halt the cooking process. Hardboil the eggs, then peel and slice or quarter them. Slice the tomatoes into lengthwise quarters.

Cooking hardboiled eggs with no gray ring around the collar is as simple as setting the timer. Bring a pot of water to the boil, then add the eggs, making sure they are immersed in the water. Set the heat to almost, but not quite, boiling. (Boiling toughens the protein and causes rubbery eggs.) Set the timer for 12 minutes for large eggs. As soon as it sounds, pour off the water and run cold water over the eggs to cool them promptly. Crack each shell with a rap from the back of a spoon to rapidly dissipate the heat. Peel the eggs, rinse well and store covered with cold water in the fridge, changing the water daily. Keep them no more than 3 days.

Preheat the grill to medium-high and grill the tuna until it is just cooked through, about 7 minutes per inch (2.5 cm) of thickness. Remove the steaks and set aside for a few minutes. Toss the cooked potatoes onto the grill to crisp the outside. Slice the steaks thickly against the grain. Assemble each salad by arranging the sliced tuna, roasted potatoes, quartered egg, quartered tomato and steamed whole green beans on the lettuce or greens. Garnish with olives and an anchovy filet, and drizzle with dressing.

Snapper Pan-Steamed with Sugar Kelp

Serves 4

The gentle action of pan-steaming results in a soft, tender exterior without the color and crispness of grilled or sautéed food. This is a perfect attribute to combine with the sweet, briny taste of sugar kelp and the citrus bite of lemon zest. It works well with fresh halibut, tilapia, catfish, cod or salmon. A grain salad provides a good textural contrast.

A Sauvignon Blanc with lots of fruit would be a good accompaniment.

6 cloves	garlic, minced	6 cloves
4 Tbsp.	minced fresh oregano or thyme	60 ml
1/2 cup	dried sugar kelp, crumbled	125 ml
2	lemons, zest only	2
	hot chili flakes to taste	
4 5-oz.	snapper filets, boneless	4 150-g
2 tsp.	canola oil or butter	10 ml

Combine the garlic, oregano or thyme, kelp, lemon zest and hot chili flakes. Rub evenly over the filets. Heat the oil or butter in a nonstick sauté pan over low heat. Cook the fish covered tightly with a lid that sits down inside the edge of the pan. Turn frequently and moderate the heat to avoid browning. When just cooked, about 8 minutes, remove the snapper to plates and serve.

Sugar kelp is harvested off the west coast in small coves and inlets. Add it to seafood stew and sauces, crumble it on top of steamed or poached fish, and remember to lick your fingers after; the seaweed is sweet and mild, only gently redolent of the sea. Sugar kelp can be found in most health food stores.

Tuna Grilled on Rosemary Skewers

Serves 4

This is a spectacular dish to take to a potluck or barbecue. All the work is done in advance, leaving just the oohs and aahs to be savored with the dish. Swordfish or salmon work equally well in this recipe, or you can go entirely to vegetables; Asian eggplant, peeled and cut into 1/2" (1-cm) coins, is great cooked on rosemary twigs.

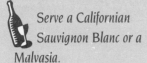

Serve a Californian Sauvignon Blanc or a Malvasia.

4 5-oz.	tuna steaks	4 150-g
24	fresh rosemary twigs	24
4	garlic cloves, minced	4
1	shallot, minced	1
1	lemon, zest only	1
	freshly cracked pepper	
1 Tbsp.	olive oil	15 ml
1 head	radicchio	1 head
1 head	escarole or curly endive	1 head
1 head	Belgian endive	1 head
1/2 cup	Maple Thyme Vinaigrette (page 47)	125 ml

Slice each tuna steak into six 1" (2.5-cm) strips. Strip the rosemary needles from the twigs, leaving a few needles at the top and being careful not to break the twigs. Thread the tuna onto the skewers of rosemary.

Mince the rosemary needles and combine with the garlic, shallot, lemon zest, pepper and olive oil. Brush onto the tuna and marinate for about 20 minutes to 1 hour.

Wash the greens.

Preheat the grill to medium-high. Grill the tuna, being careful not to overcook it. Brush it with vinaigrette as soon as it comes off the grill. Toss the greens in vinaigrette, arrange on plates, top with 6 tuna skewers per plate, and serve.

To successfully skewer food on rosemary, you need fairly woody, straight lengths of herb stalk. My rosemary is so well used and frequently picked that I end up buying skewers of rosemary and stripping the needles. If you just can't find anything that looks like it would work, use bamboo skewers, well soaked to prevent their torching, and tuck a short tuft of rosemary at each end to give the herbal impression. Creative cheating is an artform to cultivate.

Catfish with Fennel Seed on a Bed of Braised Fennel

Serves 4

This dish uses several ingredients that boast licorice flavor in varying degrees. It is a spinoff of the classic Oysters Rockefeller that originated at Antoine's in The Big Easy. The original dish is a marvel of richness and fabulous textures, from a time when luxury meant lashings of cream and heaps of butter. Try substituting oysters, salmon, scampi or monkfish in this recipe. If you feel totally indulgent, pour in a dollop of heavy cream at the very end, but the dish really does not need it. Serve this with Bean Salsa (page 20) and Dirty Rice (page 163).

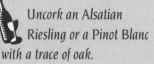

Uncork an Alsatian Riesling or a Pinot Blanc with a trace of oak.

1 tsp.	fennel seed	5 ml
1 lb.	catfish, cut into 1" (2.5-cm) cubes	450 g
3 bulbs	fennel	3 bulbs
1 Tbsp.	unsalted butter	15 ml
1	onion, minced	1
3 cloves	garlic, minced	3 cloves
1/2 tsp.	dried marjoram	2.5 ml
1/2 tsp.	dried basil	2.5 ml
1/2 tsp.	cayenne	2.5 ml
1/2 cup	dry white wine	125 ml
1/2 cup	fresh orange juice	125 ml
3 Tbsp.	minced fresh tarragon	45 ml
2	green onions, minced	2
1	lemon, juice and zest	1
1/4 cup	Pernod, Herbsaint, ouzo or anisette	60 ml
	salt and hot chili flakes to taste	
	watercress sprigs for garnish	

Crack the fennel seed in a mortar, then lightly dust some over the catfish cubes. Set aside.

Finely slice the fennel bulbs, discarding the stalks but saving the fronds for garnish. Melt the butter. Add the fennel slices, remaining cracked fennel seed, onion and garlic and cook gently without browning for 4 to 5 minutes. Stir in the dried herbs, wine and orange juice. Simmer, allowing to cook down and reduce until the fennel is meltingly tender.

Add the catfish cubes, cover and steam over gentle heat until the fish is opaque. Add the tarragon, green onions, lemon juice and zest and alcohol. Briefly return to a boil, and adjust the flavors with salt and hot chili flakes. Garnish with fresh watercress sprigs and the fronds from the fennel bulbs.

Apple Cider and Ginger Seafood en Papillote

Serves 4

*T*his is quick and painless, with no splatters on the stove and no sweat on your brow. Save it for a day with special demands on your time—an unscheduled visit to the vet, soccer practice, parent-teacher meetings. Choose mild fish. It can be firm, such as cod, or tender, fine-textured fish like sole because there is no turning, no flipping, no fussing, and no breaking up the fish. Use sole, snapper, mullet, trout, cod, pollock, tilapia, catfish, or something of similar texture. Make a green salad with impeccably fresh greens, buy a good loaf of bread, and call it dinner.

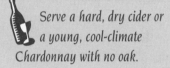 Serve a hard, dry cider or a young, cool-climate Chardonnay with no oak.

I	apple, preferably tart and firm	I
I lb.	fish filets	450 g
I	lemon, zest only	I
I Tbsp.	minced ginger root	15 ml
1/4 cup	apple cider	60 ml
	freshly ground black pepper to taste	

Set the oven at 450°F (230°C) and cut 4 circles of baking parchment, each 10–12" (25–30 cm) in diameter. Core and thinly slice the apples. Slice the fish filets on the bias into 1-ounce (30-g) pieces of even thickness, about 1/2" (1 cm). Arrange 4 slices on each parchment circle. Evenly divide the lemon zest, apple slices, ginger root and apple cider, sprinkling all on top of the fish slices. Top with pepper. Fold the paper in half over the fish and flavorings so that the round edges meet evenly. Beginning at the center of the curve, make small folds in the paper, each successive fold beginning in the middle of the previous fold so that it forms a solid seam to keep everything enclosed. When you reach the straight edge, go back to the middle and work your way down the other curved edge.

If you are working in advance, stop now and put the sealed packages on a tray in the fridge. (Remember to remove them 10 to 15 minutes before you want to cook them—to take off the chill and keep the cooking time from ballooning.) Bake until the parchment puffs up, about 10 minutes. Carefully transfer each serving onto plates and serve in the paper, with warnings about the steam contained in the packages.

Serving food baked in parchment is an olfactory thrill for all at the table. Slice open each paper and inhale the fragrant steam that suddenly blooms forth. For variety, try lime or grapefruit zest, cracked star anise, ground nutmeg, minuscule pinches of saffron, rehydrated slivers of morita chili, rehydrated and chopped dried cranberries, or any other aromatic herbs and spices you enjoy.

Halibut on Warm Greens with Miso-Gari Vinaigrette

Serves 4

Influenced by Japanese cookery, this features sweet, salt, hot and pickled all in one dish. Everything except grilling the fish can be done ahead, so the time until dinner is on the table just nudges my personal goal of half an hour. If halibut is too expensive or out of season, substitute catfish, trout, salmon, tilapia or swordfish. The flavors in this dish need little other than a pot of steamed basmati rice and some fresh asparagus or broccoli for accompaniment.

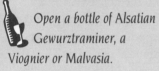 *Open a bottle of Alsatian Gewurztraminer, a Viognier or Malvasia.*

4 5-oz.	halibut steaks	4 150-g
1 cup	Miso-Gari Vinaigrette (page 40)	250 ml
2 bunches	bok choy or other mild Asian greens	2 bunches
4	blood oranges, tangerines or mandarins, peeled and sliced	4
	GARNISHES:	
1 Tbsp.	sesame seeds	15 ml
1 bunch	cilantro sprigs	1 bunch
	Pickled Red Onions (page 16)	

Brush the halibut steaks with 1/4 cup (60 ml) of the vinaigrette and set aside for 20 minutes. Preheat the grill to medium-hot and wash and finely chop the bok choy. Do not spin dry! Grill the halibut until just done in the center, about 7 minutes per inch (2.5 cm) of thickness.

Toss the greens in a hot nonstick sauté pan over high heat until they wilt. Add the remaining Miso-Gari Vinaigrette and toss well. Top with the grilled halibut.

Garnish with the sliced citrus and a sprinkle of sesame seeds. Drape a few curls of Pickled Red Onion alongside.

Fish Wrapped in Spinach with Black Bean Steam

Serves 4

The fish and the wrapping medium are your choice. If your garden is producing prodigious amounts of beet greens, use them with salmon. Or wilt Savoy cabbage for salmon or halibut; try Chinese greens, leek tops, sorrel leaves or big spinach leaves. Be sure to pair your greens with a tightly textured fish that won't flake apart into messy little pieces inside the package of greens. Consider cod, smoked black cod, tilapia, halibut, salmon, tuna, swordfish, marlin, sea bass or monkfish.

Depending on the fish and greens you serve, pour a full-fruit Sauvignon Blanc, a Pinot Noir with good extracted fruit flavors, or a Gewurztraminer or Pinot Gris.

4 5-oz.	fish filets	4 150-g
1 bunch	large-leaf spinach, chard, sorrel or other firm green	1 bunch
2 cups	Black Bean Sauce (page 18)	500 ml
	sesame seeds for garnish	

Trim the filets into tidy pieces of even thickness. Wash the greens, discarding the stems. In a large nonstick sauté pan, quickly cook the greens over high heat, using just the water clinging to the leaves and turning the greens over several times with tongs. Cook just long enough to wilt. Spinach will take mere seconds, while the chard leaves will take longer.

Spread the wilted leaves out flat on the cutting board, overlapping edges to form a wrapper large enough to encase each piece of fish. Wrap the fish filets in the greens, tucking the ends under to form tidy packages. Pour the Black Bean Sauce into the sauté pan and bring to a boil. Place the wrapped fish packages in the sauce, cover and steam over medium-high heat until just done, allowing about 8 minutes per inch (2.5 cm) of thickness. If you are in doubt, remove the largest filet and use a small sharp knife to slit a small hole in the center, checking for doneness.

To serve, ladle a quarter of the sauce onto each large shallow bowl or plate and arrange a wrapped filet on top. Sprinkle with sesame seeds. Serve with basmati rice, a wedge of Noodle Pancake (page 174), plain rice noodles or egg noodles.

Variation
If all the fussing, wilting and wrapping is more than you can face, pan-steam the fish; set it aside, covered, and quickly wilt the greens in the same pan. Turn the greens onto a platter, drizzle with the sauce, top with the fish and more sauce and then sprinkle with sesame seeds to garnish. For an extra bite of flavor, add strands of Pickled Ginger (page 17) for garnish.

Oven-Roasted Cod with Judy's Carrot, Apple and Basil Coulis

Serves 4

A t Foodsmith, the restaurant I operated, we changed part of the menu daily. As a result, every cook learned to think quickly on his or her feet to create thoughtful daily features using what we had on hand. One of my favorite sous-chefs, a tiny young Asian woman with an amazing streak of creativity, created this light and intensely flavored sauce to go with my roasted fish. Thanks, Judy.

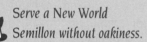

Serve a New World Semillon without oakiness.

2	sweet carrots, finely grated	2
2	apples, finely grated	2
1 Tbsp.	puréed ginger root	15 ml
1	lemon, juice and zest	1
1–2 Tbsp.	honey, melted	15–30 ml
3 Tbsp.	finely shredded fresh basil	45 ml
1/2 cup	apple cider	125 ml
	salt and hot chili flakes to taste	
1 lb.	cod or snapper filets	450 g
1 Tbsp.	mustard seeds	15 ml
2 Tbsp.	mustard	30 ml
1 Tbsp.	mustard oil or olive oil	15 ml
	salt and hot chili flakes to taste	

To make the coulis, combine the grated carrots and apples with the ginger, lemon, honey, basil and apple cider. Add salt and chili flakes and set aside.

Sprinkle the fish filets with the mustard seeds, smear on the mustard and oil, and sprinkle with salt and hot chili flakes. Roast in a 450°F (230°C) oven for about 10 minutes, or until just flaky and cooked through. Serve on a pool of carrot-apple coulis.

Clams and Mussels in Black Bean Sauce

Serves 4 as a starter

G reat alone in copious *amounts for serious fans, this dish is equally good on linguini or basmati rice. If you want rice or pasta, have it cooked and waiting; these little molluscs steam open in minutes. Use clams and mussels together, or choose one or the other.*

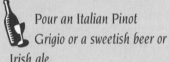 *Pour an Italian Pinot Grigio or a sweetish beer or Irish ale.*

1 lb.	clams in the shell	450 g
1 lb.	mussels in the shell	450 g
1	leek, slivered	1
1	red bell pepper, slivered	1
1 cup	Black Bean Sauce (page 18)	250 ml
	minced cilantro for garnish	

Wash the clams and mussels in running water, pulling off and discarding any beards that protrude from the mussels. Place the sliced leek and red bell pepper into a heavy-bottomed stockpot with a little water. Bring to a high boil and cook the vegetables until they are just tender. Add the Black Bean Sauce and return to a boil. Add the clams once the sauce is boiling, and cover with a tight-fitting lid. Cook on high heat for about 3 minutes, shaking the pot every minute or so to redistribute the clams. Peek after 3 minutes, and if the shells are beginning to open, add the mussels and replace the lid. Cook another 3 minutes, or until all the shellfish have opened. Toss or shake well to move the shells on the top of the pile to the bottom of the pot so that everything cooks evenly. Discard any clams or mussels that do not open when it is evident that the rest are all open.

Serve in large bowls garnished with cilantro, with empty bowls close by for empty shells, and finger bowls at the ready.

Remember to wash the clams and mussels just before you plan on cooking them. Like most wise creatures, they are not fond of chlorinated tap water, and will perish promptly if they are stored in tap water or washed too soon. It's best to buy and cook these perishable creatures all in one day, but if you have to store them, the best way is to transfer them to a colander or sieve and suspend that over a large bowl. Cover the shellfish with a damp cloth, and place ice on top of that. They drown if you put them directly into a bath of fresh water.

Clams or Mussels with Ale and Leeks

Serves 4 as a starter

These shellfish are fairly delicate and briny in taste. To avoid overwhelming the sweet, mild flavor, choose a medium ale, preferably a microbrew. If you want to use both clams and mussels, start the clams and add the mussels 2 minutes later. Serve with lots of bread to mop up all the juices.

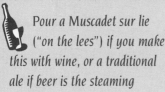

Pour a Muscadet sur lie ("on the lees") if you make this with wine, or a traditional ale if beer is the steaming medium.

2 1/4 lbs.	clams or mussels in the shell	1 kg
1	leek, slivered	1
2 cloves	garlic, minced	2 cloves
1 Tbsp.	minced fresh thyme	15 ml
1/2 cup	ale or wine	125 ml

Wash the clams or mussels, pulling off any beards that protrude from the mussel shells. Put the remaining ingredients in a large, heavy-bottomed pot. Bring to a boil, add the molluscs, and cover tightly. Cook on high for several minutes, shaking the pan vigorously, until the shells open. Discard any that do not open. Serve.

Healthy clams and mussels should be clamped tightly shut. Any that are gaping open should be tossed into the garbage right away, but if the shell is only slightly open, rap it sharply on a hard surface; sometimes molluscs like to take the air and just need a reminder to tuck themselves in. If the shell closes, go ahead and cook it.

Martini Shrimp

Serves 4 as a starter or 2 as a main course

Classic drinks are back, with cutting-edge flavors. For cooks, this is a good thing. Infused vodka adds a wonderful punch to food, especially fish. I like to heap these shrimp in oversized martini glasses, layered with olives, for a tongue-in-cheek presentation.

Choose a good vodka, mix a drink, and serve dinner before the chill is off the ice. Or pour a light white Frascati or a frizzante Chardonnay.

1 lb.	raw shrimp, peeled	450 g
1	lemon, juice and zest	1
2 Tbsp.	minced fresh lemon thyme or thyme	30 ml
1/4 cup	flavored vodka	60 ml
1 Tbsp.	freshly cracked pepper	15 ml
2 tsp.	olive oil	10 ml
	salt to taste	

If the shrimp are in the shell, peel them, freezing the shells for another purpose, such as shrimp stock. In a shallow pan, toss the shrimp with the lemon juice and zest, thyme, vodka, pepper and olive oil. Mix well to coat each shrimp, then set aside for 15 minutes to 1 hour. Heat the grill to high and cook the shrimp until pink or white, depending on the type of shrimp.

Lila's Cioppino

Serves 6 very generously as a main course

My aunt Lila has spent most of her adult life living in the San Francisco Bay region. This is my version of her version of the Italian fishermen's stew that originated in the Bay area. To determine how much fish to buy, calculate it per person: 4 shrimp or prawns, 4 clams, 4 mussels, 4 ounces (120 g) crab in the shell, 3 ounces (90 g) firm-textured white fish, such as snapper, cod, monkfish or halibut. Buy and use shellfish in the shell; the flavor is better, and it contributes to the messy, hands-on casual feeling that conjures up crowded North Beach diners, counters strewn with wine glasses and bowls of shellfish. Cioppino doesn't reheat well—the fish tends to overcook, so cook only as much as can be eaten in one meal. Don't forget to buy several loaves of the best crusty sourdough bread you can find.

Serve this with bottles of California Zinfandel, choosing a light fruity style with good acidity. Or open a French Chinon or Cabernet Franc.

1	onion, finely sliced	1
1	leek, finely sliced	1
12 cloves	garlic, minced	12 cloves
2 stalks	celery, finely sliced	2 stalks
1 bulb	fresh fennel, finely sliced	1 bulb
1 Tbsp.	olive oil	15 ml
1 tsp.	fennel seed, cracked	5 ml
1 tsp.	dried basil	5 ml
1 tsp.	dried oregano	5 ml
1 tsp.	dried thyme	5 ml
1	bay leaf	1
1/8 tsp.	saffron threads	.5 ml
1 Tbsp.	cracked peppercorns	15 ml
1 cup	dry red wine	250 ml
1	lemon, juice and zest	1
2 28-oz. tins	Italian plum tomatoes	2 796-ml tins
2 Tbsp.	tomato paste	30 ml
2 Tbsp.	honey	30 ml
	salt and freshly ground pepper to taste	
1 1/2 lbs.	firm-textured white fish	675 g
24	shrimp or prawns, shell on	24
24	clams in the shell	24
24	mussels in the shell	24
1 1/2 lbs.	crab in the shell	675 g
	minced green onions for garnish	
	minced fresh basil for garnish	

Make the sauce first; it can be made several days in advance and left to mellow in the fridge. In a large, heavy-bottomed pan, cook the onion, leek, garlic, celery and fennel with the olive oil until the vegetables are tender, adding small amounts of water as needed. Stir in the dried herbs and spices, add the red wine and bring to a boil. Stir in the lemon juice and zest, tomatoes and tomato paste. Simmer until the sauce is thickened slightly and add honey, salt and pepper to balance the flavors. Cool, then cover and refrigerate until needed.

On the day you plan to serve the cioppino, scrub the clams and mussels, pulling off and discarding any beards that protrude from the mussels. Cut the fish into bite-size pieces. Chop the crab into manageable lengths. Put large soup plates or bowls into the oven on low heat to warm up. Set out finger bowls of lemon-infused water, bowls for the shells, and copious napkins. Remind your friends and family not to wear silk—this is a messy meal.

In a large, preferably shallow pan, bring the sauce to a boil. Add the cubed fish, cover and reduce the heat. Three minutes later, check to see if the fish is about half done; if it is, add the shrimp or prawns for about 3 minutes, then add the clams, and 2 minutes later add the mussels and crab. Be sure to put the lid back on after each addition, and don't let the temperature drop too low—return briefly to a boil each time you add to the pot. Do not overcook!

Ladle into heated bowls, evenly distributing the various types of fish. Garnish with green onions and basil. Serve hot with lots of bread and wine.

Seafood stews proliferate along the coastlines of every maritime nation. It becomes a question of how the stew is seasoned and what fish is locally available. In varying parts of the world, try bouillabaisse, oyster stew, zarzuela, bourride, matelote, kakavia, ttoro, chaudree or caldeirada. On the west coast of North America, the cioppino born on the docks of San Francisco sets the standard.

Seared Scallops on Pear Slices with a Cider Glaze

Serves 4

*N*ot many fruits combine well with seafood, but pears are one of the few that do. If you like, choose Asian pears; they will remain crisp even after grilling. I prefer using Bartletts, Packhams or Anjous that are just beginning to ripen. Too ripe, and the pear will turn to mush on the grill, so choose carefully.

Thread each portion of the scallops onto two skewers to avoid having to flip half a million tiny pieces in a hurry. The use of two skewers prevents the scallops from swinging madly about on a single axis. This dish is very good when salmon is used in place of scallops.

 Open an Australian Semillon or a Chardonnay with no trace of oak.

3 cups	apple or pear cider	750 ml
I	lemon, juice and zest	I
I tsp.	peppercorns, cracked	5 ml
4 Tbsp.	minced fresh lemon balm or lemon thyme	60 ml
1/2 tsp.	ground star anise	2.5 ml
I lb.	sea scallops	450 g
2 Tbsp.	minced fresh thyme	30 ml
	salt and pepper to taste	
I Tbsp.	canola oil	15 ml
2	pears, peeled and sliced in eighths	2
	thyme, lemon thyme or lemon balm sprigs for garnish	

Place the cider in a shallow pan with the lemon juice, half the lemon zest, the peppercorns, lemon thyme or balm and star anise. Bring to a boil, then simmer to reduce the cider to a syrupy glaze totalling about 1/2 cup (125 ml). Strain it and set aside.

Preheat the grill to high. Sprinkle the scallops with the remaining lemon zest, the fresh thyme and salt and pepper. Drizzle the oil over the scallops and the sliced pears. Thread skewers through the scallops. Grill, turning once, and when the scallops are nearly done, brush the top of each with some of the reserved glaze. Grill the pears just long enough to mark the slices, then transfer to plates, arranging in a fan of 4 slices per portion. Place the skewers next to or slightly on top of the grilled pear slices. Spoon the remaining glaze in front of the slices to form a pool. Garnish with sprigs of thyme, lemon thyme or lemon balm.

Lemon thyme and lemon balm combine the best of the best—tart citrus and herbal green in a single plant! Both are easily grown perennials, so buy seeds and grow your own patch. Once you cook with them, you'll need your own to keep up.

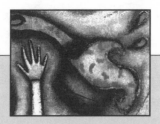

Poultry and Meat

I spent 13 years as a vegetarian; in the end, when I put meat back into my diet, it was sausage and roasted chicken and crusty lamb that I missed. Now, although we don't have meat on the table every day, or even every week, I still enjoy the outer crusty bits from a leg of lamb, or a well-grilled and spicy sausage sliced into my soup or risotto.

I rarely cook meat without marinating it first. I like to put red meat into a marinade for at least 8 hours, although I have left flank in a marinade for several days at a time, and the entire concept of sauerbraten revolves about an intense marinade. Red meat, such as beef and lamb, will gain flavor if it is in marinade for anywhere upwards of 8 hours. Breast of poultry needs only 4 to 8 hours in marinade, while thighs and drumsticks will be fine for up to 24 hours.

Finding free-range and organically raised poultry is the best thing you can do for yourself and your family. Independent butchers, always the best bet for high-quality meats, are now becoming reliable sources for free-range chicken and turkey. In addition, health food stores and co-ops tend to bring in chemical-free foods, including meat and poultry.

Breast of Turkey Rolled Around Cranberry-Sage Stuffing

Serves 4 to 8, depending on size of turkey breast

Traditional flavors deserve to stay together, but sometimes, as with any relationship, they need a little shake-up to bring out their best qualities. Turkey and stuffing, hold the cranberries, while endearing, has an enduring reputation as a slightly stodgy soporific, guaranteed to put thousands to sleep twice a year. This recipe gives a new form and a new method of cooking to this seasonal favorite, delivering it in a lighter style that is likely to make it to the dining table more often than the old stuffed bird. This dish is great with a seasonal Fresh Fruit Salsa (page 19) and Summer Grain Salad (page 160).

 Pour a Gewurztraminer, a dry rosé or a Pinot Blanc.

1/2 cup	root vegetables, julienned	125 ml
1	onion or leek, julienned	1
4–6 cloves	garlic, minced	4–6 cloves
1/2 cup	minced fresh herbs, your choice of sage, chives, thyme, parsley or lemon thyme	125 ml
1	lemon, zest only	1
1 cup	breadcrumbs	250 ml
1/2 cup	grated Parmesan, optional	125 ml
4	egg whites	4
	salt and pepper to taste	
1/2 cup	dried cranberries	125 ml
1/3 cup	minced fresh sage	80 ml
1/2	turkey breast, boneless and skinless	1/2
1 tsp.	canola oil	5 ml
1/2–1 cup	stock, water, cider or white wine	125–250 ml

To make the filling, steam the root vegetables, onion or leek, and garlic in a small amount of water until tender. Drain well. When they are cool, toss them in a bowl with the minced herbs, lemon zest, breadcrumbs and Parmesan. Stir in the egg whites (or 2 whole eggs), salt and pepper and the dried cranberries and sage.

Butterfly the half breast by slicing in half horizontally to end up with a flat, roughly rectangular piece about 1/4" (.6 cm) thick. Spread the filling over the turkey, roll it up like a jelly roll and tie at regular intervals with butcher twine.

Place on a lightly oiled baking sheet, with the seam of the filled breast facing down. Lightly oil the exposed top surfaces. Brown under the broiler until blistered and lightly browned. Add the liquid to the pan, cover and cook in a medium-hot oven (375°F/190°C) until tender, about 45 minutes. Check for doneness, and remember, there is no absolute cooking time: cook until done. The turkey juices should run clear without the meat being dried out. Cool before slicing.

Herb-Smoked Turkey Breast

Serves 6 to 8

The smokiness of the herb stems is a wonderful counterpoint to the mild, sweet flavor of turkey. Chicken breast is a good alternative if you have difficulty finding turkey. I love to pair this with juicy, spicy Fresh Fruit Salsa (page 19), Mango Sauce (page 17) or Bean Salsa (page 20) and greens tossed in your choice of vinaigrette. Cook the meat until it is just done and still juicy; overcooked turkey breast is a first cousin to shoe leather.

The wine you pour is dictated by the sauce you choose to accompany the mild turkey. For Bean Salsa, pour a Riesling or Gewurztraminer; for Fresh Fruit Salsa, open a fruity, unoaked New World Chardonnay or an Alsatian or German Pinot Blanc; for Mango Sauce, serve a fruity Semillon or Chardonnay.

2 Tbsp.	minced fresh rosemary	30 ml
2 Tbsp.	puréed garlic	30 ml
I tsp.	cracked fennel seed	5 ml
I	orange, zest only	I
2 Tbsp.	cracked white peppercorns	30 ml
2 tsp.	olive oil	10 ml
2 1/4 lbs.	whole turkey breast	I kg
2 cups	herb stems, soaked in water	500 ml

Blend together the rosemary, garlic, fennel seed, orange zest, peppercorns and olive oil. A mortar and pestle is most efficient, or stir together into a paste in a small bowl. Smear over the turkey breast, being sure to cover all the flesh on both sides, and set aside while you preheat the grill. Set the temperature controls so that one side of the grill is very slow and the other is at medium heat.

Drain the soaking herb stems and wrap them in aluminum foil with several holes poked in it. Place the package directly on the rocks or coals of the cooler side of the grill. Close the lid to allow smoke to develop for about 10 minutes, then quickly place the meat on the other side of the grill and close the lid. Turn once, and try to avoid peeking, or the smoke will be lost, and too much oxygen will be introduced into the enclosed area, increasing the chance of the twigs burning instead of smoking. Do not overcook; this is a low-fat cut of meat that will toughen and dry out if overdone. Cooking time will vary from grill to grill, but allow 10 to 15 minutes before you turn the meat.

When the turkey is done, remove it from the heat and let it stand a few minutes before carving it thinly against the grain.

If you like, make a compound butter by blending softened unsalted butter with the paste. Mix together double the amount of each ingredient, then stir into 1 cup (250 ml) of butter. Form the blend into a small log, wrap it well and chill or freeze. Slice a very small amount onto each portion when you serve it.

Chicken Cacciatore

Serves 8

This Italian version of "hunter's chicken" is not a new dish, but it is loaded with fresh flavors. The traditional start to a braised dish, the dredging of the meat in flour and sautéing in hot oil, has been left out, which marginally increases the cooking time and heightens the fresh, light quality of the dish. Use only thighs and drumsticks for this braise, as breast meat will dry out and toughen in the time it takes to reach tenderness with dark meat. If you can get wild mushrooms, do, but field mushrooms are fine too. Serve with rice or noodles.

 Keep the Mediterranean theme alive by pouring an Italian Chianti Riserva or a Spanish Rioja.

1	onion, diced in 1/2" (1-cm) cubes	1
1	leek, sliced	1
1 head	garlic, peeled and sliced	1 head
2 cups	fresh mushrooms, quartered	500 ml
2 tsp.	olive oil	10 ml
1 stalk	fresh rosemary	1 stalk
1 tsp.	dried thyme	5 ml
1 tsp.	dried oregano	5 ml
1 tsp.	dried basil	5 ml
1 28-oz. tin	canned tomatoes	1 796-ml tin
2 Tbsp.	tomato paste	30 ml
1 Tbsp.	Worcestershire sauce	15 ml
8	chicken legs, bone in	8
	salt and hot chili flakes to taste	

Set the oven at 375°F (190°C). Choose a braising dish that can be used on the stovetop and in the oven, and cook the onion, leek, garlic and mushrooms until translucent in the olive oil, adding small amounts of water as needed to prevent browning. Add the herbs, tomatoes, tomato paste and Worcestershire sauce. Bring to a boil, chop up the tomatoes with a wooden spoon if you like, and add the chicken pieces in a single layer. Spoon the sauce over and around each piece to cover as much as possible, then place in the oven, covered. Cook until tender, about 2 hours. Season with salt and hot chili flakes.

Grilled Stuffed Leg and Breast of Chicken

Serves 10 to 12 as a starter or 6 as a main course

In the late summer, this is great served on a bed of new corn kernels and peppers simmered in olive oil. Otherwise, serve on mesclun, wilted red chard or any sturdy, slightly bitter lettuce. Prairie Sage Vinaigrette is called for in this recipe, but a number of vinaigrettes would enhance this dish, such as Roasted Pepper and Cilantro Vinaigrette (page 36) or Roasted Tomato and Basil Vinaigrette (page 39).

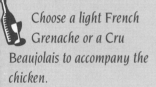

Choose a light French Grenache or a Cru Beaujolais to accompany the chicken.

1 5-lb.	chicken	1 2.2-kg
1	lemon, zest and juice	1
1 Tbsp.	honey, melted	15 ml
2 tsp.	olive oil	10 ml
2 Tbsp.	minced fresh lemon thyme or thyme	30 ml
2 tsp.	cracked peppercorns	10 ml
4 cloves	garlic, minced	4 cloves
3 cups	Cornbread (page 191)	750 ml
1–2	eggs	1–2
1 head	lettuce or chard	1 head
1/4 cup	Prairie Sage Vinaigrette (page 46)	60 ml

Bone the chicken into 2 breasts, 2 thighs and 2 drums, all bones removed and skin still attached. Freeze the wings for another purpose. Mix together the lemon, honey, oil, minced herbs, pepper and garlic. Spread it on the chicken pieces and marinate overnight.

Crumble the cornbread (make it a day in advance if you like; it keeps well). Whisk together the eggs and mix with the cornbread. Tuck the cornbread stuffing under the skin of the chicken pieces. Preheat the oven to 425°F (220°C) or heat the barbecue. Grill or roast the chicken pieces, turning once or twice, until the juices run clear. Remove from heat and let stand 5 to 10 minutes. Toss the greens with the vinaigrette, reserving a little vinaigrette. Slice the chicken. Arrange the greens and the chicken slices on the plates. Drizzle a little vinaigrette on each slice.

In the high days of summer, try this dish with juicy raspberries in the vinaigrette and on the plate, adding their color and bite to this beautiful dish. In the fall, roasted peppers in several colors or grilled eggplant contrast with the sweet undertones of the cornbread stuffing. In winter, when food seems to match the sullen sky, reach for the jars of summer on pantry shelves. Red Bell Pepper Rhumba or Chili Cha-Cha won't change the color of the sky, but they might lighten your mood.

Velvet Chicken Thighs to Sigh For

Serves 4

We should all have thighs to sigh for now and then. This delicious dish has a soft, supple texture that makes it the envy of less well-endowed meals. Sigh.

 Pour a Californian Chenin Blanc or Gewurztraminer with this sexy little number.

4	chicken thighs	4
1/4 cup	light soy sauce	60 ml
4 tsp.	cornstarch	20 ml
1/4 cup	rice vinegar or sake	60 ml
2 bunches	spinach	2 bunches
2 tsp.	canola oil	10 ml
3 Tbsp.	puréed ginger root	45 ml
3 Tbsp.	puréed garlic	45 ml
2–3 cups	water or stock	500–750 ml
2	red bell peppers, cut into 2" (5-cm) squares	2
2 bunches	green onions, cut into 2" (5-cm) lengths	2 bunches
3 Tbsp.	minced cilantro	45 ml
1 tsp.	hot chili paste	5 ml
1 Tbsp.	sesame oil	15 ml
1	lemon, zest only	1
	GARNISHES:	
	toasted sesame seeds	
	or cashews	

Remove the skin and bones from the chicken thighs. Cut the chicken into bite-size pieces. Make a marinade of soy sauce, cornstarch and vinegar or sake and toss with the chicken. Set aside for 30 minutes while you prepare the vegetables.

Wash and stem the spinach, but do not spin it or pat it dry. When the chicken has marinated for 30 minutes, heat your sauté pan or wok without any oil. Add the spinach with just the residue of its washing water and quickly toss with tongs until it wilts. Remove it immediately to a platter and cover loosely.

Tip out any spinach water and reheat the pan with the oil. Cook the ginger and garlic briefly, then add the cut-up chicken thighs and marinade. Cook, stirring, over high heat, while slowly adding the water or stock, thinning as needed. Cook until the chicken is done, about 5 to 8 minutes. Add the peppers and green onions and cook another 1 to 2 minutes.

Stir in the cilantro, hot chili paste, sesame oil and lemon zest. Pour onto the platter alongside or over the wilted spinach. Sprinkle with the toasted seeds or nuts and serve immediately.

The process of marinating less tender cuts of meat in cornstarch and acid is a Chinese tradition known as "velvetizing." Because of the cornstarch, do not double this recipe unless you put each batch into a separate bowl and cook it separately.

Darl's Honey Lemon Chicken — Bake in corning ware dish

Serves 6 growing boys

✓✓✓✓

Hockey shares pride of place with soccer in the heart of my eldest son, Darl. The small and plucky scrapper Theoren Fleury is Darl's favorite hockey player, and one day my husband brought home a cookbook, a fundraiser, that featured Theo's version of honey lemon chicken. "Make that one please, Mom," pleaded my always-starving child, so I changed it substantially to create my version. The original required a deep fryer; this works on a grill or in the oven. Use dark meet for this dish; lean white meat dries out too quickly.

Serve a Semillon-Chardonnay blend or a Chenin Blanc with this slightly sweet dish.

12	chicken legs (I used 18 thighs)	12
1/4 cup	melted honey	60 ml
1/3 cup	lemon juice	80 ml
3/4 tsp.	dried thyme	4 ml
6–8 cloves	garlic, minced	6–8 cloves
4 Tbsp.	coarse-grained mustard	60 ml
1 Tbsp.	canola oil	15 ml
	salt and freshly ground pepper to taste	

If you like, cut the thigh and drumstick bones entirely free with a boning knife. Alternatively, slice each piece of meat open along the bone so it lies flat and is of an even thickness.

Combine the remaining ingredients in a small bowl. Lay the chicken on a baking tray in a single layer and drizzle the paste over it, spreading it evenly with the back of a spoon. Bake, uncovered, at 325°F (165°C), until the chicken is tender, 1 to 2 hours, depending on the size of the legs. Turn the chicken once or twice to evenly brown all surfaces. If you prefer, grill the chicken over medium heat until tender. Be warned—no matter how you cook this dish, the skin will darken and char from the honey, but for some of us that is a large part of the attraction.

Turn to 350° ½ way through & then 400 to brown.

Chicken and Duck in Apple Cider and Molasses

Serves 10 to 12 as a starter or 6 as a main course

This dish is a funky, rich concoction of chicken and duck braised in a pungent marinade. Remove the breast meat and use it elsewhere; it will dry out during the cooking time needed for the legs. You can use either duck or chicken but it will be a slightly different dish.

I also like to serve this as a pasta sauce, with rice pilaf and salsa, with a simple steamed vegetable and a grain salad, or as a cold salad on a picnic.

This complex dish will shine with a rich, buttery, toasty Chardonnay or a Reserve Pinot Noir from Oregon.

I	chicken	I
I	duck	I
4 Tbsp.	minced fresh thyme	60 ml
I	lemon, juice and zest	I
I cup	unfiltered apple cider	250 ml
1/2 cup	unsulfured molasses	125 ml
6 cloves	garlic, sliced	6 cloves
I Tbsp.	cracked black peppercorns	15 ml
4 Tbsp.	shredded fresh basil	60 ml
2–3 twigs	rosemary	2–3 twigs
2	shallots, minced	2
I	yellow onion, finely sliced	I
2	apples, sliced and cored	2
I cup	Caramelized Apple Vinaigrette (page 45)	125 ml
4 cups	mixed greens	I litre

Cut up the birds, saving the carcasses for stock and discarding as much fat as you can. Separate the drums from the thighs and set the breast meat and wings aside for another purpose. Make the marinade by mixing together the thyme, lemon juice and zest, apple cider, molasses, garlic, peppercorns, basil, rosemary, shallots and onion. Smear over and around the chicken and duck pieces. Marinate for about 12 hours, covered and chilled.

Cover the poultry with tinfoil, leaving the marinade on the meat. Braise until tender at a temperature of 450°F (230°C), about 90 minutes. Remove from the oven, shred the meat, and toss it with the sliced apples in a small amount of vinaigrette. Toss the greens with the vinaigrette, arrange on the plates, and top with the sliced apple and shredded meat mixture. Serve warm or cold.

New Wave Chicken in Zin Vin

Serves 4 as a main couse or 8 as a side dish

This is an ideal summer salad. It doesn't take long, it doesn't heat up the kitchen, it provides fresh, juicy, crunchy textures, and it is fun; try saying Zin Vin without grinning!

This dish began as an idea for a wine and food pairing class, and it became an instant favorite. It is made to be served with wine.

Choose a white Zinfandel, or try a fruitier Californian rosé or Chenin Blanc.

4	chicken breasts, skinned and boned	4
2	Granny Smith apples, sliced	2
2 stalks	celery, sliced	2 stalks
1 bunch	green onions, chopped	1 bunch
4 Tbsp.	minced fresh thyme	60 ml
1/2 cup	diced zucchini	125 ml
1/2 cup	Caramelized Pecans (page 24)	125 ml
4 cups	mixed greens	1 litre
1 cup	White Zinfandel Vinaigrette (page 44)	250 ml

Pan-steam the chicken breasts until cooked, about 5 to 7 minutes. Slice or shred the cooled chicken into bite-size pieces. Toss in a large bowl with the remaining ingredients except for the greens and half of the dressing. Toss the greens separately with the reserved vinaigrette, arrange the greens on individual plates, and top with the chicken mixture.

Chicken Legs Roasted in Black Bean Sauce

Serves 8 as a main dish

The black bean sauce that forms the heart of this dish has had a place in my heart for years. It shows up in numerous guises and this one is at the top of the list. The slightly sweet edge works well on mild chicken, but it shines with duck, so substitute duck legs if you can.

Choose a cool-climate Gewurztraminer or Chenin Blanc, or a full-fruit Californian or Pacific Northwest Riesling.

1	onion, thickly sliced	1
1	red bell pepper, diced	1
1 cup	Black Bean Sauce (page 18)	250 ml
8	chicken drumsticks or thighs	8
	cilantro and sesame seeds for garnish	

Mix together the onion, red bell pepper and black bean sauce. Smear over the chicken pieces and place in a shallow roasting pan or baking dish with a lip. Roast in a slow oven, about 325°F (165°C), until the chicken is tender and the juices run clear, about 1 1/2 hours. Alternatively, grill over medium heat for 15 to 20 minutes. Serve hot or cold.

Chicken in Yoghurt

Serves 6

This is a spinoff from the classic Indian approach. It's fast, lends itself to a variety of cooking techniques, and the end result is meltingly tender, even more so if the chicken is allowed to marinate overnight. Choose a yoghurt that doesn't have gelatin as a stabilizer. For more pungently flavored chicken, rub the meat with generous amounts of North African Berber Spice Blend (page 25). Serve with Green Tomato Mincemeat (page 34), Cucumber Raita (page 149), any rice pilaf you particularly love, and fresh apple or fruit slices.

 Open a bottle of Riesling or Chenin Blanc, or opt for beer—a sweet brown ale or India pale ale.

6	chicken breasts, skinned and boned	6
3/4 cup	plain yoghurt	185 ml
1 tsp.	ground cumin	5 ml
1 tsp.	ground coriander	5 ml
1 tsp.	garam masala or curry powder	5 ml
1	lemon or lime, zest only	1
2 Tbsp.	minced ginger root	30 ml
1 bunch	green onions, slivered	1 bunch
1 tsp.	hot chili flakes	5 ml

Trim any fat from the chicken. Mix together all the remaining ingredients and smear thoroughly over the chicken breasts. Cover and marinate in the fridge overnight if time allows, or not at all if time is short.

Preheat the oven to 450°F (230°C). Cut 6 circles of parchment paper, each about 10 to 12" (25 to 30 cm). Fold each in half and place a chicken breast, with any yoghurt that clings to it, in the center of each circle, alongside the fold. Fold the paper so the curved edges meet, and tightly fold the edges over in 1/2" (1-cm) lengths, with each successive fold beginning in the middle of the previous fold. When you reach the straight edge, return to the center of the curve and fold in the other direction; the end result should be a half-circle package with the curved edge entirely sealed by overlapping folds. The chicken can be refrigerated at this point. Otherwise, place the packages on a baking sheet and bake for about 10 minutes, or until they puff up with steam. Serve hot, with warnings to take care when cutting the packages open.

Variation
If you want a crisp exterior rather than the soft, tender texture of chicken in parchment, cook the marinated chicken on the grill. If you opt for that, you may wish to use drumsticks and thighs as well as breast meat.

Pan-Steamed Chicken with Fennel, Saffron and Onion

Serves 4 as a main course or 6 as a side dish

This is the culinary equivalent of the all-purpose little black dress. Vary the seasonings as you please, and serve the chicken sliced on a heap of greens in a sharp vinaigrette, tossed in Roasted Tomato Sauce (page 23) or the sauce from Orzo with Tangiers Sauce (page 172), on pasta or grain, or with Fennel Apple Slaw (page 146).

Open a Spanish Rioja or Portuguese Dao to serve with the saffron flavors.

4	chicken breasts	4
1 tsp.	fennel seeds	5 ml
4 cloves	garlic, puréed	4 cloves
1/8 tsp.	saffron threads	.5 ml
1/2 tsp.	dried basil	2.5 ml
1 tsp.	cracked peppercorns	5 ml
1 bunch	green onions, finely minced	1 bunch
1	orange, zest and juice	1
1 tsp.	olive oil	5 ml

Remove all fat and skin from the chicken. Crack the fennel seeds in a mortar and pestle or electric spice mill. Smear the garlic onto the chicken, then sprinkle on the saffron, fennel seeds, basil, pepper, green onions and orange zest. Drizzle with the orange juice and olive oil. Cover and marinate in the refrigerator from 15 minutes to overnight.

Heat a nonstick sauté pan to low, remove the chicken from the fridge, and pan-steam, covered tightly with a lid, until the chicken is cooked through, from 7 to 10 minutes. Remove the chicken from the pan and slice thinly against the grain. Serve warm.

Any chicken that can be pan-steamed can be grilled for an entirely different textural finish. Never hesitate to try a different cooking technique, particularly in the summer when it's too hot to turn on the stove, even when the entire crew is famished.

Braised Beef with Garlic, Leeks and Ale

Serves 8 to 10 with lots of leftovers

Pot roast, as earthy as they come, is economical, needs little attention, and invariably yields leftovers for another day's meal. This one is flavored with ale to reinforce that earthy quality. Choose a microbrew with character and a dark, slightly bitter edge to it.

Serve a Cru Beaujolais or a full, rich, high-alcohol beer with this meat.

1 Tbsp.	olive oil	15 ml
2 1/4 lbs.	cross-rib, blade or chuck roast	1 kg
1	onion, diced	1
1	leek, diced	1
4	carrots, diced	4
2 stalks	celery, diced	2 stalks
1 head	garlic, split horizontally	1 head
1 tsp.	dried thyme	5 ml
1 tsp.	dried oregano	5 ml
1 tsp.	dried savory	5 ml
1 sprig	fresh rosemary	1 sprig
1 Tbsp.	freshly ground pepper	15 ml
1 lb.	diced potatoes	450 g
2 cups	raw green lentils	500 ml
4–6	Roma tomatoes, diced	4–6
12 oz.	dark ale	340 ml
2 cups	beef stock	500 ml
2 Tbsp.	cornstarch (optional)	30 ml
	salt and freshly ground pepper to taste	

Set the oven to 375°F (190°C). Heat the oil in a nonstick sauté pan and brown the meat on all sides. Transfer the beef to an ovenproof dish and brown the onion, leek, carrots, celery and garlic in the oil. Stir in the dried herbs, rosemary, pepper, potatoes, lentils and tomatoes, then spread the mixture around the meat.

Deglaze the sauté pan with the ale and stock, bring it to a boil and pour over the meat. Cover tightly and place in the oven. Cook until tender, checking after 2 1/2 hours.

When it's done, remove the meat and let it rest, loosely covered. Skim off any fat on the roasting juices, then bring the juices to a boil. Thicken with cornstarch if desired. Adjust seasoning with salt and pepper. Serve the tender lentils and vegetables as part of the sauce.

Variation

For **Braised Chicken**, substitute chicken thighs and drumsticks on the bone for the beef in this recipe. If you like, leave out the browning of the meat, and replace the lentils with 2 cups (500 ml) cooked beans, adding them along with the ale (or cider, if you prefer). The chicken should be tender and ready to eat inside an hour and a half.

The type of lentil dictates the texture of the finished dish. Red lentils cook into a thick purée, good for soup but not ideal for salad or curry. Brown lentils hold their shape even better, but my favorites are the fine little green French lentils.

Marinated Flank Steak

Serves 4

The strong and assertive seasonings in this dish work best on beef. Use flank steak, tenderloin, or a blade roast cut into steaks and grilled quickly to medium-rare. Do not overcook! Serve it sliced on greens with Ponzu Vinaigrette (page 41), with grilled baby vegetables on the side, or on sliced crusty baguette with the aioli from Grilled Vegetable Cornbread Sandwich with Herb Aioli (page 140). This is enough marinade for one or two flank steaks; double or triple the proportions for larger volumes.

Serve a full-fruit Zinfandel or an Australian Shiraz.

1/2 cup	dark soy	125 ml
2 Tbsp.	sesame oil	30 ml
4 Tbsp.	minced green onion	60 ml
6–8 cloves	garlic, minced	6–8 cloves
1 Tbsp.	minced ginger root	15 ml
2 Tbsp.	melted honey	30 ml
1 Tbsp.	toasted and ground sesame seeds	15 ml
1	orange, juice and zest	1
1/2 tsp.	hot chili flakes	2.5 ml
1 lb.	flank steak	450 g

Combine all the ingredients but the beef, mix well, and pour over the beef. Cover securely and refrigerate overnight, or for up to 3 or 4 days. The longer it marinates, the more tender the finished texture. Remove the meat from the fridge 20 minutes before grilling. Grill over high heat until medium-rare, about 10 minutes, although the exact time will vary with the size of the steak. Let rest a few minutes after cooking, then slice thinly against the grain.

Flank steak is an underappreciated cut that deserves to be enjoyed more often. It is almost entirely lean, and most people see it as a prime candidate for tough old-boot styles of cooking. Long marinating combined with quick cooking to medium-rare can change that perception with one bite.

Honey-Herb Cured Beef with Fresh Mango Sauce

Serves 12 to 16 as a starter, 6 to 8 as a main course

This can be a showstopper for special-occasion meals. Tenderloin is expensive, but it is also virtually fat-free and blessed with a texture the quality of good butter. For a change of texture, serve a mango-based Fresh Fruit Salsa (page 19) in place of the mango sauce.

Serve a Southern Californian Zinfandel with a light, soft style and baked fruit characteristics.

2 1/4 lbs.	beef tenderloin, whole	1 kg
1/2 cup	honey, melted	125 ml
4 cloves	garlic, puréed	4 cloves
1 Tbsp.	olive oil	15 ml
2	shallots, minced	2
2 stalks	fresh rosemary, finely minced	2 stalks
2 Tbsp.	minced fresh thyme	30 ml
1 Tbsp.	minced fresh marjoram or oregano	15 ml
	hot chili flakes or freshly ground pepper to taste	
2 cups	Mango Sauce (page 17)	500 ml

Clean the beef by carefully stripping off all the silverskin and fat with a sharp knife; leave the steak in one large piece. Combine the remaining ingredients except the Mango Sauce. Smear the mixture generously over the beef to cover it. Place on a rack with a drip tray below and refrigerate, uncovered or very loosely covered, for 1 to 3 days.

When you are ready to cook, remove the meat from the fridge to warm up at room temperature while you make the sauce. Turn on the grill or heat the oven to 425°F (220°C) and grill or roast the tenderloin to medium-rare, about 30 minutes, or to taste. (Bear in mind that such a lean cut of meat will be tougher if cooked to well-done.) Remove from the heat, cover loosely and let rest 10 minutes before carving. Serve in thin slices with the sauce.

Whenever my dad grilled steaks when we were all growing up, he would carefully trim off the little skirt of tenderloin from each cooked T-bone and collect them on his plate. It was a mystery. Why would my great big dad want those little scraps instead of his own big steak? Now, on the rare occasion I grill a T-bone for my boys and myself, I trim off the little skirt of tenderloin for me, and the guys share the rest. Father sometimes does know best.

Mom's Sauerbraten

Serves 6 to 8 generously, or 4 growing teenagers

Every book needs at least one recipe from Mom, so here is my Mom's seven-day marinade for my favorite childhood memory. Serve this classic with noodles or Garlicky Mashed Potatoes (page 134), Braised Leeks (page 143), Glazed Root Vegetables (page 142) or Roasted Vegetables in Roasted Pepper Vinaigrette (page 133).

To complement this meat, open a bottle of German Riesling or Gewurztraminer, or opt for a good German Pilsner.

1 cup	dry red wine	250 ml
1 Tbsp.	red wine vinegar	15 ml
1 tsp.	cracked peppercorns	5 ml
2 tsp.	mustard	10 ml
1	bay leaf	1
1 tsp.	dried thyme	5 ml
1/4 tsp.	ground cloves	1.2 ml
1	onion, finely minced	1
2 1/4 lbs.	blade roast	1 kg
1 Tbsp.	cornstarch	15 ml
2 Tbsp.	whipping cream (optional)	30 ml
	salt and pepper to taste	

To make the marinade, combine the wine, vinegar, pepper, mustard, bay, thyme, cloves and onion. Immerse the roast in the marinade, turning daily, for a minimum of 48 hours, and up to a week for the biggest flavor.

Place the roast and marinade in an ovenproof pan with a snug lid and braise, covered, at 350°F (180°C) for 2 hours or until tender. Remove the roast to a plate, cover loosely and strain the braising liquid, discarding the solids. Bring the liquid to a boil, thicken with cornstarch dissolved in cold water, and return briefly to a boil until the starch is clear. Add the cream if desired, then adjust the seasoning with salt and pepper. Slice the meat very thinly against the grain.

Herb-Crusted Leg of Lamb with Red Wine Glaze

Serves 6 to 8

I'd love to lay claim to this robust marinade/glaze, but I can't . . . it originates with Lesley Stowe, owner of the fabulous Vancouver-based Lesley Stowe Fine Foods, and I thank her for giving me permission to use her recipe here. I have, however, tinkered with it in an attempt to make a good thing even better.

If you have not yet acquired a taste for lamb, this may be the dish that converts you. . . . In the meantime, you can substitute a piece of lean beef for the lamb in this recipe. This is great with grilled vegetables, Garlicky Mashed Potatoes (page 134) or a potato gratin.

To accompany this big, intense dish, choose a rich, gutsy Gigondas, an Australian Shiraz or a powerful Californian Cabernet Sauvignon.

1 leg	lamb	1 leg
2 cups	dry red wine	500 ml
2	oranges, juice and zest	2
1/2 cup	light soy	125 ml
1/2 cup	balsamic vinegar	125 ml
1/2 cup	brandy	125 ml
1/4 cup	honey, melted	60 ml
2 Tbsp.	Dijon mustard	30 ml
2 tsp.	peppercorns, coarsely cracked	10 ml
6 cloves	garlic, puréed	6 cloves
6 Tbsp.	minced fresh herbs, your choice of rosemary, thyme, oregano, sage, parsley	90 ml

Ask your butcher to remove the bone from the leg of lamb and butterfly it. Trim off the fell (membrane-like covering) and any fat. Mix together all remaining ingredients. Set half aside for the glaze. Immerse the lamb leg in the remaining mixture, cover and refrigerate overnight. Remember to turn the leg once or twice if it is not completely immersed.

The next day, remove the lamb from the fridge 30 minutes before you plan to roast it. Pat it dry and discard the marinade. Heat the grill to medium-high or set the oven at 450°F (230°C). Roast or grill the lamb until medium-rare, about 45 minutes, depending on the size. Remove from the heat, cover loosely and let rest 20 minutes before carving.

Bring the reserved marinade to a boil, and serve it with the lamb. (Don't allow the liquid to reduce at all in the process of heating it; reduction will drastically affect the balance of the sauce, bringing the soy into focus.)

Summer Lavender Lamb

Serves 10 generously, with leftovers

O ne memorable summer holiday was spent with close family friends on Saltspring Island, home to artists and artisans, in the group of Gulf Islands nestled off the inside southern end of Vancouver Island. Most nights, I cooked, and one of the best things we ate was a leg of Saltspring lamb. I created the marinade en passant, using what we had hauled along to eat and drink, and raiding the owner's herb garden for fresh lavender. The result was impressive, so I wrote it down. Even Janet said, "dee, did you write that one down?" And I did, but where? The travel journal I think I used is hidden somewhere on my bookshelves, so I had to dust off my memory, recalling what we had on hand. This is it.

To stand up to this flavorful dish, pour a big Californian or Pacific Northwest Cabernet Sauvignon or a Merlot with plenty of extracted fruit flavor.

4- to 5-lb.	lamb leg	2- to 2.2-kg
1/4 cup	hoisin sauce	60 ml
1/2 cup	dry vermouth	125 ml
1 Tbsp.	olive oil	15 ml
6 cloves	fresh garlic, sliced	6 cloves
1/4 cup	light soy sauce	60 ml
2 Tbsp.	honey, melted	30 ml
2 Tbsp.	puréed ginger root	30 ml
1 Tbsp.	minced fresh lavender	15 ml
1/2 tsp.	cinnamon	2.5 ml
1 tsp.	hot chili paste	5 ml

Clean the lamb, removing excess fat, silverskin and the bones. Mix together all the remaining ingredients and smear over the meat, covering all the surfaces. Cover tightly with plastic wrap and refrigerate overnight or for up to 8 hours. Remove from the marinade, heat the grill to medium-high and grill the lamb to medium-rare, or your preference.

Variation

For **Lamb with Port and Rosemary**, leave out the hoisin, replacing it with 1 cup (250 ml) port and adding 1 Tbsp. (15 ml) minced fresh rosemary.

Lavender is most familiar as a talcum for grandmothers, as a cosmetic oil, or as a sachet for lace-trimmed lingerie. It works well in the kitchen also, adding a haunting, nearly sweet herbal undertone to many dishes. Like other things with close-twined roots, lamb and lavender have a natural affinity, as evidenced by centuries of Provençal cooking.

If you can, grow a plant of your own. Failing that, buy fresh sprigs and flowers as they show up at your market, and hang them to dry for use throughout the fall and winter. Buying pink lavender petals from a health food store is my final fallback, but be sure to ask if the lavender is organically grown and free of sprays and pesticides. As always with dried herbs, use but a pinch or whisper of dried lavender as a replacement for fresh.

North African Lamb

Serves 4 as a main course

This springs from one African meal I cooked years ago under the watchful eye of a transplanted Algerian. Together we spitted and roasted a goat, mopping it frequently with North African Berber Spice Blend. Then, when the entire thing was in danger of falling off, bones and all, we hauled it down, shredded it and served it with flatbread and couscous. I've re-created the flavors here using lamb shoulder, braised long and slow. You can also use a leg, and grill or roast it to medium-rare. Chicken legs will work as well, but like the shoulder, they should be braised until very tender. Serve this dish with a grain salad or pilaf, flatbread and grilled vegetables.

To complement the fruit in this dish, serve a southern Californian Zinfandel or a warm-climate Shiraz.

3-lb.	lamb shoulder	1.3-kg
4 Tbsp.	North African Berber Spice Blend (page 25)	60 ml
1 head	garlic, split horizontally	1 head
2	onions, thickly sliced	2
2	bell peppers, thickly sliced	2
1/3 cup	dried apricots	80 ml
1/2 cup	white wine	125 ml
2 cups	chicken stock	500 ml
1 19-oz. tin	chickpeas	1 540-ml tin
1	orange, zest only	1
	salt and freshly ground pepper to taste	

Rub the lamb shoulder generously with the spice blend. If time allows, cover and marinate it overnight in the fridge. Place the meat in a roasting pan and strew the garlic, onions, peppers and apricots around the meat. Add the wine and stock, mix in the chickpeas and orange zest, cover with tinfoil and cook at 325°F (165°C) for 3 hours, or until the lamb is tender enough to shred.

Let the cooked shoulder cool for 10 to 15 minutes, then shred or slice the meat. Skim any fat from the roasting pan and season the pan juices with salt and pepper.

Grilled Lamb Chops with New Mint, Peppercorns and Lemon

Serves 4

This is a play on the classic Italian garnish, gremolata. In this version I substitute mint, lamb's perennial sidekick, for the traditional parsley, and add ginger to the mix. If you are blessed with a prolific mint patch (and all mint patches are prolific), try this with Fresh Mint Chutney (page 21) and Fresh Fruit Salsa (page 19) on the side.

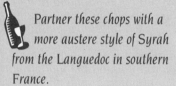 Partner these chops with a more austere style of Syrah from the Languedoc in southern France.

8 3-oz.	lamb chops	8 90-g
1/2 cup	finely minced fresh mint	125 ml
2 Tbsp.	puréed fresh garlic	30 ml
2 Tbsp.	puréed ginger root	30 ml
2 Tbsp.	freshly cracked pepper	30 ml
1	orange, zest only	1
1	lemon, zest only	1
1 Tbsp.	olive oil	15 ml

In a mortar and pestle or small bowl, combine all ingredients except the chops. Mix well to form a paste. Spread evenly over both sides of the chops, and set aside while the grill or broiler heats.

Cook the chops over high heat to medium-rare, or to your taste, turning once.

Cassoulet

Serves 8 hungry friends generously, with leftovers

*N*ot many kitchens boast the aroma of this intoxicating peasant dish, but it surely deserves to be resurrected. Traditionalists may blanch, but this dish reinvented leaves the winter cook much room for ingenuity and experimentation. Choose beans, already cooked, that you like. Choose a link or two of flavorful sausage (kielbasa is good), get a duck (barbecued, from Chinatown) and pinch your rosemary plant. The whole, as you expected, is greater than the sum of its parts, and like any dish of this nature, is best made in advance and allowed to mellow. Serve this hearty dish with simple greens, crusty bread and wine.

Pour a full-bodied Chateauneuf du Pape or a Côtes du Rhône such as a Syrah, Grenache or Carignane.

2	onions, thickly sliced	2
2	leeks, chopped coarsely	2
2	carrots, chopped coarsely	2
2	celery stalks, chopped coarsely	2
8 cloves	garlic, sliced	8 cloves
1 Tbsp.	olive oil	15 ml
2 links	sausage, sliced	2 links
2	bay leaves	2
2–3 sprigs	fresh rosemary	2–3 sprigs
4–5 sprigs	fresh thyme	4–5 sprigs
2–3 sprigs	fresh sage	2–3 sprigs
1 tsp.	dried oregano	5 ml
1 tsp.	dried basil	5 ml
1 or 2	whole star anise	1 or 2
1/2 stick	cinnamon, broken	1/2 stick
1 Tbsp.	cracked peppercorns	15 ml
1/2 tsp.	cracked allspice berries	2.5 ml
4–6	whole cloves	4–6
1	lemon, zest only	1
1 cup	red wine	250 ml
1/2 cup	unsulfured molasses	125 ml
9 cups	cooked beans or lentils	2 litres
1	barbecued duck, boned and shredded	1
4 cups	chicken or beef stock	1 litre
	salt and freshly ground pepper to taste	
1–2 Tbsp.	herb-infused wine vinegar	15–30 ml

In a heavy-bottomed ovenproof pot, cook the onions, leeks, carrots, celery and garlic in the olive oil, adding small amounts of water as needed to prevent browning. Once the vegetables are tender, allow the water to evaporate and the vegetables to brown for color and flavor. Add the remaining ingredients except for the salt, pepper and vinegar. Stir well, bring to a boil, then cover snugly and pop into a medium oven, 375°F (190°C), for 2 hours, or until all the flavors are mingled and mellowed. Skim any fat from the surface, taste, and add salt, pepper and a splash of vinegar as needed to balance the flavors.

Pork Medallions Crusted with Oregano, Ginger and Pepper

Serves 6

This is a quick, pan-steamed meal that takes advantage of synergistic flavors and tender textures. Serve it with grilled apples or pears and a salad dressed in Caramelized Apple Vinaigrette (page 45) or Pear and Chive Vinaigrette (page 46). Add a pot of steamed basmati rice and it begins to look a lot like dinner.

Ask your butcher to clean, slice and pound out the tenderloin into medallions if you aren't inclined to do it yourself. A good butcher will be glad to do it for you.

 Pour a dry, full-flavored, higher acid rosé or a Pinot Noir.

2 8-oz.	pork tenderloins	2 240-g
1/4 cup	minced fresh oregano	60 ml
1/4 cup	minced ginger root	60 ml
1/4 cup	cracked peppercorns	60 ml
1/2 cup	orange juice	125 ml
2 tsp.	canola oil	10 ml
1	lime, juice and zest	1
2 Tbsp.	whipping cream (optional)	30 ml
1 Tbsp.	orange liqueur (optional)	15 ml
	salt to taste	

Slice each tenderloin against the grain into 1- or 2-ounce (30- to 60-g) slices. Using a mallet or the blunt side of your French knife, pound the slices between plastic or parchment paper layers to flatten each into a thin medallion that will cook in next to no time.

Mix a tablespoon (15 ml) each of the oregano, ginger, and peppercorns into the orange juice and set it aside to infuse. Use the rest of the oregano, ginger and peppercorns to coat the pork medallions on both sides. Heat a pan to medium-low, add the oil, and pan-steam the pork, snugly covered, for several minutes, until just cooked through.

When the meat is cooked, remove it from the pan to a platter or plate and cover loosely. Return the pan to the stove over high heat. Add the juice-herb mixture. Bring to a boil and add the lime juice and zest. Stir in the cream and the orange liqueur, if desired. Add the liqueur carefully—it may ignite once it gets hot. Taste, add salt and return the pork medallions to the pan just long enough to reheat them and coat them with the sauce. Divide the pork and the sauce evenly among the plates and serve.

Neon Greens

Serves 4 as a side salad or light lunch

This is a bright and irreverent-looking salad that is as much fun to eat as it is quick to make. Use tender lettuce, in two-toned colors if possible. For the dressing you could use the Ponzu Vinaigrette specified here, or choose Ginger Zin Vin (page 44), Roasted Beet and Dill Dressing (page 39), Cranberry Vinaigrette (page 43) or Citrus Vinaigrette (page 42).

If you don't have access to a Chinese market that sells barbecued duck or pork, use Pan-Steamed Chicken (page 107).

Serve this salad with a Gewurztraminer or Alsatian Reisling.

1 head	red lettuce	1 head
1 cup	snow peas, trimmed	250 ml
1/4 cup	dried apricots, sliced finely	60 ml
1/2 lb.	barbecued pork or duck, sliced finely	225 g
8	kumquats, quartered lengthwise	8
1/4 cup	toasted and chopped peanuts	60 ml
1/2 cup	Ponzu Vinaigrette (page 41)	125 ml
	cilantro or mint sprigs for garnish	

Wash and dry the lettuce. Arrange the leaves as a bed on a platter or individual plates. Steam the snow peas briefly in a small amount of boiling water, then quickly immerse them in cold water. When they are cool enough to handle, finely sliver them on an angle. Combine the slivered snow peas with the apricots, pork or duck, kumquats, peanuts and half the vinaigrette and toss well. Drizzle the remaining dressing over the greens, then heap the mixed fruit, vegetables and meats into the center of each plate or the platter. Garnish with the herb sprigs.

Finding a good source of barbecued Asian pork and duck is a fairly easy task in most North American cities. Vietnamese and Chinese meat markets seem to be the best bet. Buy your duck whole instead of having it chopped up with the big cleaver. That way, you can slice off the portions as you want them to look, and still have the intact carcass of the duck for great stock.

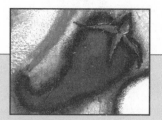

Vegetables and Legumes

Vegetables and legumes are frequently misunderstood and often maligned. "Eat your vegetables" has become a threat, while legumes are the cause of jokes, misunderstanding and embarrassment. Vegetables may be common, but that needn't lessen their value. Legumes may be peasant fare, but they can still be delicious.

Legumes are becoming more popular and more accessible as old, near-forgotten varieties are reseeded. Some of the names of heirloom varieties are amusing, such as Jacob's Cattle, Speckled Trout, Painted Pony and Appaloosa. In the end, though, they are still beans, and they need thorough cooking and generous seasoning.

There are several schools of thought on how to cook beans. Some people advocate soaking the beans in cold water overnight. The soaking water, filled with carbon dioxide from the beans, is drained off and discarded, and the beans are rinsed well. But the soaking water can leach out vitamins and minerals, and from my experience the cooking time isn't altered significantly for most bean varieties.

I prefer to dump the beans in a big pot with a heavy bottom, rinse them and discard stones and any beans that float, then add four times as much water. Bring the pot to a boil, cover, and simmer for several hours, checking periodically that the beans do not run out of water. Burnt beans are not salvageable. Salt will toughen the protein and inhibit the beans from becoming tender, so save the salt until the beans are cooked. Tender is where you want your beans to end up, not crunchy or even almost crunchy. To test if the beans are tender, take one out of the pot and squeeze it between your fingers. It should be soft enough to squish; if not, check the water level, replace the lid and put the beans back on the stove.

Chickpea and Mint Salad

Serves 6 as a side salad

I always seem to make this salad with chickpeas, but you could use any type of cooked bean that you like and have on hand. This is a dish that improves with sitting for a few hours or overnight, so make extra to enjoy the next day.

Serve this minty salad with a bottle of Muscat or Malvasia.

2 cups	cooked chickpeas or beans	500 ml
1/2 cup	Pickled Red Onions (page 16)	125 ml
1/2 cup	pitted and chopped Kalamata olives	125 ml
3	green onions, finely sliced	3
1/2 cup	diced red bell pepper	125 ml
1/4 cup	diced celery	60 ml
2 cups	Fresh Mint Chutney (page 21)	500 ml
	salt and hot chili flakes to taste	

Combine all the ingredients and season to taste. Wait at least 4 hours before serving if possible.

The issue of gas from eating beans is a sensitive one. The truth is, although I know people who scoff, that your body can become acclimatized to eating beans, learning how to digest them more efficiently with time (although the indigestible sugar molecules that are the culprit will always be present). The secret is to cook beans until they are well-done, eat them often and in small amounts, and consider seasoning the pot with any of a handful of carminatives from several cultures. In Mexico and Central America, beans are cooked with epazote, a wild cousin of oregano. In Central Europe, beans have fennel, caraway or anise seed added to the pot. Adding any member of the mint family to the finished dish can also help lessen gas.

Lentil Salad

Serves 4 to 6 as a side dish

Lentils have the immense advantage of cooking relatively quickly. They take about 45 minutes to an hour, depending on the variety of lentil, but there is no absolute cooking time. If pineapples aren't available, use oranges, kumquats, peaches or apples instead. Like any salad, the dressing can be varied to suit your whim or the weather. Other dressings worth considering are Pear and Chive Vinaigrette (page 46) and Roasted Pepper and Cilantro Vinaigrette (page 36).

Partner this dish with Basmati Rice Pilaf with Lemon (page 162), Couscous with Currants and Cumin (page 159), Cedar-Planked Salmon with Honey and Mustard (page 78) or North African Lamb (page 114).

An Australian white Frontignac would suit this dish admirably.

2 tsp.	canola oil	10 ml
1	onion or leek, minced	1
1	carrot, finely diced	1
2 cloves	garlic, minced	2 cloves
1 Tbsp.	puréed ginger root	15 ml
1/2 tsp.	mustard seed	2.5 ml
1 tsp.	ground cumin	5 ml
1/2 tsp.	garam masala	2.5 ml
1 cup	green lentils	250 ml
2 cups	water, or more as needed	500 ml
1/2	ripe pineapple, peeled and diced	1/2
1/2 cup	Citrus Vinaigrette (page 42)	125 ml
2 Tbsp.	minced cilantro or chives	30 ml
	salt and hot chili flakes to taste	

Heat the oil in a heavy-bottomed pot and wilt the onion or leek, carrot, garlic and ginger with the mustard seed, cumin and garam masala. Cook until the vegetables are tender, about 5 minutes, adding small amounts of water as needed to prevent the spices sticking or the vegetables burning. Add the lentils and water; cover and bring to a boil. Reduce the heat and simmer, adding more water as needed, until the lentils are completely tender, about 45 minutes.

Carefully drain any excess water from the cooked lentils. Stir in the pineapple, vinaigrette, cilantro or chives, salt and hot chili flakes. Serve hot or cold. Season the lentils with a generous hand if you plan on serving them cold, remembering that the flavor of chilled food is muffled by the cold.

Black Bean Chili

Serves 18 to 20 generously

Every year I listen to the arguments and battles that ensue over whose chili or chili con carne is best. Every firefighter and chef from Toledo to Timbuktu claims the edge. Well, I won't enter the fray, except to state categorically that this one is not too shabby in spite of its slightly disreputable appearance. It has the added benefits of being quick to assemble and amenable to freezing. Don't be put off by the rather daunting volume—make this in your biggest heavy-bottomed pot, enjoy it for as many meals as you can, then freeze the remnants for another dark and stormy night. Of course you could use any type or combination of beans that you have on hand in the freezer. I particularly enjoy black turtle beans because they hold their shape when cooked, and their color adds a raffish character.

Open a bottle each of a red Spanish Rioja, a Chilean Cabernet Sauvignon, and an Australian or South African Shiraz. With 18 or 20 hungry friends, three bottles is no problem.

2 tsp.	canola or olive oil	10 ml
2	onions, roughly chopped	2
6 cloves	garlic, puréed	6 cloves
3 stalks	celery, chopped	3 stalks
1	leek, chopped	1
2	bell peppers, diced	2
1 link	Italian sausage, diced (optional)	1 link
1 Tbsp.	cumin	15 ml
1 Tbsp.	coriander	15 ml
4 Tbsp.	chili powder	60 ml
1 Tbsp.	Hungarian sweet paprika	15 ml
1/4–1/2 tsp.	hot chili flakes or cayenne	1.2–2.5 ml
1 Tbsp.	dried basil	15 ml
1 Tbsp.	dried oregano	15 ml
1 Tbsp.	dried thyme	15 ml
1 tsp.	cracked fennel seed	5 ml
2 Tbsp.	Worcestershire sauce	30 ml
1 28-oz.tin	canned Roma (plum) tomatoes	1 796-ml tin
1/2 cup	tomato paste	125 ml
1/4 cup	molasses	60 ml
8 cups	cooked black turtle beans	2 litres
1 Tbsp.	apple cider vinegar	15 ml
	salt to taste	

GARNISHES:

minced flat-leaf parsley or cilantro
Savory Yoghurt Cheese (page 50)

Heat the oil and sauté the onion, garlic, celery, leek and peppers in the oil, adding small amounts of water as needed to prevent sticking or browning. Stir in the chopped sausage if you are using it and cook until all trace of pink is gone. Add the cumin, coriander, chili powder, paprika and chili flakes or cayenne. Cook, stirring, for a minute or two until the spices smell toasty. Add the dried herbs and cracked fennel seed.

Stir in the Worcestershire sauce, canned tomatoes, tomato paste, molasses and black beans with any remaining bean-cooking liquid. Simmer until thick, stirring frequently to prevent sticking or burning. Adjust the seasoning with vinegar, salt and additional hot chili flakes if needed.

Garnish with chopped parsley or cilantro and Savory Yoghurt Cheese.

When you choose your chili powder, search out the pure ground chili from New Mexico, and in particular Chimayo. Look in health food stores and upscale food markets, and pay the extra; this stuff is the best, with no fillers or extras.

White Bean and Smoked Trout Salad

Serves 2 as a main dish and 4 as a side dish

This salad can be dinner all on its own, or it can play second fiddle, although it doesn't deserve to. Dress this combination of tender textures in either a brash and forthright style with the Pear and Chive Vinaigrette specified here, adding extra wasabi, or in a light and subtle style with Roasted Beet and Dill Dressing (page 39). Substitute hot-smoked salmon for the trout if you prefer. Serve with crusty bread and a grain or a dairy-based dish.

 Open yet another bottle of Sauvignon Blanc.

2	leeks, chopped	2
1	onion, sliced	1
4–6 cloves	garlic	4–6 cloves
3	shallots, minced	3
4	green onions, sliced	4
2	carrots, diced	2
2 cups	cooked white beans	500 ml
8 oz.	smoked trout	240 g
1/2 cup	Pear and Chive Vinaigrette (page 46)	125 ml

Steam the raw vegetables in a small amount of water. Toss with the warm beans, trout and vinaigrette. Serve warm.

Variation

For **White Bean Salad with Pistachio-Mint Vinaigrette,** add 1 cup steamed green beans, omit the smoked trout and change the dressing to Pistachio Mint Vinaigrette (page 48). Served warm, with toast, this makes a piquant dish on its own, or a great accompaniment to Herb-Crusted Leg of Lamb with Red Wine Glaze (page 112).

Not-Quite Tuscan Beans with Tea-Smoked Eggplant Tapenade

Serves 8 generously as a side dish

This had a traditional beginning, just another potful of beans in the Italian style. But my brain threw up a roadblock and decided that a sensual eggplant purée with a whiff of smoke might be an interesting side road. Herewith, a detour on the culinary highway.

Serve a light Chianti, just to keep the map-readers happy.

1	medium onion, diced	1
2	carrots, diced	2
2	celery stalks, diced	2
4 cloves	garlic, minced	4 cloves
2 tsp.	olive oil	10 ml
4 cups	cooked beans	1 litre
2 cups	spelt berries, cooked	500 ml
3 Tbsp.	minced fresh thyme	45 ml
1	bay leaf	1
1 Tbsp.	minced fresh oregano	15 ml
	stock or water as needed for thinning	
	salt and hot chili flakes to taste	
6–8	Asian eggplants, washed and trimmed	6–8
1/4 cup	white sugar	60 ml
1/4 cup	loose black tea	60 ml
1/4 cup	raw white rice	60 ml
	salt and hot chili flakes to taste	
	extra-virgin olive oil (optional)	

Sauté the onion, carrots, celery and garlic in the oil until tender. Add the beans, spelt berries and herbs, reheat, and stir. Thin to the desired texture with stock or water and adjust seasoning with salt and hot chili flakes.

To make the eggplant purée, line the bottom of a wok or old baking pan with a piece of tinfoil about 6" (15 cm) square. Put the sugar, tea and rice on the tinfoil and mix it around. Place a wire rack in the wok, and position it so that it does not touch the tea mixture. Lay the eggplants on the rack. Put the lid on, then dampen and roll up two kitchen towels. (Don't use your best ones!) Place the rolled towels where the lid meets the wok, being sure to cover the gap all the way around. (This will contain the smoke and not alert your smoke detector to your doings.)

Put the wok, on its ring, on high heat and cook, covered, until the eggplant is just done, about 30 to 45 minutes. (The more eggplant you use, the longer it will take.) You can turn off the heat and remove the rolled towels and lid to check whether it is done without compromising the smoking. Once the eggplant is cool enough to handle, remove the skins and purée the remaining pulp. Season with salt and hot chili flakes. To enrich this purée, add extra-virgin olive oil, stirring it in a bit at a time until you think it's time to stop. It becomes immeasurably richer.

To serve, top each bowl of beans with a dollop of eggplant purée. (When thinned with stock it can be served as a soup, or it can be a side or main dish when left thicker.) Traditionalists top each serving with olive oil; our eggplant purée replaces that.

Spelt, or farro, an ancient cousin of wheat, has newly reappeared on the grain scene. Raymond Sokolov, author of *With the Grain,* calls the flavor of spelt "healthy." Draw your own conclusions! Spelt is most easily available in bulk at health food stores. If you cannot locate it, use wheat berries.

Tea-smoking is a traditional Chinese method of cooking usually used for duck, poultry and some seafood. It seemed to me an ideal flavor to partner with eggplant. The fuel, as explained to me by Barbara Tropp, chef of China Moon in San Francisco, is the rice and sugar, while the tea, mixed in with the fuels, provides the flavor. I have tried pungent Lapsang Souchong as well as various less assertive black teas; my favorite is Russian Caravan. Just be sure to use a good loose tea; trying to use tea emptied from teabags doesn't give good results! You can use this technique to smoke scallops threaded on skewers, plump big shrimp, duck or chicken breasts, and even pork tenderloins.

Green and Gold Curry

Serves 6 to 8 as a main course

*T*his is a quick dish that needs only a pot of rice, Pickled Red Onions (page 16) and a chutney from your cold room to set the table for a weeknight dinner. Serve it with warm tortillas so people can roll up the various components, or just use plates or bowls.

If you want to serve a classic combination, substitute peas for the cauliflower. For a richer sauce, stir in some coconut milk at the very end.

 Try a fruity Chilean Sauvignon Blanc with this curry.

I	onion or leek, sliced	I
2 Tbsp.	puréed garlic	30 ml
2 Tbsp.	minced ginger root	30 ml
I Tbsp.	canola oil	15 ml
I Tbsp.	ground cumin	15 ml
2 tsp.	ground coriander	10 ml
1/2 tsp.	turmeric	2.5 ml
1/4 tsp.	ground fenugreek	1.2 ml
1/2 tsp.	mustard seed	2.5 ml
1/4 tsp.	fennel seed, cracked	1.2 ml
I head	cauliflower, trimmed into florets	I head
2 cups	diced potato	500 ml
I cup	cooked chickpeas or beans	250 ml
	lime or lemon, juice and zest	I
1–2 Tbsp.	honey	15–30 ml
1/2 tsp.	hot chili paste	2.5 ml
I	small zucchini, diced	I
	salt to taste	
	chopped cilantro for garnish	
	toasted cashew nuts for garnish	

In a heavy-bottomed sauté pan or shallow pot, cook the onion or leek with the garlic, ginger and canola oil until the vegetables are tender, about 5 minutes. Add small amounts of water as needed to prevent the vegetables from burning. Stir in the cumin, coriander, turmeric, fenugreek, mustard seed and fennel seed and cook for a minute until the spices smell toasty. Add the cauliflower, potato, chickpeas or beans and enough water to just cover the vegetables. Cover and cook over medium heat until the vegetables are tender, about 20 to 45 minutes, depending on the size of the dice and florets.

When the potatoes and cauliflower are tender, stir in the lime or lemon juice and zest, honey, hot chili paste and diced zucchini. Replace the cover and steam for several minutes, until the zucchini is tender. Add salt as dictated by your tastebuds. Serve topped with chopped cilantro and toasted cashews.

White Bean Pot

Serves 4 as a main dish or 6 as a side dish

This recipe, which started out as a tongue-in-cheek play on traditional peasant food, reinforces my belief that beans needn't be boring. Substitute chickpeas for the beans if you prefer. Carnivores will enjoy this beside Mom's Sauerbraten (page 111) or Herb-Smoked Turkey Breast (page 99), while vegetarians could serve it with Dirty Rice (page 163), Winter Waldorf Salad (page 161), any of the pilafs or Roasted Mushrooms (page 138).

A Marsanne or Viognier would complement this rich dish.

1	large onion, minced	1
1	leek, sliced	1
2	carrots, cut in 1/2" (1-cm) dice	2
8 cloves	garlic, minced	8 cloves
1/2 tsp.	fennel seed, cracked	2.5 ml
2 tsp.	olive oil	10 ml
2 Tbsp.	paprika	30 ml
1/2 cup	dry white wine	125 ml
2	medium potatoes, cut in 1/2" (1-cm) dice	2
1 tsp.	dried dillweed	5 ml
2 cups	cooked white beans	500 ml
1 cup	water or stock	250 ml
2 Tbsp.	heavy cream	30 ml
1	lime, zest only	1
2 tsp.	white wine vinegar	10 ml
	salt and hot chili flakes to taste	
	minced fresh mint for garnish	

In a large, heavy-bottomed pot, cook the onion, leek, carrots, garlic and fennel seed in the olive oil, adding small amounts of water as needed to keep the vegetables from browning. When the vegetables are tender, add the paprika, stirring it in well, and then the white wine. Bring to a brief hard boil, then add the potatoes, dillweed, cooked beans and water or stock. Return to a boil, stirring well, then stir in heavy cream and lime zest. Cover and simmer until the potatoes are tender. Taste and add the vinegar, salt and hot chili flakes until the broth is balanced. Serve garnished with fresh mint.

The smartest way to cook beans, regardless of how you do it, is in volume. Because they take so long to cook, it is wise to cook a lot, once in a while, then freeze what you don't immediately need in small tubs, labelled and dated, in useful sizes. It's much quicker to thaw beans than it is to cook them, so make it easy on yourself. If the beans are on hand, cooked and ready, you'll use more of them, more often.

Maple-Basted Bitter Greens with Sausage

Serves 6

Choucroute Garni is an Alsatian sauerkraut dish that is generously garnished with a variety of meats, many of them pork. My variation crossed the Atlantic and headed west across the Prairies, making detours at all the usual places of interest. The end result is light and seasonal, with lots of herbs and hardly any meat. Serve this with crusty bread or little Bintje potatoes cooked in their jackets. You can vary the greens according to the season and your tastes.

 Pour an Alsatian Reisling, Pinot Gris or a Gewurztraminer, and transport your taste buds.

3 bunches	bitter greens or spinach	3 bunches
1	onion, sliced	1
2 Tbsp.	puréed ginger root	30 ml
2 links	Savoy sausage, sliced	2 links
4 cloves	garlic, minced	4 cloves
1/2 cup	dry white wine	125 ml
1 cup	Maple Thyme Vinaigrette (page 47)	250 ml
1 bunch	green onions, minced	1 bunch
1 Tbsp.	minced fresh thyme or lemon thyme	15 ml
4 Tbsp.	shredded fresh basil	60 ml
	lemon, juice and zest	1
	salt and pepper to taste	

Wash and slice the greens. Simmer the onion, ginger, sausage and garlic in a small amount of water until the onion is tender, then add the white wine. Bring to a boil, add the greens and cook quickly, stirring, until they wilt. (Spinach will cook in just a minute or so, but sturdier greens with more structure will take longer.) Add the remaining ingredients and balance the flavors, using a generous amount of fresh pepper to balance the sweet of the syrup and the acid of the lemon juice.

Warm Winter Greens

Serves 4 to 6 as a main dish or 6 to 8 as a side dish

Some years, winter seems reluctant to give way to spring, and cooks find themselves chafing at the bit to begin the light, sensual cooking that makes warmer weather so entrancing. In years when the cold chases us, I find myself coming up with food that combines warm-weather lightness with winter flavors. This is lovely with a rice pilaf.

 Think spring and open a full-flavored Sauvignon Blanc.

2–3 bunches	winter greens (kale, spinach, beet greens, chard, mustard greens, bok choy)	2–3 bunches
1 bunch	asparagus	1 bunch
1 cup	Miso-Gari Vinaigrette (page 40)	250 ml

Wash and chop the greens. Do not spin dry. Snap the brittle ends off the asparagus and discard. Chop the asparagus into 1" (2.5-cm) lengths, cutting on the angle. Put the vinaigrette into a small pot and heat gently. Mix well and keep warm. In a large, nonstick sauté pan, briefly steam the asparagus in a small amount of water.

Set the asparagus aside, then wilt the greens in the water that clings to their leaves from washing. Add the hot cooked asparagus and the vinaigrette, toss well and serve.

If there are growers and producers following organic practices in your neighborhood, support them. The world is small, and shrinking rapidly; all the effluent dumped into the ground will wash into our backyard eventually. Feeding ourselves and our families foods laced with chemicals can do little but harm in the long run.

Most organic farmers are in their fields because they believe in clean food, not because they expect to make anything other than a hard living at farming. Frequently it is the organic grower who is more willing to seed heirloom varieties of fruits and vegetables; these old varieties are usually not designed for ease of transport or prolonged storage, but they are often the varieties that deliver the best, and truest, flavors.

Wilted Bitter Greens with Warm Dressing and Baked Goat Cheese

Serves 8 as a main course or 12 as a side dish

If you dislike or can't find bitter greens, try this on spinach, Chinese greens, chard, or nappa or Savoy cabbage. It is hearty and sustaining, a winter approach to salad when romaine is imported and expensive. Serve it with crusty bread.

The goat cheese would pair well with a Sauvignon Blanc.

2 heads	radicchio, sliced	2 heads
2 heads	Belgian endive, leaves separated	2 heads
1 head	escarole or curly endive, sliced	1 head
3/4 lb.	soft creamy goat's cheese	350 g
1/2 cup	sesame seeds or bread crumbs	125 ml
1 cup	Puréed Peasant Vegetable Vinaigrette (page 38)	250 ml

Wash the greens and slice or separate the leaves. Shape the cheese into 8 or 12 tidy round patties about 1 1/2" (3.5 cm) across. Dredge the cheese in the sesame seeds or breadcrumbs, then bake on a parchment-lined baking sheet in a hot oven (450°F/230°C) for about 10 minutes, or until the cheese is hot and softened. Let the patties stand a few minutes before you try to move them, or they will break.

Heat a sauté pan, and add the greens, with whatever water still clings to their leaves. Cook just until they begin to wilt. Add the vinaigrette and toss well. Arrange on plates, and top with a baked cheese round.

Wilted African Greens

Serves 6 as a side dish

Years ago, I was involved in a celebration for a couple who had spent many years in Africa. We spent hours analyzing their memories of the meals they had enjoyed while there. This is the closest we got to re-creating her favorite vegetable dish.

Choose something with a touch of sweetness, like a South African Chenin Blanc or Riesling.

3 bunches	sturdy greens (bok choy, sui choy, kale, spinach)	3 bunches
1	onion, sliced	1
4 cloves	garlic, puréed	4 cloves
1 tsp.	turmeric	5 ml
1 tsp.	ground cumin	5 ml
1 tsp.	ground coriander	5 ml
1/2 tsp.	mustard seed	2.5 ml
1/2 tsp.	fenugreek	2.5 ml
1/4 tsp.	ground cinnamon	1.2 ml
1/4 tsp.	ground allspice	1.2 ml
1/4 tsp.	fennel seed	1.2 ml
1/4 tsp.	hot chili flakes	1.2 ml
1/4 cup	butter, melted	60 ml
1 cup	ricotta	250 ml
	salt to taste	

Wash the greens. Simmer the onions in a small amount of water until tender, then add the greens and wilt them. Dry-roast the spices, then add about 2 tsp. (10 ml), or to taste, to the butter. Mix well, stir in the ricotta and salt, then pour over the greens. To give a crisp, crusty top, pop it under a hot broiler.

Grilled Vegetables on Romaine Hearts with Balsamic Vinaigrette

Serves 4 to 6 as a main course or 8 as a side dish

*T*his is best in the fall, when peppers flood the farmers' markets in an array of colors, shapes and varieties. Use fresh thyme for the cleanest flavor, and hot or mild peppers, as you like.

For a straight-up vegetable dish, omit the salad greens. Try dropping the finished and flavored vegetables onto pizza or into pasta sauce, stirring them into a grain dish or placing them atop a piece of crusty bread.

Enjoy this with a Rioja or Valpolicella.

1 lb.	Asian eggplant	450 g
1 lb.	fresh peppers	450 g
1 lb.	Roma tomatoes	450 g
1 lb.	Portobello or shiitake mushrooms	450 g
1 lb.	young zucchini or crookneck squash	450 g
1	sweet onion, like Spanish or Vidalia	1
	oil as needed	
1 cup	Roasted Pepper and Balsamic Vinaigrette (page 36)	250 ml
3 hearts	romaine	3 hearts
	feta cheese and olives for garnish (optional)	

Slice the eggplant and peppers into batons or slices. Split the tomatoes in half lengthwise and wash the mushrooms, slicing them if Portobellos. Slice the zucchini or squash. Peel and slice the onion, leaving a little of the root attached to each slice to hold it together. Lightly oil the cut surfaces of all the vegetables. Heat the grill.

Grill the vegetables over medium-high heat for several minutes, tossing them in vinaigrette as soon as they are cooked. Arrange them on a large platter and set aside until needed. Serve warm or at room temperature with romaine hearts. If desired, garnish with feta cheese and olives.

Grilled New Potatoes and Tomatoes with Quark-Tarragon Dressing

Serves 4 as a side dish

Much as I enjoy spuds, I really don't want another serving of good old potato salad with commercial mayo. This is potato salad with an attitude. In the absence of Quark, use cottage cheese, ricotta or yoghurt.

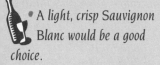

A light, crisp Sauvignon Blanc would be a good choice.

1 lb.	tiny new potatoes	450 g
1 lb.	Roma tomatoes	450 g
1 Tbsp.	canola oil	15 ml
	salt and pepper to taste	
1 cup	Quark Tarragon Dressing (page 49)	250 ml

Cook the tiny new potatoes in their jackets until tender, then thread them onto skewers. Slice the tomatoes into halves lengthwise. Lightly oil the potatoes and the sliced side of the tomatoes, dust with salt and pepper and grill.

Put the dressing in a bowl or spread it on the surface of a large platter. Arrange the grilled vegetables on or in the dressing and serve hot or warm.

Roasted Vegetables in Roasted Pepper Vinaigrette

Serves 8 to 10 generously

This salad is dressed with a bright, citrusy vinaigrette that entirely avoids the issue of mayonnaise. Substitute any vinaigrette you prefer, but remember to add it to the potatoes while they are still warm to get the best flavor. And if spuds aren't to your liking this week, turn this into a pasta salad, with penne or fusilli.

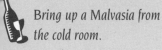

Bring up a Malvasia from the cold room.

2 lbs.	potatoes	900 g
2 each	red and green bell peppers	2 each
3	Asian eggplants	3
2	zucchini	2
1/2 cup	Kalamata olives, pitted and chopped	125 ml
1 bunch	green onions, thinly sliced on the bias	1 bunch
2 cups	Roasted Pepper and Dried Chili Vinaigrette (page 36)	500 ml

If the potatoes are small, cook them whole in their jackets. If they are large, slice or cube them before cooking. Preheat the grill to medium-high. Slice the peppers into narrow strips, and slice the eggplant and zucchini thinly on the bias. Grill the vegetables over high heat. Combine the grilled vegetables with the olives, green onions and vinaigrette.

Garlicky Mashed Potatoes

Serves 6 to 8 generously

2 lbs.	potatoes	900 g
1–2 heads	garlic, peeled	1–2 heads
1/2 cup	liquid for thinning, as needed	125 ml
	salt and hot chili flakes to taste	
	butter or olive oil to taste	
	minced chives for garnish	

*T*his dish is so simple to make and as lean as you please. I invariably select Yukon Gold potatoes because I enjoy their flavor and rich golden color, but use any variety you like. If it isn't the middle of winter, when potatoes show their age with thick skins and bruises, simply wash the potatoes and cook them in their skins for maximum nutrition and a slightly rustic look. If you are avoiding dairy products entirely, use the cooking water from the potatoes to thin them as they are being mashed, and add a little olive oil at the end. I have successfully added buttermilk, sour cream, yoghurt, whipping cream, crème fraîche, milk and, of course, butter. Each has its own flavor and fat content. For a sinus-clearing potful of mashed potatoes, add a tablespoon or two (15 to 30 ml) of horseradish or rehydrated wasabi.

If you are intent on mashed spuds and wine for dinner, serve a Rhône wine.

Cook the potatoes with the garlic, starting with cold water to ensure even cooking. When all is tender, drain the liquid, keeping it for soup or to add to the mashed potatoes. Mash by hand or with a food mill or ricer, slowly adding your choice of liquid to thin the purée. Add salt, hot chili flakes and butter or olive oil. Garnish with minced chives.

Variation

For **Maritime Lobster Hodge Podge**, top each serving with 2 ounces (60 g) shredded cooked lobster meat. Drizzle with Pear and Chive Vinaigrette (page 46), broil briefly and serve hot, with salad.

In Ireland, mashed potatoes are, of course, green. Called champ, and textured and flavored with generous amounts of finely minced chives, the herbal tint of the Irish mash can elevate the dullest plate, and has a flavor to match.

A cooking scholarship sent me to Ireland several years ago. I spent a week at Darina and Tim Allen's beautiful and efficient Ballymaloe Cookery School in East County Cork, then a week driving through the green countryside of Ireland in May. It was an enchanted tour through an enchanted land still haunted by piskies, and my memories are wispy in places where I'm sure the hand of Faery reached through and smudged the ink of time.

Twisted Potato Torte

This recipe calls for Yukon Gold potatoes, but you could use new potatoes and simply toss them in this flavorful mélange for equal flavor and less fuss. This is a do-ahead dish, great to take to potlucks and barbecues. Serve it with greens and crusty bread.

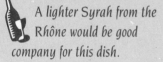

A lighter Syrah from the Rhône would be good company for this dish.

1 lb.	Yukon Gold potatoes, sliced	450 g
3	Asian eggplants, thinly sliced on the bias	3
3	leeks, finely sliced	3
6 cloves	garlic, minced	6 cloves
1–2	ancho or morita chilies	1–2
1 1/2 cups	mild creamy chèvre	375 ml
4 Tbsp.	minced fresh thyme	60 ml
1 twig	minced fresh rosemary	1 twig
1 bunch	green onions, minced	1 bunch
1/2 cup	slivered sun-dried tomatoes	125 ml
	salt and hot chili flakes to taste	

Cook the potatoes in salted boiling water until just tender and not yet falling apart. Drain, reserving the cooking water. Grill or broil the eggplant and set aside. Steam the leeks and garlic in a small amount of water. Rehydrate the dried chilies in hot water, discard the stems and seeds, and chop or purée the flesh. Crumble the chèvre into a bowl, then add the leek-garlic mixture, fresh herbs and onions, tomatoes and chili purée. Thin with some of the potato cooking water to a saucelike consistency.

In a baking dish, layer the potatoes, eggplant and chèvre mixture in several layers, finishing with chèvre. Add a little of the potato-cooking water to the assembled gratin. The dish can be covered and refrigerated for one or two days. To cook, place it on a baking sheet to minimize spillage, and bake uncovered at 375°F (190°C) for 45 to 60 minutes, until hot throughout.

Black Market Eggplant with Walnuts and Fennel

Serves 4 to 6 as a side dish

Eggplant, the most elegant vegetable in the world, is at its best when it is grilled or braised. This simmered dish shines in the fall and winter when root vegetables are sweet and tender, and the new crop of nuts has been harvested. Serve it with basmati rice.

Pour a Provençal red with a bit of tannin.

1 Tbsp.	olive oil	15 ml
1 lb.	Asian eggplant, julienned	450 g
1	onion, sliced	1
1	leek, julienned	1
1	carrot, thinly sliced or julienned	1
1	fennel bulb, thinly sliced	1
6 cloves	garlic, sliced	6 cloves
1/2 tsp.	cracked fennel seeds	2.5 ml
1 cup	white wine	250 ml
2 Tbsp.	minced fresh thyme	30 ml
1 Tbsp.	cracked white pepper	15 ml
1 lb.	ripe tomatoes, diced	450 g
1/2 bunch	cilantro, chopped	1/2 bunch
1	lemon or lime, juice and zest	1
1 Tbsp.	honey	15 ml
	salt to taste	
	toasted walnuts for garnish	

In a nonstick sauté pan, heat the oil, then add the raw vegetables, garlic and fennel seed. Simmer until tender, adding small amounts of water as needed. Add the wine, thyme, pepper and tomatoes, and simmer until all the flavors meld, about 10 to 15 minutes, adding more water if it dries out. Stir in the cilantro, lemon or lime, honey and salt. Garnish with toasted walnuts.

Roasted Mushroom Muffaletta with Olive Salad

Serves 16 as a starter or 8 as a main dish

I've given this takeoff on a messy New Orleans classic an Asian slant, in part because Italians and Japanese share a love of pickled vegetables. Choose any combination of fresh wild mushrooms mixed with cultivated; if the mushrooms that are available locally are less than stellar, use cultivated mushrooms with rehydrated dried wild mushrooms of quality. If using Chinese black mushrooms, remember how pungent and overwhelming they can be, and use them sparingly.

Pickled vegetables can be from your own kitchen or Italian-style, usually called giardinaria and available at Italian markets. For Asian pickled vegetables, search out stores carrying Japanese, Philippine and Korean foods.

 Serve a bottle of dry Chenin Blanc.

4 cups	Roasted Mushrooms (page 138)	1 litre
1	red bell pepper, thinly sliced	1
1/2 cup	chopped pimento-stuffed olives	125 ml
1/2 cup	pitted and chopped Kalamata olives	125 ml
1/2 cup	chopped pickled vegetables	125 ml
1 cup	Pickled Red Onions (page 16)	250 ml
2 Tbsp.	minced garlic	30 ml
2 Tbsp.	puréed ginger root	30 ml
3	green onions, minced	3
1/4 cup	minced cilantro	60 ml
3 Tbsp.	light soy sauce	45 ml
3 Tbsp.	rice vinegar or lemon juice	45 ml
2 tsp.	Japanese sesame oil	10 ml
	salt and hot chili flakes to taste	
10" loaf	round crusty Italian-style bread loaf	25-cm
2–3 Tbsp.	hot mustard, wasabi or horseradish	30–45 ml

Drain the roasted mushrooms in a colander. (If they aren't thoroughly drained, the muffaletta will be soggy rather than just messy.) To make the olive salad, toss the red bell pepper with the olives, pickled vegetables and pickled onions. Stir together the garlic, ginger, green onions, cilantro, soy sauce, vinegar or lemon juice and oil. Mix with the olives and vegetables, then add salt and hot chili flakes.

To assemble the muffaletta, slice the top off the bread and cut or tear out the bread inside, creating a bowl. Be sure to leave a 1/2" (1-cm) wall at the sides and bottom. Brush the inside of the loaf with the hot mustard, wasabi, or horseradish, then layer the roasted mushrooms and olive salad inside the loaf, packing it all down firmly. Replace the bread lid, wrap well and chill for 1 to 2 hours before slicing into wedges.

Olives with the pit have much more flavor than pitted olives. The most effective way to remove pits is to put the olives onto a chopping block, and, depending on their firmness, squish each with the heel of the hand or with thumb and forefinger held together. The olives will flatten, making it easy to pick out the pits.

Roasted Mushrooms

Makes about 4 cups (1 litre)

This is a goofproof dish with many uses—on pasta or rice pilaf, on flatbread, sandwiches or pizza, in soup, and as a warm salad tossed in Maple Thyme Vinaigrette (page 47). If you make more than can be enjoyed at one sitting (hard to imagine), chill the leftovers and reheat with a small amount of water. Combine more than one variety of mushroom or use just one for intense flavor. Try oyster, crimini, Portobello, shiitake, morel and chanterelle, or in a pinch, good old field mushrooms. If you don't have miso in your fridge, you can leave it out. The dish will still be delicious.

 To complement this dish, serve an earthy Pinot Noir with good fruit.

2 lbs.	mushrooms	1 kg
4 Tbsp.	minced fresh thyme	60 ml
1 head	garlic, separated and peeled	1 head
6	shallots, peeled and sliced	6
2	onions, peeled and sliced	2
1 Tbsp.	olive oil	15 ml
1 Tbsp.	white miso	15 ml
1/2 cup	red or white wine	125 ml
	salt and freshly ground black pepper	

Wash and slice the mushrooms. In a large roasting pan, toss them with the thyme. Sprinkle the garlic, shallots and onions on top and drizzle with the olive oil and miso dissolved in the wine. Roast, uncovered, at 450°F (230°C), until the onions are tender and browned around the edges, about 45 minutes. Add salt and pepper, stir and serve.

Variation

Add an extra splash of sherry or wine to the roasting pan before you add the mushrooms. After the vegetables are cooked, remove them from the pan and add a little more wine or sherry to deglaze the pan. Scrape up any browned or crunchy bits, and pour into a smaller pan if necessary. Bring to a boil, and whisk in a little heavy cream, or stir in crumbled blue cheese or a flavorful vinaigrette. Toss with the mushrooms.

Roasted Vegetables with Stock and Honey

Serves 6 to 8 generously with leftovers

Root vegetables are mundane, and that makes them easy to ignore or mistreat. They hang about so patiently in the fridge, like old boyfriends waiting for a second chance, but they really deserve their own opportunity for glory. Don't deny them: they will blossom into lifelong partners. Any leftovers can find their way into soups, vinaigrettes, stews, gratins or even pasta sauces, so don't shy away from the volume of this dish.

Alsatian Pinot Blanc is a happy partner with this deceptively ordinary dish.

1 head	garlic, peeled and separated	1 head
2	onions, peeled and thickly sliced	2
4	carrots, peeled and julienned	4
4	parsnips, peeled and julienned	4
2	celeriac or celery root, peeled and julienned	2
1	fennel bulb, julienned	1
2	small turnips, peeled and julienned	2
4 stalks	celery, julienned	4 stalks
2	leeks, julienned	2
1 Tbsp.	freshly cracked pepper	15 ml
3 Tbsp.	minced fresh thyme	45 ml
1–2 cups	chicken stock	250–500 ml
1 Tbsp.	olive oil	15 ml
2 Tbsp.	honey	30 ml
	salt to taste	
	minced fresh chives for garnish	

Toss all the ingredients together in a shallow ovenproof casserole dish, omitting only the salt and fresh chives. Cover snugly and place in a hot oven, about 450°F (230°C), for 1 1/2 hours or until the vegetables are tender. (Cooking time may vary with the age and woodiness of the vegetables.) When the vegetables are cooked, remove the lid and return to the oven to allow the top surface to brown. Before serving, sprinkle with salt and top with the minced chives.

Grilled Vegetable Cornbread Sandwich with Herb Aioli

Serves 6 generously

This tender-textured cornbread is a winner with black bean chili. Leftover bread makes great croutons and even better savory bread pudding. Leftovers topped with grated cheese make a more than adequate cheese melt with hot salsa and pickled onions on the side. Like any fresh mayonnaise, aioli is perishable and must be eaten within a day or two of being made. The chopped vegetables give it a chunky, relishlike texture that adds interest to any sandwich. Leftovers can also be used on hot pasta, potatoes or grilled vegetables.

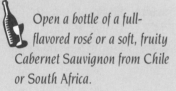 Open a bottle of a full-flavored rosé or a soft, fruity Cabernet Sauvignon from Chile or South Africa.

1 Tbsp.	grainy Dijon mustard	15 ml
4 cloves	garlic, puréed	4 cloves
1 Tbsp.	minced fresh oregano or basil	15 ml
2 Tbsp.	minced fresh parsley	30 ml
1 tsp.	minced fresh rosemary	5 ml
2	green onions, minced	2
1 Tbsp.	lemon juice	15 ml
1	egg yolk, raw or hard-boiled	1
1/4 cup	olive oil	60 ml
1 cup	canola oil	250 ml
2 Tbsp.	herb-infused vinegar	30 ml
3 Tbsp.	pitted and minced Kalamata olives	45 ml
1 Tbsp.	capers	15 ml
1 Tbsp.	Worcestershire sauce	15 ml
1 tsp.	hot chili paste	5 ml
	salt to taste	
2	Asian eggplants, thinly sliced	2
1	sweet bell pepper, thinly sliced	1
1/2	Spanish or other mild onion, sliced	1/2
1	Portobello mushroom, sliced	1
1	zucchini, thinly sliced	1
6	Roma tomatoes, sliced in half lengthwise	6
	oil for the vegetables	
1 recipe	Cornbread (page 191)	1 recipe
	sliced cheese for garnish (young Gorgonzola, mild goat cheese, old cheddar, Fontina or ripe Brie)	

To make the aioli, whisk together the mustard, garlic, herbs, onion, lemon juice and egg yolk. Slowly add the oil, whisking constantly, to form an emulsion, thinning with water or more lemon juice as needed. Whisk in the vinegar, olives, capers, Worcestershire sauce, hot chili paste and salt. Refrigerate until ready to use.

Preheat the grill or broiler. Lightly oil the cut surfaces of the vegetables. Grill the vegetables, turning once, until tender and lightly charred, about 3 to 5 minutes.

To serve, slice the cornbread into 3" (7.5-cm) squares, and split them horizontally. Layer with aioli and vegetables and top with cheese. Eat with a knife and fork. If desired, make the sandwiches open-faced and pop them under the broiler to melt the cheese.

Eggplant Szechuan

Serves 4 as a side dish

You can never have too many good eggplant dishes! Serve with a chutney or salsa and some rice or pasta for a quick and glamorous meal. To add a little color, grill some peppers.

A fruity Malvasia, Riesling or Chenin Blanc would do the job with this dish.

1 1/2 lbs.	Asian eggplant	675 g
2	onions, in 1" (2.5-cm) dice	2
12 cloves	garlic, sliced	12 cloves
2 Tbsp.	minced ginger root	30 ml
2 Tbsp.	light soy sauce	30 ml
4 Tbsp.	hoisin paste	60 ml
1/4 cup	sherry	60 ml
1 Tbsp.	hot chili paste	15 ml
1 tsp.	honey	5 ml
1	orange, juice and zest	1
1/4 tsp.	ground anise seed	1.2 ml
2 tsp.	roasted sesame oil	10 ml

Peel the eggplant and slice or cube it into bite-size pieces. Set aside. In a nonstick sauté pan, mix together the onion, garlic and ginger. Add a small amount of water and cook until the vegetables are transparent and tender. Stir in the eggplant and all the remaining ingredients, add a little more water as needed, and cover. Simmer until tender, stirring well, and serve hot.

Glazed Root Vegetables

Serves 4 as a side dish

*T*his classic method of cooking dense-textured root vegetables is still one of the best. Its beauty lies in the fact that all the chopping and trimming can be done in advance, then all the ingredients except the fresh herbs can be set aside until ten minutes before dinner.

Sprinkle it with chopped, toasted nuts for an added crunch of a different style. Add leftovers to pasta sauces and soups, or stir them into any rice dish.

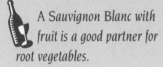 *A Sauvignon Blanc with fruit is a good partner for root vegetables.*

I lb.	carrots, parsnips or turnips	450 g
I	small onion or shallot, finely minced	I
I Tbsp.	puréed garlic	15 ml
I Tbsp.	minced ginger root (optional)	15 ml
1/2 tsp.	cumin seed (optional)	2.5 ml
I Tbsp.	butter	15 ml
I Tbsp.	honey or sugar	15 ml
I	lemon, zest only	I
I cup	cold water	250 ml
	salt and hot chili flakes to taste	
I Tbsp.	minced chives	15 ml
I Tbsp.	minced fresh dillweed	15 ml
2 Tbsp.	lemon juice or herb-infused white wine vinegar	30 ml

Peel and slice the carrots, parsnips or turnips into even batons or thin slices of regular size for even cooking. Place them in an uncovered sauté pan. Add the onion, garlic, ginger, cumin, butter, honey or sugar, lemon zest, cold water, salt and hot chili flakes. Bring to a boil. Cook, uncovered, until the water is evaporated, the vegetables tender and the remaining ingredients form a light glaze, about 7 minutes. Add small amounts of water if it evaporates before the vegetables are done. Stir in the chives, dillweed and lemon juice or vinegar. Serve hot or cold.

Variation
For a dressier version, add green beans in the last few minutes of cooking, and top with Caramelized Pecans (page 24).

Braised Leeks

Serves 4 as a side dish

Make this on top of the stove on a cold and blustery day. It's the perfect accompaniment to Herb-Crusted Leg of Lamb with Red Wine Glaze (page 112). If you're so inclined, make extra, then turn it into soup with leftover lamb.

4	leeks	4
2 tsp.	butter	10 ml
12 cloves	garlic, peeled	12 cloves
1/2 cup	dry white wine	125 ml
2–3 sprigs	fresh thyme	2–3 sprigs
1 cup	chicken or vegetable stock	250 ml
1 Tbsp.	minced fresh thyme	15 ml
1/2	lemon, juice and zest	1/2
1 Tbsp.	heavy cream (optional)	15 ml
	salt and freshly cracked pepper	

Trim the leeks to 6" (15 cm) in length, then split them lengthwise. Melt the butter and spread it over the surface of a large shallow pan, preferably nonstick. Arrange the leeks flat side down with the garlic in a single layer. Brown the leeks, cooking them about 5 to 7 minutes, then add the wine and thyme sprigs. Bring briefly to a boil, add the stock, return to a boil and cover. Reduce the heat to low and simmer until the leeks are tender, about 45 minutes. Add more water or stock if needed.

When the leeks are fork-tender, add the minced thyme, lemon and the heavy cream, if desired. Sprinkle with salt and pepper. Serve hot.

Moussaka with Roasted Tomato Sauce and Feta Cheese

Serves 6 to 8 as a main course

Any fan of moussaka knows and values the amount of time and effort that goes into creating a single pan of this vegetable dish. Try to plan ahead and have the tomato sauce already made—that alone will save considerable time. The other vegetables are delicious grilled, but if time is scarce you may want to quickly steam them instead. Add a layer of poached, sliced, spicy sausage (two sausages is generous), if you wish. In the interest of time and to keep things light, I leave out the layer of white sauce or ricotta on top, replacing it with a sprinkle of feta. I like to serve this dish with simple greens and bread.

Select a fruity Zinfandel or a softer-style Chilean Merlot.

1 lb.	Asian eggplant	450 g
2	onions	2
3	zucchini	3
3	red bell peppers	3
2 heads	garlic, split horizontally	2 heads
1 recipe	Roasted Tomato Sauce (page 23)	1 recipe
2	spicy sausages, poached and sliced (optional)	2
1 bunch	green onions, sliced	1 bunch
	salt and freshly ground black pepper to taste	
1 1/2 cups	feta cheese, crumbled finely	375 ml

Slice the vegetables into 1/4" (.5-cm) slices. Grill or broil the vegetables, being sure that the eggplant is cooked at least three-quarters through. Grill or broil the garlic halves and pop the slightly blackened half-cloves out of the papery cover.

In a 9" x 13" (22.5 x 33 cm) baking dish, layer the tomato sauce, vegetables and garlic, starting with the sauce and distributing the vegetables evenly through each layer. If you're using the sausage, place it somewhere in the middle. Sprinkle each layer with green onions, salt and pepper. Finish with the feta cheese. Place the dish on a baking sheet to catch the drips. You can refrigerate it at this point if you are working in advance. Bake at 375°F (190°C) for 45 minutes, or longer if it has been refrigerated, until it is hot and bubbly.

Roasted Beets in Citrus

Serves 4 as a side dish

C ooking beets in the oven is the tidiest and tastiest way of dealing with these messiest of all vegetables. The juice and the flavor is all contained within the beet, as opposed to bleeding all over counters, pots and stovetops. Rubber gloves, in spite of their hint of sterile hospitals, remain the best bet when you peel beets, especially the red ones. The tops can be steamed and drizzled with a little herb-flavored Citrus Vinaigrette.

To turn this into a dinner salad, serve a slice of ripe young Gorgonzola alongside.

2 lbs.	fresh beets, leaves attached	900 g
1/3 cup	Citrus Vinaigrette (page 42)	80 ml
1 Tbsp.	finely minced chives	15 ml
1 Tbsp.	finely minced fresh thyme	15 ml
	salt and freshly ground pepper to taste	
1 head	red or green leaf lettuce or radicchio	1 head
1	tart apple, sliced	1
1/4 cup	Caramelized Pecans (page 24)	60 ml

Scrub the beets well and cut off the tops, leaving a 1/2" (1-cm) stub attached to the beet roots. Trim off the root ends if they are long. Wrap the beets in a double layer of tinfoil, in packages of 4 or 5 beets each. Make sure to fold the ends securely to prevent leaking as the beets cook. Put the packages into a medium-hot oven of about 400°F (200°C), and cook until tender. The time will vary, depending on the size and age of the beets, but expect young, small beets to take at least 1 hour, while larger, older beets can take up to 2 hours. The only way to check is by carefully unwrapping the beets and piercing the biggest with a fork. When the beet gives easily and the fork slides back out willingly, they are likely cooked through.

Don your rubber gloves if you like, then slide the beet skins off, working at the sink with cold water running. Slice or quarter the beets, and toss them in the vinaigrette and minced herbs while the beets are still warm. Season with salt and pepper. Arrange leaves of lettuce or radicchio on plates, top with the beets, fan the sliced apples beside the beets, and sprinkle the pecans on top.

This salad is incredibly vibrant when made with both red and gold beets. Toss it as little as you can to minimize the red beets coloring everything, or toss them in separate bowls and serve them side by side. Lay the golden beets on red leaf lettuce or radicchio, and the red beets on green leaf or with spears of Belgian endive. Then choose a red-skinned apple to slice beside the golden beets, and a green-skinned apple to pair with the red beets.

Fennel Apple Slaw

Serves 4 as a side dish

The texture of the ingredients in a slaw helps determine the success of the salad. A coarse-bladed grater sometimes does the trick, but usually the best tool is patience and a sharp French knife.

This salad works best as young fennel bulbs are being harvested in the fall. Mature, large bulbs are too strong and stringy. Choose apples with a degree of sweetness under a tart edge, like Jonagolds, Galas, Northern Spy or Cox's Yellow Pippin. Add as much or as little vinaigrette as you like. Some people like their slaw juicier than others. This salad is good with pork dishes, Black Bean Chili (page 122) or North African Lamb (page 114).

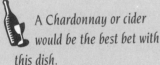

A Chardonnay or cider would be the best bet with this dish.

2 bulbs	young fennel	2 bulbs
3	apples, peeled and grated	3
2 stalks	celery, finely slivered	2 stalks
3	green onions, minced	3
1 Tbsp.	minced fresh tarragon	15 ml
1 Tbsp.	minced dried cranberries	15 ml
1/2 cup	Citrus Vinaigrette (page 42)	125 ml
	salt and hot chili flakes to taste	

Trim the stalks and fronds off the fennel. Discard the stalks, as they tend to be hollow and stringy. Keep the wispy fronds for garnish. Grate or finely slice the raw fennel, keeping all the pieces uniform. Combine all the ingredients with the vinaigrette, cover and refrigerate for 2 hours if possible. Taste the slaw, adding salt and hot chili flakes, and more vinaigrette if it needs it. Garnish with the fennel fronds.

Variation

For **Pineapple Apple Slaw**, omit the fennel, replacing it with one ripe diced pineapple.

One of my all-time favorite slaws is my Grandma Sarah's. She uses simple autumn ingredients, just cabbage, onion and carrots, but she shreds them finely and dresses it all in heavy whipped farm cream mixed with mustard and a little vinegar. I couldn't eat it every day, but I love to eat it every time my Grandma sets it on her old table.

Appley-Dappley Salad

Serves 4 as a side salad

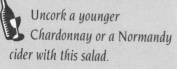

For a more substantial salad, make it with Caramelized Apple Vinaigrette (page 45) or Hazelnut Vinaigrette (page 48), and serve wedges of cheese on or beside it. Try old cheddar, good Swiss or Emmenthal, young chèvre, young Gorgonzola or Cambozola, ripe Brie.

Uncork a younger Chardonnay or a Normandy cider with this salad.

4	apples, all different varieties	4
1/2 cup	Rhubarb Lime Vinaigrette (page 45)	125 ml
2 cups	mesclun or mixed greens	500 ml
1/2 cup	Caramelized Pecans (page 24)	125 ml

Slice the apples thinly, leaving the skins on for color contrast. Toss them in half the vinaigrette.

Toss the greens in the remaining vinaigrette. Heap the greens onto plates and top with the apple slices and pecans.

Late Summer Salad

Serves 6 as a side dish

This is a farmers' market special, changing with what is available. I love it as a cool and refreshing nibble when the long light of a late summer evening is moving across my front yard.

Dry cider is a good autumn choice.

1/2 cup	sliced almonds, oven-toasted	125 ml
1 cup	diced zucchini	250 ml
2	tart apples, diced	2
6 ears	corn, steamed and shucked	6 ears
1 cup	Prairie Sage Vinaigrette (page 46)	250 ml
1 head	lettuce	1 head

Toss all the ingredients except the lettuce in a bowl. Arrange lettuce leaves on each plate or on a platter, creating a cup effect to hold the salad. Spoon the mixed vegetables, apples and nuts onto the lettuce.

Almonds are easily toasted in the oven. Spread them in a thin layer on a baking sheet. For evenly colored nuts, set the oven at 300°F (150°C) and toast them for 10 minutes, or until they are golden. For variegated tones of brown, set the oven at 425°F (220°C) and expect to stir the nuts several times as they toast.

Spinach Salad with Pistachios

Serves 4 as a side salad

Green on green is hard to resist when it's your favorite color. I'm so fond of green, and it is such a good food color, that I find myself drawn to monochromatic plates featuring shades and tones of green. This is one. For a lighter, punchier dressing, choose Kumquat Tahini Vinaigrette (page 42).

1 bunch	spinach	1 bunch
2	avocados	2
1 cup	Greenhouse Dip (page 52)	250 ml
1/4	Long English cucumber, cut in 1/2" (1-cm) dice	1/4
1/2 cup	jicama, peeled and cut in 1/2" (1-cm) dice	125 ml
1/2 cup	coarsely chopped pistachios	125 ml

Wash the spinach and remove the stems. Spin or otherwise dry the leaves and set them aside.

Split the avocados in half lengthwise. Remove the pit, then carefully scoop out the flesh, keeping the halves intact. Set each avocado half on a salad plate, cut side down. Using a sharp small knife, make a series of vertical slices, as close together as possible, to within 1/2" (1 cm) of the tapered end without severing the top. Gently place your fingers on top of the slices and push them over, fanning them out.

Toss the spinach with half the dressing and arrange it around the avocado halves. Sprinkle the cucumber and jicama dice over the spinach, then sprinkle the pistachios over everything. Spoon a puddle of dressing over and beside the avocado.

Jicama is a tuber native to Mexico and Central America. It is a brown oval that looks slightly squashed. The thick brown skin is cut off with a large knife to reveal a nearly white interior that is crunchy and sweet. The flesh of the jicama is as dense as that of carrots and, like carrots, it is easily stored in water in the fridge. Be sure to change the water daily; jicama is starchy, and the starch will leach out into the water. One of the best ways to eat raw jicama is dipped in lime juice, with salt, cilantro and hot chili flakes.

Cucumber Raita

Makes 2 cups (500 ml)

As a cooling accompaniment to hot curries, this salad has no equal. To convert it into a pita sandwich filling, stir in leftover curried lamb or chickpeas.

1 1/2 cups	Savory Yoghurt Cheese (page 50)	375 ml
1	cucumber, peeled and seeded	1
1/4 cup	raisins or dried cranberries	60 ml
1 Tbsp.	mustard seed	15 ml
1/4 tsp.	fennel seed, cracked	1.2 ml

Grate the cucumber and wring out all water from it by wrapping the gratings in a kitchen cloth and twisting tightly over the sink. Add the dry cucumber to the drained yoghurt and stir in the raisins or dried cranberries, mustard and fennel seed.

Asparagus and Blood Orange Salad

Serves 4 as a side salad or light lunch

Two bright harbingers of spring make good companions on the plate. Blood oranges, originally from Italy, are usually dark red inside and out. They tend to be considerably tarter than normal oranges, and add an exotic look to any plate. Asparagus is the light at the end of the tunnel after long, cold winters.

For a frivolous look, make Berry Vinaigrette (page 43) for this plate. You'll have to use frozen berries, but for the dressing, that is fine. As the season progresses, use fresh berries on the plate in place of the blood oranges.

1/2 lb.	asparagus spears	225 g
4	blood oranges	4
1 head	butter lettuce	1 head
1/2 cup	Citrus Vinaigrette (page 42)	125 ml
	poppy seeds for garnish	

Snap off the thick ends off the asparagus wherever they willingly snap and discard the ends. Bring 1/2" (1 cm) water to a boil in a large sauté pan. Cook the asparagus spears for a couple of minutes, just until their color is heightened to bright green. Remove them from the heat, drain off the hot water, and place them under cold water to stop the cooking.

Peel and slice the oranges. Wash and spin dry the lettuce, arranging whole leaves on a flat platter. Cluster the asparagus spears at one end of the lettuce and scatter the orange slices over or around. Drizzle with vinaigrette and sprinkle with poppy seeds.

Grapefruit and Avocado Salad on Mango Sauce

Serves 4 as a side or light lunch

Choose pink grapefruit, firm and heavy for their size, and near-black Hass avocados for this salad. It's easy to vary the components in this dish to make it more or less filling as each season rolls by. For instance, in the summer, serve grilled scallops and steamed green beans with avocado on mango sauce with a mango-based Fresh Fruit Salsa. In the fall, try avocado garnished with steamed shrimp and broccoli. In the winter, go back to citrus fruits as they come into season, pairing them with crabmeat or pan-steamed chicken to counterpoint the avocado.

2	grapefruits, preferably pink	2
2	ripe avocados	2
1 cup	Mango Sauce (page 17)	250 ml
2 cups	Bean Salsa (page 20)	500 ml
2 cups	Fresh Fruit Salsa (page 19)	500 ml

Peel the grapefruit as you would any citrus fruit. Slice or segment. Split the avocados in half. Remove and discard the pits, and scoop out the avocado halves from their skins.

Pool 1/4 cup (60 ml) of the sauce on each plate. Set the grapefruit slices on the plates with one avocado half per person, cut side up. Fill the cavity with 1/2 cup (125 ml) Bean Salsa and 1/2 cup (125 ml) Fresh Fruit Salsa. Serve immediately.

Broccoli, Jicama and Leek Salad

Serves 4 as a side salad

This is a quintessential winter salad, robust and sturdy textured. It is good warm or cold. If serving it hot, try to time it so the broccoli, leeks, garlic, red bell pepper and beans are all hot within a minute or two of each other, and make sure to remove the dressing from the fridge to take off the chill. This also makes a good sauce for cold pasta salad.

Like most salads, this one is influenced by the vinaigrette that binds it together. Blue Cheese Dressing (page 57) makes a richer salad, which has its attractions in the winter.

1 lb.	broccoli	450 g
1 small head	jicama	1 small head
1 Tbsp.	olive oil	15 ml
4	leeks, sliced thinly	4
4 cloves	garlic, minced	4 cloves
1/2	red bell pepper, julienned	1/2
1 cup	cooked white beans	250 ml
1 1/2 cups	Buttermilk Dressing (page 51)	375 ml
	salt and hot chili flakes to taste	
	crumbled blue cheese (optional)	

Trim the broccoli, cutting it into bite-size florets. Peel the stalk and slice it thinly on the bias.

Peel and dice the jicama into 1/2" (1-cm) cubes. Place it in a bowl and cover with cold water to prevent discoloring.

In a nonstick sauté pan, heat the olive oil and add the leeks, garlic and red bell pepper. Cook over medium-high heat until the vegetables are tender, adding small amounts of water as needed to prevent the vegetables browning. Add the beans, stirring to prevent sticking.

Cook the broccoli in 1/2" (1 cm) of boiling water, covered, for several minutes, just until bright green. Drain and place in a large bowl. Drain the jicama. Add the hot leek-bean mixture, jicama and the dressing to the broccoli and toss well. Season with salt and hot chili flakes. Serve hot or cold, topping with crumbled blue cheese if you like.

Piquant Vegetable Toss with Blue Cheese Dressing

Serves 6 to 8 generously

This travels well, keeps well, works as a side or main dish, translates into a wonderful sandwich or pasta topping, and generally earns its keep. Vary the vegetables as they come in and out of season.

Pour a Chardonnay with a bit of body.

2	red bell peppers	2
4	Asian eggplants	4
2	small zucchinis	2
1	red or sweet onion	1
1 cup	Blue Cheese Dressing (page 51)	250 ml
3	small carrots	3
1	small broccoli	1
1/2 head	cauliflower	1/2 head
	crumbled blue cheese (optional)	

Cut the peppers, eggplant, zucchini and onion into 1/4" (.6-cm) slices. Grill them over medium-high heat. Toss with the dressing while the vegetables are still hot from the grill.

Slice the carrots thinly on an angle and cut the broccoli and cauliflower into florets. Blanch them briefly in boiling water if you don't want them raw, and add them to the bowl. Mix thoroughly to coat the vegetables with dressing. If desired, top with additional blue cheese.

Grains and Pastas

Grains and pastas are the current heroes of the menu, both at home and in restaurants. Both can provide heartwarming comfort or light, untroubling dishes. Both deserve their starring roles.

The dishes in this section can be used as accompaniments, but in my busy home, they frequently form the backbone of dinner, unadorned and simple, with a salad or vegetable accompaniment.

Having a good assortment of grains on hand makes it easy to quickly put together a wide array of grain-based dishes. If some of the grains used here are new to you, buy them in small amounts until you become familiar with them.

Layered Baked Polenta with Quark and Herbs

Serves 8 as a starter or side dish

*S*tirred polenta is a soft and sticky food evocative of nurseries and babies. But this grown-up version will provide comfort of a different sort with its layers of flavors and textures. This dish works well on its own as an entrée, or you can use it as an accompaniment to grilled meats, fish or vegetables. (If you are using the grill, quickly grill the sliced zucchini and pepper before chopping them up.) Serve with a salad and crusty bread.

For an earthier collection of flavors, add grilled eggplant slices and top with a blue cheese such as Ermite, Saga Blue or young Gorgonzola.

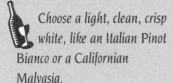 Choose a light, clean, crisp white, like an Italian Pinot Bianco or a Californian Malvasia.

1 1/2 cups	cornmeal	375 ml
5 cups	water	1.2 litres
2 cups	corn kernels	500 ml
2 cups	quark	500 ml
1	lemon, zest only	1
2	eggs (optional)	2
1 bunch	green onions, minced	1 bunch
4 Tbsp.	minced fresh herbs (basil, thyme, savory, dillweed or marjoram)	60 ml
1	red bell pepper, cut in 1/2" (1-cm) dice	1
1	zucchini, cut in 1/2" (1-cm) dice	1
	salt and hot chili flakes to taste	
1 cup	grated Parmesan cheese	250 ml

Set the oven at 375°F (190°C) and lightly oil or butter a baking dish. Measure out the cornmeal and set aside, then put the water in a large pot and bring to a boil. Add a pinch of salt to the water if you like.

Meanwhile, mix together the corn, quark, lemon zest and the eggs, if desired, adding a little of the minced green onions and herbs as well.

Once the water is boiling, add the cornmeal in a slow, steady stream, stirring constantly. Cook over medium heat, stirring until tender, about 10 minutes, depending on the coarseness of the cornmeal. Be careful—polenta will spit as it cooks! (Traditional cooks wear long sleeves to protect their wrists.) When a short-handled wooden spoon will stand up in the polenta, it is done.

To assemble, spread half the polenta onto the bottom of the prepared baking dish. Cover with the corn-quark-egg mixture, then with the red pepper, zucchini, onion and herbs. Sprinkle each layer with salt and hot chili flakes as you go along. Add the remaining polenta, smooth the top and dust with the Parmesan. Bake for 30 to 40 minutes, until hot, bubbly and crisp.

Wild Rice and Millet Salad with Currants and Pine Nuts

Serves 6 as a side salad

This grain salad rescues millet from the ignominy of the bird feeder, where it has languished in most North American homes. Aside from that, millet has a long and honorable history, feeding millions in Asia and Africa for millennia. Millet is very alkaline, making it a wise first food for babes ready to advance beyond mother's milk, as well as being ideal for persons with digestive disorders. This recipe introduces Eastern Mediterranean flavors with the studding of currants and pine nuts throughout the grain.

1/2 cup	wild rice	125 ml
1 1/2 cups	water	375 ml
1/2 cup	millet	125 ml
1/2 cup	currants	125 ml
1/4 cup	dried apricots, slivered	60 ml
1	apple, finely diced	1
1 bunch	green onions, finely minced	1 bunch
1/2 cup	herb-infused vinaigrette (page 47)	125 ml
	toasted pine nuts for garnish	

Simmer the wild rice, covered, with about 2 cups (500 ml) of water, for about 45 minutes, or until the rice cracks open and is tender to the bite. Don't let the rice boil dry!

Measure the 1 1/2 cups (375 ml) water into a separate pot and bring to a boil. Add the millet, currants and apricots and stir well. As soon as the water has returned to a boil, reduce the heat and cover the pot with a snug lid. Set the timer for 45 minutes. Don't peek and don't stir the grain.

When both pots of grain are cooked, drain any water left on the wild rice, mix the contents of the two pots, and add the apple, green onions and vinaigrette. Toss well and serve hot or warm, sprinkled with the toasted pine nuts.

Variations

Use toasted chopped hazelnuts in place of the pine nuts. Substitute dried cherries for the apricots, and dried cranberries for the currants. Use any flavor of vinaigrette that strikes your fancy.

For a meat-based alternative, stir in sliced leftover cooked chicken before leaving the millet on the stove to steam.

Make **Warm Millet and Black Bean Salad** by adding 1 cup (250 ml) cooked black beans and 4 Tbsp. (60 ml) minced cilantro.

Wild Rice and Lobster Fritters

Serves 8 as a starter or 4 to 6 as a main dish

Large or small, these make a snappy base; spread with a compote, a soft cheese or just plain crème fraîche or lemon yoghurt cheese. Heap them high with roasted mushrooms, a warm salad, or flakes of grilled fish. Make small fritters and serve them with Mint Chutney (page 21) as an hors d'oeuvre. Substitute or add any other cooked grain—mixed grains make this even better. If you like, leave out the lobster.

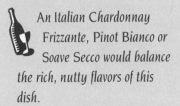

An Italian Chardonnay Frizzante, Pinot Bianco or Soave Secco would balance the rich, nutty flavors of this dish.

1 cup	wild rice	250 ml
1/2 cup	shredded lobster meat (optional)	125 ml
4	eggs, lightly whisked	4
3 Tbsp.	arrowroot powder	45 ml
4 Tbsp.	minced fresh oregano, dill or thyme	60 ml
1 bunch	green onions, minced	1 bunch
	salt and pepper to taste	

Cook the wild rice in about 4 cups (1 litre) of water, covered, until split open and tender, about 45 minutes. Drain and cool. Add the lobster meat, mix well, then add remaining ingredients.

Heat a griddle or large, nonstick sauté pan, add a small amount of canola oil, and drop the fritter mixture onto the hot surface in small spoonfuls. Flatten with the back of the spoon. When brown and crispy, turn and cook the other side. Keep warm in the oven or make them in advance and reheat before serving.

As an alternative to sautéing, form the patties and place them on a baking sheet in a single layer. Bake at 450°F (230°C) until hot and crispy.

Variation

For **Curried Chickpea and Basmati Fritters**, omit the lobster and wild rice. Add 1 cup (250 ml) cooked basmati rice, 1/4 cup (60 ml) peas, 1 tsp. (5 ml) toasted cumin and 1/2 cup (125 ml) coarsely crushed chickpeas. Serve with Fresh Mint Chutney (page 21).

My sister Lee has spent her entire life coping with a multitude of allergies. These fritters arose out of a meal for her. The binding agent, arrowroot, can be replaced by flour or cornstarch if your kitchen doesn't have arrowroot powder.

Wild Rice with Roasted Garlic and Leeks

Serves 6 to 8 as a side dish

Serve this hot or cold; it works well either way. The nutty, chewy nature of wild rice makes it a great contrast to the soft textures of pan-steamed fish or chicken dishes. If there are leftovers, add stock and lemon juice for a delicious and filling extemporaneous soup. Or make fritters by binding the cooled leftovers with eggs and arrowroot (see opposite page).

I cup	wild rice	250 ml
2–3	leeks, finely sliced	2–3
1/2 tsp.	dried thyme	2.5 ml
2 Tbsp.	sugar	30 ml
I Tbsp.	unsalted butter	15 ml
1–2 Tbsp.	sherry vinegar	15–30 ml
I head	roasted garlic (page 69)	I head
I bunch	green onions, minced	I bunch
I cup	pitted and chopped olives	250 ml
4 Tbsp.	shredded fresh basil	60 ml
	salt and freshly ground pepper to taste	

Simmer the rice in about 4 cups (1 litre) of water until it cracks open and is tender, about 45 minutes. Keep an eye on the water level—wild rice quadruples in volume. Cook until tender and drain excess water.

Combine the leeks, thyme, sugar, butter and vinegar in a large sauté pan. Cook until the leeks are tender, adding water as needed to prevent the leeks from browning. Squeeze in the roasted garlic and mix well. Stir the remaining ingredients, adding salt and pepper. Serve hot or cold.

Variation
For a bright and tangy note to this dish, add 4 to 6 thinly sliced kumquats to the leeks while they are simmering.

Use roasted garlic anywhere you don't want the sting of raw garlic. Serious garlic lovers squeeze roasted garlic out of its paper and smear it directly onto crusty bread to help keep body and soul together until dinner is ready. But you don't have to be quite so blatant; whisk mashed roasted garlic into salad dressings, put it onto fajitas and other flatbreads, and stir it into sauces. If you can't use it up all at once, wrap it, still in its paper casing, and refrigerate for several days. Use the cooking water in soups or sauces.

Ethiopian Vegetable Stew

Serves 8 generously

This quick stew transcends its simple ingredients. I learned it from a transplanted Algerian, the owner, with his Marseillaise wife, of a small French bistro where I cooked for a while. A simpler version of this recipe, along with Maryse's plum clafouti recipe, was handwritten for me, in sloping European script, in my battered kitchen notebook. So saturated with wine and sauce was this particular page that it eventually caused me to encase the entire book, page by page, in splashproof plastic sleeves. Even so, some of the writing is almost smudged off the page.

Serve a Provençal red or a full-flavored white, like Marsanne or Rousanne.

1 Tbsp.	olive oil	15 ml
1	onion, chopped	1
2 stalks	celery, chopped	2 stalks
2 or 3	carrots, sliced	2 or 3
1 or 2	bell peppers, diced	1 or 2
1	cinnamon stick	1
1/8 tsp.	saffron threads	.5 ml
1 tsp.	coriander	5 ml
1/2 tsp.	cumin	2.5 ml
1/2 tsp.	ground ginger	2.5 ml
1 tsp.	paprika	5 ml
1/2 cup	dry red or white wine	125 ml
1	orange or lemon, zest only	1
1 cup	cooked chickpeas	250 ml
1 cup	diced squash	250 ml
1/2 cup	currants	125 ml
1/2 cup	sliced dried apricots	125 ml
3 1/2 cups	diced canned or fresh tomatoes	875 ml
2 cups	diced potatoes	500 ml
8 cups	water or stock	2 litres
2 Tbsp.	chopped mint	30 ml
2 Tbsp.	minced parsley	30 ml
2 Tbsp.	minced cilantro	30 ml
2	hot green chilies	2
	salt and pepper to taste	
2 cups	couscous or bulgur	500 ml

In a large, heavy pot, heat the olive oil, then add the onion, celery, carrots and peppers, simmering them with small amounts of water to prevent browning. Stir in the dried herbs and spices and cook briefly until the spices smell toasty, a minute or so. Stir in the wine, citrus zest, chickpeas, squash, currants, apricots, tomatoes, potatoes and water or stock.

Bring to a boil, then reduce the heat and simmer, covered, until everything is meltingly tender.

Stir in the fresh herbs and chilies, then add salt and pepper. Remove from the heat. In a separate bowl, measure out the couscous or bulgur and pour boiling water over it, using just enough water to cover the grain. Cover the bowl with a snug lid and let it stand for 10 minutes. Fluff the steamed grain with a fork. Serve bowls of couscous topped with stew.

Variations

For **Lentil Vegetable Stew**, replace the chickpeas with 1 cup (250 ml) raw lentils and simmer an hour, or until the lentils are tender.

To make **Chicken or Beef African Stew**, add sliced chicken thighs or diced blade roast and simmer until tender, about 2 hours.

Couscous with Currants and Cumin

Serves 4 as a side dish

This side dish is typically served with a sauce or with cooked meats and their cooking juices. For that authentic experience, serve it with North African Lamb (page 114). Use it anywhere you might otherwise serve a rice dish.

1 cup	couscous	250 ml
1/2 cup	currants	125 ml
1	small onion, minced	1
2 cloves	garlic	2 cloves
1 Tbsp.	puréed ginger root	15 ml
2 tsp.	olive oil	10 ml
1 tsp.	cumin seeds, toasted	5 ml
	salt and hot chili flakes to taste	
1	orange, zest only	1
1 Tbsp.	minced cilantro	15 ml

Mix the couscous and currants and add boiling water to cover. Cover with a lid and let stand while you prepare the rest of the ingredients. In a nonstick sauté pan, simmer the onion, garlic and ginger in the oil, adding small amounts of water as needed to prevent browning. Add the cumin.

Remove the lid from the couscous and currants, and fluff with a fork. Add the cooked onion mixture, then stir in the remaining ingredients.

Summer Grain Salad

Serves 8 to 10 as a side dish

I love to make this breezy salad in advance and take it to a potluck. It feeds a crowd easily and inexpensively, looks festive with all the bright and colorful vegetables and fruits, and people feel so righteous when they eat it! Small fruits like dried cranberries, raisins or currants are easiest, but you could chop up dried apricots or pears if you prefer.

Choose a crisp, lively Sauvignon Blanc from Chile, California or southern France.

1 cup	basmati rice	250 ml
1 cup	couscous	250 ml
1 cup	bulgur, medium grade	250 ml
1/2 cup	dried fruit (dried cranberries or currants)	125 ml
1/2 cup	asparagus, sliced on the bias	125 ml
1/4 cup	minced red bell pepper	60 ml
3	minced green onions	3
3 Tbsp.	minced fresh basil or mint	45 ml
1	carrot, grated or finely diced	1
1	orange, zest only	1
1/2 cup	finely minced celery	125 ml
1/2 cup	Citrus Vinaigrette (page 42)	125 ml
1/2 cup	toasted and chopped pecans	125 ml
	salt and hot chili flakes to taste	

Bring 2 cups of water to a boil, add the rice, and cover. Reduce the heat to low and steam for 16 minutes. Pour boiling water to cover over the couscous, bulgur and dried fruit. Cover and let stand for 10 minutes, then remove the lid and fluff with a fork.

Briefly steam the asparagus until just bright green. Drain and refresh with cold water to stop the cooking process. Toss all the ingredients together. Season generously with salt and hot chili flakes. Serve warm or cold.

Learning to identify grains needn't be as intimidating as it seems. Bulgur, which is cracked parboiled wheat, is irregularly shaped and is some shade of brown or reddish brown. It comes in several grades, which indicate size rather than quality. Choose the size you prefer if your market carries more than one grade.

Couscous, really a pasta in disguise, is made of tiny rolled balls of semolina or durum flour, and it is more golden than brown. In addition, couscous refers to the well-travelled Berber dish of any grain steamed over a sauce. When it is stale, couscous granules smell distinctly of rancid oil. Most of the couscous we get in North America, like bulgur, is parboiled and needs only to have boiling water and ten minutes under a lid in order to be edible.

Winter Waldorf Salad

Serves 6 as a side salad

Waldorf Salad, soggy with mayo, cream and discolored apples, was a luncheon staple of a bygone era. This approach contains all the essential elements of the original, but discards the soggy mayo dressing. It is a great way to use leftover basmati rice, but for maximum flavor, assemble and dress the salad while the rice is still warm. Choose an organic variety of apple if possible, and leave the peel on for a little more color.

To vary the salad replace the Cranberry Vinaigrette with Hazelnut Vinaigrette (page 48), Caramelized Apple Vinaigrette (page 45), or Ponzu Vinaigrette (page 41). Each will subtly influence the character of the finished salad.

 Serve with a dry southern French rosé.

1/2 cup	wild rice	125 ml
1 cup	basmati rice	250 ml
1/4 cup	Thompson seedless raisins	60 ml
1 cup	Cranberry Vinaigrette (page 43)	250 ml
2	apples	2
1/2 cup	diced celery	125 ml
1/2 cup	toasted chopped pecans or hazelnuts	125 ml
1 bunch	green onions, slivered	1 bunch
2 Tbsp.	minced fresh basil (optional)	30 ml
	salt and hot chili flakes to taste	

Simmer the wild rice, covered, in about 2 cups (500 ml) of water until tender, about 45 minutes. Check the pot several times to make sure the water hasn't all been absorbed; add more water as needed to keep the rice immersed.

In a separate small pot, steam the basmati rice and the raisins, covered, for 16 minutes over low heat. When the rice is cooked, remove the lid and turn off the heat.

Meanwhile, make the vinaigrette you have chosen. Make the dressing a little more acidic (the starch of the grain will mute the flavors somewhat) by adding an extra tablespoon (15 ml) or so of acid to the vinaigrette. Core and dice the apples, then promptly toss the apple dice in a tablespoon (15 ml) of the vinaigrette to prevent browning.

After 45 minutes, check the wild rice to ensure it is cooked through. The kernels should all be split open. Drain the rice well. (You can dump the leftover cooking water along with a handful of the cooked grain into any handy pot of soup.)

Toss all the ingredients together in a large bowl, coating well with the dressing. Add salt and hot chili flakes generously.

Basmati Rice Pilaf with Lemon

Serves 4 as a side dish

Some grains deserve to be eaten on their own. Basmati rice, the fragrant queen of long-grain rices, deserves an uncluttered plate from time to time to allow its flavor and unmistakable aroma to shine through cleanly. This simple pilaf makes an easy accompaniment to fish, any grilled dish, or just about every vegetable dish in the world.

1	onion, minced	1
2 tsp.	olive oil	10 ml
1 cup	basmati rice	250 ml
1/4 cup	dry white wine	60 ml
2 cups	chicken or vegetable stock, boiling	500 ml
2	green onions, minced	2
2 Tbsp.	minced fresh thyme or lemon thyme	30 ml
1	lemon, zest only	1

In a heavy-bottomed pot, sauté the onion in the olive oil. When the onion is tender, add the rice and stir in. When each grain is lightly coated with olive oil and smelling toasty, add the wine and the hot stock. Bring to a boil, cover and reduce the heat. Set the timer for 16 minutes. No peeking and no stirring. When the rice is cooked, mix in the remaining ingredients and serve hot.

Variations

For **Red Bell Pepper Pilaf**, add 1/2 cup (125 ml) diced red bell pepper to the onion, along with 1/2 tsp. (2.5 ml) New Mexican or Chimayo chili powder (see page 123).

For **Leek and Rosemary Pilaf**, add 1 minced leek to the onion, along with 2 tsp. (10 ml) finely minced rosemary.

For **Pine Nut and Corn Pilaf**, add 1/2 cup (125 ml) untoasted pine nuts and 1 cup corn kernels to the onion.

Things to do with leftover rice . . . for a cold salad, add a flavorful herb vinaigrette to the leftover pilaf, preferably while the rice is still warm. Turn the rice into fritters or stuffing, adding onion, seasonings, egg, and herbs. Make rice pudding out of plain steamed leftover basmati rice by reheating it with a little milk, cinnamon and brown sugar for a lighter approach to a nursery dessert.

Dirty Rice

Serves 6 as a side dish

A classic of Cajun/Creole cooking is a delicious, badly named rice dish that incorporates chicken livers into a pilaf with delightful results. My version has adopted the name and the muddy color of the original, due here to black turtle beans. This dish is particularly good with North African Lamb (page 114).

3 Tbsp.	minced ginger root	45 ml
2 tsp.	olive oil	10 ml
I cup	basmati rice	250 ml
I	lime, zest only	I
I tsp.	mustard seed	5 ml
1/2 tsp.	dried thyme	2.5 ml
1/2 tsp.	dried basil	2.5 ml
1/4 cup	finely sliced dried apricots	60 ml
2 cups	chicken stock	500 ml
1/2 cup	cooked black beans	125 ml
	salt and freshly ground pepper to taste	

In a heavy-bottomed pot, gently cook the ginger in the olive oil without allowing the ginger to brown, adding small amounts of water as needed. Add the rice and stir well, then stir in the lime zest, mustard seed, thyme, basil and dried apricots. Add the stock and the cooked beans and bring to a boil. As soon as the liquid is boiling, reduce the heat to the minimum, put a snug lid on the pot and cook for 16 minutes. Check the rice for doneness. Stir in salt and pepper and serve hot.

For perfectly cooked rice every time, measure your rice and measure your water. Brown rice, like millet, requires three times as much water as rice and takes 45 minutes to cook. White rice, such as basmati, requires twice as much water as rice, and it cooks in 15 minutes. For either type of rice, bring the water to a boil, add the rice, stir well, and return to a boil. As soon as the liquid is boiling, put a snug-fitting lid on the pot, reduce the heat to the lowest setting on your stove and set the timer. Do not remove the lid for a peek to see if it's done yet—all the steam that is cooking the rice will be lost.

Wehani and Basmati Pilaf with Ginger and Kumquats

Serves 8 as a side dish

This is a spicy, chewy dish full of texture, color and snap. Cooking the pilaf in the oven allows grains with differing cooking times to be cooked in the same pot without overcooking. Serve it with curries, strongly seasoned dishes or foods with Asian flavors to complement the orange flavor of the kumquats.

1 Tbsp.	olive oil	15 ml
1	onion, minced	1
4 Tbsp.	puréed ginger root	60 ml
8–10	kumquats, puréed	8–10
1 cup	wehani rice	250 ml
1 cup	basmati rice	250 ml
5 cups	chicken or vegetable stock	1.2 litres
1	lemon, zest only	1
2 Tbsp.	minced fresh tarragon	30 ml
	salt and pepper to taste	

In a heavy-bottomed pan, heat the oil, then add the onion, ginger and kumquats. Cook until tender and transparent, then add both rices and stir well. Stir in the stock, bring to a boil and cover. Transfer to a hot oven, 400°F (200°C), for 45 minutes. No peeking or the steam being generated will dissipate, increasing the cooking time.

When the rice is cooked, stir in the lemon zest, tarragon, and salt and pepper. Serve hot. If there are leftovers, add vinaigrette while the grain is still hot, then cover and refrigerate for the next day's salad.

Kumquats are a miniature orange that are eaten, skin and all, in one or two nibbles. They have an intriguing sweet and sour flavor; sliced into quarters or tiny rounds, kumquats are a vibrant addition to any sauce or dish that has an affinity for citrus flavors. Not only that, but they are cute, and little kids find them enchanting.

Wehani rice is a shortgrain rice with a reddish-brown hue and a chewy, nutty texture. It is a California-bred hybrid, a cross of Indian basmati and brown rice. It takes 40 to 45 minutes to cook. Sometimes I'll toss a small handful of wehani rice into a risotto for interest's sake. It is readily available at health food stores. In its absence, use brown rice or red "Christmas" rice.

Barley Pilaf with Tarragon and Great Northern White Beans

Serves 4 as a main course or 6 as a side dish

This is hearty fall food that beckons on a crisp, cold afternoon. The tarragon and lemon give the dish a deceptively light finish that belies its other, more rustic ingredients. Think of it as a stew and serve it in solitary splendor, or match it with grilled lamb chops, a warm salad of wilted greens, or roasted vegetables.

Drink a Chilean Sauvignon Blanc or a light Gamay or Pinot Noir.

1	onion, minced	1
1	leek, minced	1
1	celery stalk, minced	1
2	carrots, diced	2
4 cloves	garlic, puréed	4 cloves
1 Tbsp.	canola oil	15 ml
2 cups	pearl barley	500 ml
1	bay leaf	1
1 tsp.	dried thyme	5 ml
1/2 cup	dry white wine	125 ml
8 cups	water or vegetable stock	2 litres
1 cup	cooked Great Northern white beans	250 ml
1	lemon, juice and zest	1
1–2 Tbsp.	honey	15–30 ml
	salt and hot chili flakes to taste	
3 Tbsp.	minced fresh tarragon	45 ml

Cook the vegetables and garlic in the oil until tender and transparent. Add the barley, bay leaf and thyme, stir well to coat with oil, then add the wine and water or stock. Bring to a boil, cover and reduce heat to a simmer. Cook until tender, about 45 minutes.

Check for tenderness, cook longer if needed, then add the beans, lemon and honey. The texture should be loose enough to pour easily into a bowl; if not, thin with additional liquid. Rebalance the flavors with salt and hot chili flakes. Stir in the fresh tarragon and serve hot in soup plates.

Wheat and Barley Risotto

Serves 4 as a side dish

Definitely cold-weather fare, this nontraditional risotto is resonant of winter nights on the Prairies. To keep this dish from stodginess, I use bulgur, or cracked and parboiled wheat, instead of wheatberries.

This hearty dish can carry the main course alone; follow it with an acidic salad, such as Roasted Beets in Citrus (page 145) or Grapefruit and Avocado Salad on Mango Sauce (page 150). For a more substantial meal, add Braised Beef with Garlic, Leeks and Ale (page 108), Glazed Root Vegetables (page 142) or any grilled meat.

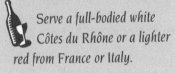

Serve a full-bodied white Côtes du Rhône or a lighter red from France or Italy.

1/2 cup	medium-grade bulgur	125 ml
1	onion, minced	1
6–8 cloves	garlic, minced	6–8 cloves
1 link	kielbasa sausage, diced (optional)	1 link
1 Tbsp.	olive oil	15 ml
1/2 cup	pearl barley	125 ml
1/2 cup	dry white wine	125 ml
3–4 cups	chicken stock	750 ml–1 litre
3 Tbsp.	minced fresh oregano	45 ml
	salt and pepper to taste	

GARNISHES:
Pickled Red Onions (page 16)
Cranberry Compote (page 15)

Cover the bulgur with boiling water, cover with a tight-fitting lid and let stand 5 to 10 minutes.

In a heavy-bottomed pot, sauté the onion, garlic and sausage in the oil. When tender, add the barley and stir. When the barley smells toasty, add the wine and one cup of stock and cook, stirring, for about 15 minutes. If the stock is absorbed too quickly, reduce the heat. Add the rest of the stock a cupful at a time, stirring continually. (You may require additional stock to cook the barley.)

Stir in the oregano, bulgur and salt and pepper. Serve garnished with Pickled Red Onions and Cranberry Compote.

The differences between pilaf and risotto hinge on the type of rice used and how the liquid is added. The long-drawn-out process of patiently adding and stirring liquid on moderately high heat over a half-hour span is what helps develop the creamy texture of risotto. The stirring helps liberate the starch from the rice's exterior, giving it a self-thickened, puddinglike texture. When making pilaf, all the liquid is added at once and the pot is covered, temperature set to low, while the rice slowly absorbs the hot liquid. The end result is a potful where each grain is separate and distinct from its neighbors.

Champagne Risotto

Serves 2 as a main course or 4 as a side dish

Risotto is made exclusively with Italian shortgrain rice, of which arborio is the most readily available. The emphasis is on the rice, but any number of vegetables, herbs, cheeses, meats or fishes can be added as garnish. Too many other ingredients, though, and everything becomes a confused muddle, so try to keep the additions focused. Risotto takes 20 to 30 minutes of nonstop stirring, so choose a day when you can lean on the stove in relative peace while you drink a glass of wine and stir. The bubbly adds a toasty, yeasty layer of flavor to this risotto. Substitute a Muscat or good chicken stock for the champagne if you prefer.

Serve a champagne or an Italian Chardonnay Frizzante.

1 Tbsp.	olive oil	15 ml
1	onion, minced	1
4 cloves	garlic, minced	4 cloves
1/2 cup	diced red bell pepper	125 ml
1 cup	arborio rice	250 ml
1 Tbsp.	minced fresh thyme	15 ml
1 bottle	champagne	1 bottle
2 Tbsp.	minced parsley	30 ml
3	green onions, minced	3
1	lime, zest only	1
	salt and pepper to taste	

Heat the oil in a heavy-bottomed pot, then add the onion, garlic and red bell pepper. Cook until the vegetables are tender, about 3 minutes. Add the rice and stir until the rice smells toasty, then add the thyme. Add the champagne, 1/2 cup (125 ml) at a time. Stir constantly, and do not add more until the previous addition is absorbed. Cook, stirring and adding champagne, until the rice is al dente. The risotto should be a little soupy; add hot chicken stock if it looks too dry. Add the remaining ingredients, adjust the seasoning, and serve immediately.

Variations

For **Spring Asparagus Risotto**, add 2 cups (500 ml) chopped raw asparagus with the onions. Replace the champagne with 3 to 4 cups (750 ml to 1 litre) hot chicken stock, add lemon zest in place of the lime zest, and proceed as above. Top each serving with grated Asiago or Parmesan cheese. For brighter green asparagus, add the asparagus halfway through the cooking time, but the risotto will have somewhat less flavor.

For **Roasted Pepper and Eggplant Risotto**, add grilled chopped eggplant and roasted peppers in generous amounts with the onion, garlic and pepper.

For **Cheese Risotto**, wait until you have four or five cheese ends in the fridge, then grate it all up and stir into the hot risotto.

Buckwheat Noodle and Eggplant Salad

Serves 4 to 6 as a main course

Soba noodles are Japanese buckwheat noodles. They have a strong, dusky buckwheat flavor that stands up well to other assertive, sharp flavors. Look for them in Asian markets or at health food stores. If you like, add sliced barbecued duck or pork. This salad is a good keeper, holding well in the fridge for a day or two.

A good wine match would be a crisp, fruity Riesling from California or the Pacific Northwest, or an Alsatian Pinot Blanc or Gewurztraminer.

1 lb.	soba noodles	450 g
1 1/2 cups	Ponzu Vinaigrette (page 41)	375 ml
1 lb.	Asian eggplant, thinly sliced	450 g
1	red bell pepper, julienned	1
1 cup	snow peas	250 ml
2	carrots, julienned	2
	GARNISHES:	
	toasted sesame seeds	
	minced green onions	
	cilantro	

Cook the soba noodles in boiling water until al dente. Drain and rinse with cold water to halt the cooking process. Toss with half the vinaigrette. Cover and set aside.

Broil or grill the eggplant slices on both sides until brown. Slice into julienne, then toss with the remaining marinade.

Bring a small pot of water to a boil. Blanch the bell peppers, snow peas and carrots until barely done. Refresh under cold water and drain well.

Heap the noodles onto a platter and surround with the blanched vegetables and the eggplant. Sprinkle with the sesame seeds, green onions and cilantro.

Eggplant exists in many varieties and colors. Asian eggplant, easily found in Asian markets and most growers' markets, are long, narrow and pointed. European globe eggplant tend to have more seeds, a thick and inedible skin, and a tendency to bitterness. Given a choice, I buy the milder Asian eggplant.

Green Herb Ravioli with Crab Filling and Mango Sauce

Serves 6 as a main course

Every New Year's Eve, 8 of us spend the evening cooking and eating, then cooking and eating some more, and then, after we toast in the New Year, we cook and eat even more. One year, I decided to make ravioli, for both our party and for our kids and their sitter. It turned into a huge afternoon party all its own, and it taught me the valuable lesson of making BIG ravioli rather than millions of tiny ravioli.

This dish is light, luxurious and almost entirely fat-free. In addition, the majority of the work is done in advance, so it's easy and tidy to take to a special event in your party clothes. If crab is too pricey, use any finely textured white fish, like sole, or coarsely chopped shrimp. This recipe calls for fresh sheet pasta, but if you don't have a pasta machine or time is marching, use won ton wrappers. (The commercial fresh pasta sheets are a little too thick.)

Pour a rich, fruity Sauvignon Blanc or a good French or Californian Viognier to accompany this indulgent dish.

1 bunch	fresh parsley	1 bunch
1–2	eggs	1–2
2 cups	all-purpose flour	500 ml
	salt to taste	
1 lb.	fresh or frozen crabmeat	450 g
3	green onions, minced	3
2 Tbsp.	minced fresh thyme	30 ml
1	whole egg or egg white	1
1	lemon, zest only	1
	salt and hot chili flakes to taste	
18 oz.	Mango Sauce (page 17)	504 ml

GARNISHES:
lemon zest
minced green onions
thyme sprigs

To make the sheet pasta, wash the parsley, and pick off all the stems, freezing them to add to stock. Thoroughly dry the parsley, then purée it and the eggs in a food processor or blender, or chop the parsley very finely by hand and add it to the egg.

If you are using a food processor, change to the plastic blade to avoid breaking your steel knife. Add the flour and salt; allow the machine to run. Little balls of pasta should form and grow into large balls, then tumble around the workbowl in one large mass for a couple of minutes. Let it; this kneading will save you work. Add flour or water as needed in very small amounts.

If you are making the pasta by hand, measure the flour and salt directly onto the counter or into a mixing bowl. Add the chopped parsley and egg and mix well.

Turn the pasta onto the counter, knead it for 2 to 3 minutes if it is not smooth and shiny, then split it into 3 equal pieces. Pat each piece flat with the heel of your hand to fit your pasta machine's aperture, and roll through the hand-cranked pasta roller, starting at the widest setting and arriving at one of the narrowest settings. Each machine will vary, but expect to finish at

Green pasta is traditionally colored and flavored with puréed cooked spinach. However, spinach has a high water content that adversely affects the texture of the pasta, making it wet and hard to roll. I use parsley for a vibrant and intense green without the worry of too much additional liquid. Other leafy herbs can be used as well—basil, dillweed, cilantro and oregano, to name a few. The resulting flavors and shades of green are dictated by how much or how little of the fresh herb you add. In addition, flat sheets can include herbs that are more coarsely chopped, for a rustic streaking of colors. If you plan on cutting your pasta into ribbons or other fine narrow shapes, it's best to finely purée any herb addition so that the pasta will cut cleanly, without any protruding herbs to clog the cutting blades.

the second-last or last setting for pasta fine enough for ravioli. Trim the sheets into 6 manageable lengths of about 24" (60 cm). Lay out in single layers on a counter that has been well dusted with flour to prevent sticking. Cover with plastic wrap.

To make the filling, stir together the crabmeat, green onions, thyme, egg, lemon zest, salt and hot chili flakes.

To assemble the ravioli, lay each long sheet out on a cutting board or other flat surface that won't be damaged by a knife. Drop 2 Tbsp. (30 ml) of the filling on the sheets at regular intervals along one long edge, leaving 2–3" (5–7 cm) between each heap, and placing the filling 1/2" (1 cm) from one long side, and 2" (5 cm) from the other long edge. Using a pastry brush or a piece of dampened paper towel, brush the outer edges of the sheets with water, then brush the pasta in between the piles of filling as well. Fold the sheet in half lengthwise, covering the heaps of filling. You should end up with one long piece of pasta, long edges joined, with a fold the entire length. Using the side of your hand, push down gently on the sheet in between each pile of filling. This should help to remove air bubbles as well as start sealing the ravioli edges. Gently push down along the two long edges, now stacked one on top of the other, to seal the pocket. Using a sharp knife, pasta roller/crimper, or a rolling pizza cutter dipped in flour, cut the folded and filled sheet into little packets between the fillings. Cut and crimp, checking the edges for seal and elimination of air pockets. Pinch the cut edges together with your fingers if they gape, and brush a little more water along the pasta to glue it shut if it dried out as you worked. Be careful not to totally soak the dough, or it will not stick together.

Line a flat baking sheet with plastic, dust it very generously with cornstarch to prevent sticking, and place the ravioli on the tray. Wrap well and store in the fridge for up to 8 hours.

If you are using won ton wrappers, place a spoonful of filling in the center of half the wrappers. Using a pastry brush, lightly brush the outer edges of the wrapper with water, then place another won ton wrapper on top. Gently pinch the seams together and place each dumpling on a cornstarch-dusted sheet. Cover and chill.

To cook the ravioli, bring a large potful of water to a boil and add a sprinkle of salt. Gently add the ravioli and cook until the pasta is al dente. Meanwhile, heat the Mango Sauce. Strain the cooked pasta into a colander, then transfer individually into large flat soup plates. Ladle 1/3 cup (80 ml) of sauce on top and sprinkle with lemon zest, green onions and thyme. Serve hot.

Orecchiette with Beans, Broccoli and Parmesan

Serves 6 as a main course

This pasta is based on a traditional Italian peasant dish. When the fridge is starting to look bare, I can still usually manage to scrape together the few ingredients for this dish. Substitute other types of cooked legumes, although I prefer Great Northern white beans for their tenderness and warm golden color.

Serve this modest dish with a light, crisp Frascati or a Portuguese Vinho Verde.

1 lb.	dried shell or "ear" pasta	450 g
1 lb.	broccoli, sliced into florets	450 g
2 Tbsp.	olive oil	30 ml
2	onions, minced	2
6 cloves	garlic, minced	6 cloves
1 cup	cooked Great Northern white beans	250 ml
1 cup	grated Parmesan cheese	250 ml
	freshly ground pepper to taste	

Cook the pasta in rapidly boiling salted water for about 10 minutes, then add the broccoli and cook until just tender. Meanwhile, heat the oil, add the onions and garlic and sauté until golden. Add the beans and toss to heat. Drain the pasta and broccoli and toss them in a large bowl with the cooked onions, garlic and beans. If it looks a little dry, add a small amount of the pasta cooking water. Top with the grated cheese and pepper. Serve hot.

Orzo with Tangiers Sauce

Serves 4

*T*his tart tomato sauce can be made with fresh, canned or frozen tomatoes. If your tomatoes are frozen, discard the skins—they pull away and are unpleasant to chew on their own. If using canned tomatoes, choose Italian plum or Roma tomatoes.

Use this sauce on pasta or grain, with pan-steamed chicken, or in layered vegetable gratins. For a change of pace, add leftover cooked lamb, pieces of raw or cooked chicken, or cooked chickpeas and orange zest. Or steam mussels or clams in the hot sauce.

Choose a fruity Rhône white wine to counter the high acid levels in this sauce.

I	onion, minced	I
6 cloves	garlic, minced	6 cloves
2 Tbsp.	minced ginger root	30 ml
I Tbsp.	olive oil	15 ml
I lb.	Roma tomatoes, cut in 1/2" (1-cm) dice	450 g
1/8 tsp.	saffron threads	.5 ml
I tsp.	dried thyme	5 ml
1/2 cup	dry white wine	125 ml
2 cups	chicken or vegetable stock	500 ml
I	lemon, juice and zest	I
2 Tbsp.	minced fresh cilantro	30 ml
I Tbsp.	minced fresh parsley	15 ml
	salt and pepper to taste	
3/4 lb.	orzo	350 g
	Kalamata olives for garnish	

Sauté the onion, garlic and ginger in a pan with the olive oil until the vegetables are transparent and tender. Add the tomatoes, saffron, thyme, and white wine. Bring to a boil, then stir in the stock. Simmer, uncovered, for 20 to 30 minutes, then add the lemon juice and zest, chopped herbs, and salt and pepper.

Cook the orzo in boiling salted water for 8 to 10 minutes, or until al dente. Drain the pasta and toss with the hot sauce. Garnish each serving with a few olives.

Pasta Puttanesca

Serves 6

Pasta Puttanesca has a slightly tawdry image, being named for the hardworking women of the street. The story goes that the aroma of the sauce was enough to entice men into the woman's building, and then, of course, nature would take its course. In the early '80s, while I was going to cooking school, I bumped into James Barber as he performed a cooking demo. His description of this pasta sauce really fixed it in my memory forever. Neither mincing words nor hiding behind euphemisms are James's style; he sketched a verbal portrait of an unfaithful wife. She engaged in a midafternoon dalliance, then hurried home and tossed together this aromatic sauce to convince her husband she'd been slaving over a hot stove all afternoon. This sauce, racy history aside, makes an admirable braising medium for sturdy-textured fish, like cod or snapper.

Pour a big, gutsy Italian Barolo, a Spanish Rioja, or a Californian Rhône-style red.

2	onions, minced	2
6 cloves	garlic, chopped	6 cloves
1 2-oz. tin	anchovy filets	1 60-g tin
10–12	mushrooms, sliced	10–12
1 tsp.	dried basil	5 ml
1/2 tsp.	dried oregano	2.5 ml
1 tsp.	dried thyme	5 ml
1 28-oz. tin	Roma tomatoes	1 796-ml tin
2 Tbsp.	tomato paste	30 ml
1 Tbsp.	Worcestershire sauce	15 ml
2 Tbsp.	capers	30 ml
1/2 cup	pitted and chopped Kalamata olives	125 ml
1 tsp.	cayenne	5 ml
	salt to taste	
2 Tbsp.	parsley, chopped (optional)	30 ml
18 oz.	papparadelle or fettucine	504 g
1/2 cup	grated Parmesan cheese	125 ml

Toss the onions and garlic into a nonstick sauté pan with the anchovies and their oil. Cook over moderate heat until the onions are tender and the anchovies have cooked into invisibility. Add small amounts of water as needed to keep the onions from browning. Add the sliced mushrooms and cook until they are tender, then stir in the dried herbs, canned tomatoes, tomato paste, Worcestershire sauce, capers and olives and simmer until all is hot and the sauce has reduced slightly. Stir in the cayenne and salt, then add the chopped parsley.

Cook the pasta in boiling salted water for about 10 minutes, or until just tender. Drain and toss with the sauce. Sprinkle grated cheese on each serving.

Noodle Pancake with Barbecued Duck and Black Bean Sauce

Serves 6 generously

About 18 years ago, I was totally enchanted by a crispy noodle pancake I ate regularly at a small Vietnamese restaurant in Vancouver. The pancake had a soft interior, and it was filled with herbs and mung bean sprouts. The memory never left me, and this is what I've done with its traces. If you don't like barbecued duck, use pan-steamed chicken or grilled shrimp. If you don't want Asian flavors, serve it with Tangiers Sauce (page 172). You can use dried spaghettini or fresh fine egg noodles from the refrigerated case in your favorite market.

Pour a Gewurztraminer or Riesling to accompany this dish.

1 Tbsp.	canola oil	15 ml
1	onion or leek, julienned	1
1	red bell pepper, julienned	1
3 cups	Black Bean Sauce (page 18)	750 ml
3/4 lb.	barbecued duck, shredded	350 g
18 oz.	dried spaghettini	504 g
1 bunch	green onions, slivered on an angle	1 bunch
2 Tbsp.	minced ginger root	30 ml
	sesame seeds and cilantro sprigs for garnish	

In a sauté pan or shallow pot, heat half the canola oil, then add the onion or leek and the red bell pepper. Cook until tender, adding small amounts of water as needed to keep the vegetables from browning. Add the Black Bean Sauce and the duck, bring to a boil, then reduce the heat and keep warm until needed.

Cook the pasta in boiling salted water. Drain well without rinsing, then transfer the cooked noodles to a large bowl. Add the green onions and ginger and toss well.

Heat the other half of the oil in a 12" (30-cm) nonstick sauté pan, and add the cooked noodles. Flatten the noodles into a single flat layer, pressing them down with the back of a wooden spoon.

Cook the pancake over medium-high heat without disturbing for about 5 minutes, then gently lift the edge to see if the underside is browned and crisp. If it is, cover the pan with a large flat plate or pizza pan.

Be sure to protect your hands with oven mitts or potholders that won't stick, and grasp the handle very close to the pan with one hand. Open your other hand out flat to cover as much as possible of the covering pan, holding it firmly against the top of the sauté pan. Quickly flip the pancake over onto the plate or pan. Remove the sauté pan; you should see a nicely browned pancake surface.

Slide the pancake back into the pan, crispy side up, and brown the other side. When it is brown, slide the whole pancake onto a platter.

Slice into wedges. Ladle 1/2 cup (125 ml) sauce onto each plate and center each wedge on the sauce. Garnish with sesame seeds and cilantro.

Spaghetti with Roasted Mushrooms and Cream

Serves 4

This is luxurious in a way only roasted vegetables can be. Make it when you happen upon fresh wild mushrooms at the market. I've even made it with cultivated mushrooms inspired by traces of rehydrated dried wild mushrooms. For a less hedonistic dish, use Roasted Vegetables with Stock and Honey (page139) or Glazed Root Vegetables (page 142).

Choose a New World Merlot to balance this rich dish.

1	onion, finely sliced	1
4 cloves	garlic, minced	4 cloves
2 tsp.	olive oil	10 ml
1/2 cup	dry white wine	125 ml
1 Tbsp.	minced fresh rosemary	15 ml
2 cups	Roasted Mushrooms (page 138)	500 ml
1/4 cup	heavy cream (optional)	60 ml
1 Tbsp.	minced chives	15 ml
1/2	lemon, juice and zest	1/2
	salt and freshly ground black pepper to taste	
3/4 lb.	spaghetti	350 g
	chive blossoms for garnish	

In a sauté pan, cook the onion and garlic with the olive oil until the onion is tender and transparent, adding small amounts of water as needed to keep the vegetables from burning. Add the wine and rosemary, then stir in the roasted mushrooms. Reheat the mushrooms, then stir in the cream if desired, chives and lemon. Add salt and pepper to balance the flavors.

Cook the pasta in salted boiling water. Drain well, then toss the noodles with 1/2 cup (125 ml) of the hot sauce. Ladle onto plates, dividing the rest of the sauce among the plates. Garnish with chive blossoms.

Linguini with Scallops and Cabbage

Serves 6

If you can find fresh rather than frozen scallops, this dish will be spectacular because the scallops will actually color and enrich the sauce with their caramelized flavor. Frozen scallops, while they taste like scallops and look like scallops, are usually too soggy to color well, either on the grill or in a pan. Either way, it's important to make sure the scallops aren't overcooked, or they will resemble little pieces of rubber best suited for patching your bike tire. If you are not fond of scallops, try this sauce with salmon, shrimp, halibut, oysters or clams added at the very end to steam their shells open.

 Try a Chardonnay with tropical fruits and some oak.

1 lb.	scallops	450 g
2 slices	side bacon, minced	2 slices
1	leek, sliced	1
1 Tbsp.	puréed ginger root	15 ml
6 cloves	garlic, minced	6 cloves
2/3 cup	Savoy cabbage, shredded finely	160 ml
1	lemon, juice and zest	1
1/2 cup	dry white wine	125 ml
1 cup	fish stock, mild chicken stock or clam nectar	250 ml
1 Tbsp.	cornstarch	15 ml
1/4 cup	heavy cream	60 ml
1 Tbsp.	minced fresh thyme	15 ml
1 Tbsp.	minced chives	15 ml
1 Tbsp.	minced fresh tarragon	15 ml
	salt and hot chili flakes to taste	
18 oz.	linguini	504 g
	chive sprigs for garnish	

Clean the scallops by removing the little "foot" along the side that anchors the scallops to their homes. Cut each scallop into 2 or 3 medallions horizontally. Set them aside.

In a nonstick sauté pan, cook the bacon to well-done. Remove the bacon and discard virtually all the fat from the pan, leaving no more than 2 to 3 teaspoons (10 to 15 ml). Reheat the pan and add the scallops in a single layer. Using tongs to turn them, brown the scallops over high heat, removing them to a plate or bowl as soon as they lose their translucent quality.

Return the pan to the stove, adding the leek, ginger and garlic. Cook over high heat until tender, adding small amounts of water as needed to prevent the vegetables from burning. Add the shredded cabbage, lemon and white wine. Bring to a boil, then add the stock or clam nectar.

Dissolve the cornstarch in a little cold water. Return the reserved bacon to the pan, bring the liquid to a boil, and stir in the cornstarch. Boil briefly until the sauce is clear, then stir in the cream, herbs and scallops. Taste, adding salt, hot chili flakes and lemon juice as needed to balance the flavors.

Cook the pasta in salted boiling water. Drain it well, then toss in the pan with the sauce. Serve hot, garnished with chive sprigs.

I indulge in scallops infrequently, so any dish I make with them is special. Try the more flavorful sea scallops rather than the small calico or bay scallops. If you find swimming scallops, buy them for their sheer beauty, then scrub and save the shells. Scallops in the shell are best simply steamed like clams or mussels.

Lamb and Hazelnut Penne

Serves 4

Usually meat only makes it into my pasta sauces if I have leftovers from another meal. Leftover lamb is lucky to make it past the door of the fridge, but whenever I can scare off the scroungers, this is one way I particularly enjoy it. Stir a little of the pasta cooking water into the sauce if it seems too dry for your liking.

A full-flavored Pinot Noir or Cabernet Franc would offset the tannins in the hazelnut skins.

1	onion, cut in 1/2" (1-cm) dice	1
4 cloves	garlic, minced	4 cloves
1/2	red bell pepper, diced	1/2
2 tsp.	olive oil	10 ml
1/2 tsp.	dried oregano	2.5 ml
1/4 cup	dry red wine	60 ml
2 cups	leftover lamb, shredded	500 ml
1/2 cup	artichoke hearts, drained and quartered	125 ml
	salt and freshly ground pepper to taste	
3/4 lb.	dried penne	360 g
	GARNISHES:	
	minced chives	
	toasted and coarsely chopped hazelnuts	

In a sauté pan, cook the onion, garlic and red bell pepper in olive oil until tender, adding small amounts of water as needed to prevent burning. Add the oregano and red wine, then stir in the leftover lamb and artichoke hearts. Heat well, then season with salt and pepper. Cook the pasta in boiling salted water. Drain well and toss with the sauce. Sprinkle the nuts and chives on top for garnish.

Potstickers

Potstickers are aptly named. Anyone who has ever cooked a pan of these crusty dumplings knows the care and effort it takes to pry them up from their pot. Like other small things, though, potstickers are worth the time and effort—every bit of scraping to free them, every minute spent forming them, and every tongue-singeing second of eating them too soon, too hot, barely free of the pan's surface.

Evergrowing popularity and unending filling possibilities have seen these traditional Asian dumplings migrate from the dim sum emporiums of Chinatown to the upscale, cross-cultural menus of leading restaurants. My quest for the perfect potsticker has lured me into many restaurants of many descriptions and caused me to make heaps of the little dumplings at home.

Tips and Tricks

There are a few tricks of the trade that make it easier to assemble and cook these delicious beauties.

- Get help. Plan on making a fair amount at a time to justify the effort. Invite a friend or two to visit and drink wine or iced sake just as you begin the shaping of your dumplings. Be sure to invite them back when it's time to eat them, or your friendship may fall upon hard times.
- A potsticker is only as good as its filling, so check the seasoning before you spend any time stuffing wrappers. Drop a spoonful of filling into a nonstick pan and sauté it in a little oil to cook it. When it is done through, taste the sample to be sure the filling is well seasoned. If the sample tastes flat, add a little more salt and try again. If it's too hot, add lemon juice or mild vinegar.
- Freeze the dumplings raw after you assemble them. As you form each dumpling, place it on a tray dusted with cornstarch. Wrap the trays well and freeze. When the dumplings are frozen solid, transfer them to freezer bags. You can cook the dumplings

frozen. It takes a few minutes more steaming time and the addition of extra water, but it's actually easier because the wrappers don't have the opportunity to stick together the way they like to when they thaw completely.
- Won ton wrappers are fragile and prone to drying out when they are uncovered, so keep the main stack of wrappers covered with plastic wrap, and have a smaller stack of 8 or 10 wrappers close at hand. Fill and shape

---

All of the recipes here stipulate won ton wrappers. After much experimentation and happy tasting, I decided that these wrappers contribute that sought-after crusty bottom without being thick, stodgy or hard to work with. Other types of wrappers are out there—Japanese gyoza skins, lumpia wrappers from the Philippines, or egg roll wrappers, spring roll wrappers, or even handmade mu shu pork wrappers. There are more fragile rice noodle sheets and dried rice paper, but they are best left for another day. Poke through the cooler and freezer cases in Asian and good western markets to see what's available locally, and investigate a variety of brand names, as the quality and thickness of the wrappers varies.

them one at a time—the assembly-line approach has no advantage here. Unused wrappers can be stored in the fridge for up to a week if they are well wrapped. Don't try to refreeze them; like filo pastry, the wrappers will crack and dry if refrozen.

• Cook the potstickers in a nonstick sauté pan. This not only minimizes the amount of oil needed to create a crusty bottom, but makes it easier to pry them up at the end of the cooking time. Just make sure to use a flat-edged wooden implement to scrape and lift.

After all this, you still need to know how to shape potstickers. They are hands-on, labor-intensive, but worth it all. To assemble, place a round wrapper on the palm of your hand or on the counter. Center 1 teaspoon (5 ml) of filling on the wrapper, then, using the tips of your fingers, gently push the outer edges of the wrapper up and onto the filling, forming vertical sides, with all the wrapper in contact with the filling. This will leave an uncovered top with a diameter of about 1 inch (2.5 cm); dropping a pea into the center and gently pushing it halfway into the filling is a nice finishing touch. To establish a flat surface to allow optimal browning, gently tap the potsticker on the countertop once or twice.

Following are several different fillings. Share them wisely; many friendships have had their genesis with smaller things.

If you want totally enclosed, classic half-moon shapes, round won ton wrappers are again the best starting point. (Any square wrappers can be trimmed with a sharp knife, unfrozen and stacked up. Trim off each corner, then trim the resulting corners to almost round.) Drop a teaspoon (5 ml) of filling in the center, then brush half the outer circumference of the wrapper with water, well-beaten egg white or an edible glue made of flour whisked into whole egg. Fold the unbrushed side over the filling and gently deflate any air bubbles as you pinch together the edges. The seam can be along the top, pointing up to the sky, or curving like a spine along the side.

For stuffed dumplings in broth, be sure to entirely enclose the filling in the wrapper. Instead of sautéing them, poach the dumplings in aromatic stock, either vegetable or chicken.

Thai-Flavored Potstickers

Makes about 60 potstickers

This is my adaptation of delicious Thai flavors to dumpling wrappers. Remember to totally encase the filling if you opt for poaching instead of sautéeing. The crab can be omitted if you wish, as can either the chicken or pork. If you omit the meat or fish, be sure to replace it with the same amount of other ingredients. Serve at least one dip; choose Vinegar-Chili Dip (page 184), Sesame Dip (page 185) or Hoisin Dip (page 184).

Pour a crisp Californian Chenin Blanc, Riesling or Gewurztraminer.

1/2 lb.	raw chicken, ground or chopped	225 g
1/2 lb.	raw pork, ground or chopped	225 g
1/2 lb.	crab, shredded	225 g
4 Tbsp.	minced cilantro	60 ml
1/2 tsp.	hot chili flakes	2.5 ml
12–15 cloves	garlic, minced	12–15 cloves
2 Tbsp.	minced ginger root	30 ml
4	green onions, minced	4
4 Tbsp.	fish sauce	60 ml
4 Tbsp.	coconut milk	60 ml
2	eggs or egg whites	2
2 packages	won ton wrappers	2 packages
1 cup	fresh or frozen peas	250 ml
1 Tbsp.	canola oil	15 ml

Combine all the ingredients except for the wrappers, peas and oil. Place by spoonful on the round won ton wrappers and pinch the sides up to make round, uncovered dumplings with flat bases and an open top. Stick a single pea on the center top of each dumpling. Arrange in a single layer on a tray dusted with cornstarch.

Lightly oil a nonstick pan and pack the potstickers in a single layer. You will need to do more than one batch to cook them all. Cook until brown on the bottom, then add water to a depth of 1/2" (1 cm) and cover. Steam on high heat until the meat is cooked and the wrappers are translucent. Remove the lid for the last minute or two to cook off the water.

Serve hot with a few dips, heaps of napkins and pairs of chopsticks.

Pork and Peanut Potstickers

Makes about 40 potstickers

This recipe features amazing textural and flavor contrasts of Thai origins. Try other types of nuts if peanuts don't agree with you. If nuts are out, add finely diced jicama or water chestnut to replace the crunch. Serve these potstickers with any or all of these dips: Vinegar-Chili Dip (page 184), Sesame Dip (page 185) or Hoisin Dip (page 184).

Serve a chilled bottle of Gewurztraminer, Marsanne or Viognier.

1 lb.	ground pork shoulder	450 g
8 cloves	garlic, puréed	8 cloves
3 Tbsp.	puréed ginger root	45 ml
6 Tbsp.	roasted and coarsely chopped peanuts	90 ml
4	green onions, minced	4
4 Tbsp.	fish sauce	60 ml
1	egg	1
1/2 cup	light brown sugar or honey	125 ml
1/2 tsp.	hot chili paste	2.5 ml
1/2 tsp.	cayenne	2.5 ml
1/2 tsp.	ground anise seed	2.5 ml
4 Tbsp.	minced cilantro	60 ml
1/2	Asian pear, minced	1/2
	salt to taste	
2 packages	won ton wrappers	2 packages
1 Tbsp.	canola oil	15 ml

Combine all ingredients except the wrappers and oil, and drop by the spoonful onto round won ton wrappers. Pinch the sides up to encase the dumpling with a flat base, leaving the top open. Arrange in a single layer on a tray dusted with cornstarch.

Lightly oil a nonstick pan and pack the potstickers in a single layer. Fry until the bottoms are well browned. Add a small amount of water, cover with a lid and steam on high heat until the meat is cooked and the wrappers are translucent. Remove the lid for a minute or two to cook off any water left in the pan.

Serve hot with at least one dip.

Turkey Potstickers

Makes about 40 potstickers

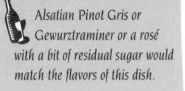

Turkey and dried cranberries combine for an amusing take on turkey and cranberry stuffing. If you prefer, leave out the shrimp (or the turkey) and make up the difference with the other meat. Choose Cranberry Apple Cider Dip (page 185) as a nontraditional grace note.

Alsatian Pinot Gris or Gewurztraminer or a rosé with a bit of residual sugar would match the flavors of this dish.

1 lb.	ground turkey	450 g
1/2 lb.	raw shrimp, peeled and chopped	225 g
1	egg	1
2 Tbsp.	minced cilantro	30 ml
1 Tbsp.	light soy sauce	15 ml
1 Tbsp.	fish sauce	15 ml
2 Tbsp.	minced chives or green onion	30 ml
2 Tbsp.	chopped dried cranberries	30 ml
1/2 tsp.	hot chili paste	2.5 ml
1 Tbsp.	minced garlic	15 ml
1 Tbsp.	minced ginger root	15 ml
1	lemon, juice and zest	1
	salt to taste	
1 package	won ton wrappers	1 package
1 Tbsp.	canola oil	15 ml

Combine all ingredients except for the wrappers and oil in a large bowl, adding the salt at the end. Spoon onto round won ton wrappers, pleat or pinch the sides up to cover but not enclose the filling, and arrange in a single layer on a tray dusted with cornstarch.

Heat a nonstick sauté pan, add a small amount of oil and a layer of potstickers. Brown the bottoms, then add 1/2" (1 cm) of water and steam until the filling is cooked and the wrappers are translucent. Remove the lid to cook off any remaining water. Serve hot.

Vegetarian Potstickers

Makes about 40 potstickers

These meatless dumplings are light and packed with flavor. If you are not an eggplant fan, simply leave it out, making up the volume with other vegetables. Virtually any combination of vegetables is possible, as long as you don't muddy the pot by using too many types at once. Choose several vegetables whose flavors and textures combine well, and stop there. If fresh shiitake mushrooms are unavailable, use field mushrooms or rehydrate and slice one or two dried shiitakes or black Chinese mushrooms. These dumplings are tender and much more fragile than those containing meat, so be gentle.

Pour a bottle of Australian or Pacific Northwest Semillon.

2–3	Asian eggplants, sliced and grilled or otherwise cooked until tender	2–3
2–3	large shiitake mushrooms	2–3
4	green onions, minced	4
1 bunch	cilantro, minced	1 bunch
2 Tbsp.	minced ginger root	30 ml
2 Tbsp.	minced garlic	30 ml
1–2 Tbsp.	light soy	15–30 ml
1 Tbsp.	light miso or hoisin sauce	15 ml
2	carrots, grated	2
1/3 cup	Nappa or Savoy cabbage, finely slivered and blanched	80 ml
1 bunch	spinach, wilted and chopped	1 bunch
1 tsp.	sesame oil	5 ml
1 Tbsp.	toasted sesame seeds or cashews	15 ml
1	lemon, zest only	1
	hot chili flakes to taste	
1–2	egg whites	1–2
1 package	round won ton wrappers	1 package
1 Tbsp.	canola oil	15 ml

Chop the cooked eggplant and add all the ingredients except the egg whites, wrappers and oil. Mix well, then add egg whites if the eggplant is insufficient to hold the mixture together.

Drop the filling by spoonfuls onto the center of the won ton wrappers. Using a pastry brush, brush the edges of the wrapper with water and gently pinch the edges together to enclose the filling. Heat a small amount of canola oil in a nonstick sauté pan, fill it with one layer of dumplings, and brown the bottoms well. Add water to a depth of 1/2" (1 cm), cover and steam until done, about 5 to 7 minutes. Remove lid and cook off any remaining water.

Serve hot with at least one dip.

Potsticker Dips

In dim sum houses, the dips are simple, usually single ingredients that can be mixed and blended to taste. Little bowls cluster together, containing hot chili oil or paste, hoisin, sweetened vinegar, and soy. Diners can pick and choose according to whim and preference. This collection takes the premise one step further by mixing together the basics into finished dips. Give each person a little bowl of each type to avoid any potstickers falling apart in a communal dip.

All of these dips keep well, refrigerated, for several days.

Vinegar-Chili Dip

Makes 1 1/2 cups (375 ml)

1 cup	rice vinegar or white wine vinegar	250 ml
1/2 cup	water	125 ml
2–3 Tbsp.	sugar	30–45 ml
1/4 tsp.	hot chili flakes	1.2 ml
	salt to taste	
	GARNISHES:	
1 Tbsp.	finely grated carrot	15 ml
1 Tbsp.	chopped toasted peanut	15 ml

Combine the vinegar, water, sugar, chilies and salt. Taste and adjust the flavors. Sprinkle with the grated carrot and peanut for garnish.

Hoisin Dip

Makes 1 1/4 cups (310 ml)

1/2 cup	hoisin sauce	125 ml
2–3 Tbsp.	lemon juice	30–45 ml
1 Tbsp.	minced cilantro	15 ml
1 Tbsp.	puréed garlic	15 ml
1 Tbsp.	puréed ginger root	15 ml
1/2 tsp.	hot chili paste	2.5 ml
1/4–1/2 cup	water	60–125 ml
	soy sauce to taste	

Combine the ingredients and adjust the balance with the soy sauce.

Sesame Dip

Makes 1 cup (250 ml)

1 cup	mayonnaise or drained yoghurt	250 ml
4 Tbsp.	toasted ground sesame seeds	60 ml
2 Tbsp.	minced green onions	30 ml
1 Tbsp.	minced cilantro	15 ml
1 Tbsp.	sesame oil	15 ml
1/2 tsp.	hot chili paste or flakes	2.5 ml
1 tsp.	light soy sauce	5 ml
1	lime, juice and zest	1

Combine and adjust the flavors with additional soy and lime juice if needed.

Cranberry Apple Cider Dip

Makes 3/4 cup (185 ml)

1/2 cup	apple cider	125 ml
1/4 cup	apple cider vinegar	60 ml
1	lemon, juice and zest	1
2 Tbsp.	chopped cranberries (dried, fresh or frozen)	30 ml
	melted honey to taste	
1 Tbsp.	minced cilantro	15 ml
	salt and hot chili paste to taste	

Combine ingredients, stirring well. Taste and add additional vinegar or lemon if the dip is too sweet.

Breads

As a lifelong breadmaker, I have difficulty with the fact that most people don't make their own bread at least occasionally. I derive so much tactile gratification from hands-on kneading, it's hard to imagine that not everyone gets the same pleasure. And bread machines? They are here to stay, but half the pleasure of making bread is the thrill of feeling the living dough change beneath your fingers. It's a shame and a pity, but reality speaks; bread-making is not a big item in most North American homes.

As a result, the bread-making here is limited to a basic bread dough and numerous variations, including a list of suggested Skinny Feast recipes for pizza and flatbread. The rest of the savory baking focuses on quickbreads, which rely on baking soda and baking powder for leavening.

Basic Bread

Makes 2 loaves

I have friends who think that bread-making is alchemy, and bread-makers are magicians. Much as I appreciate the sentiment, I believe that anyone can learn to make good bread with their own hands. The most important thing is to keep doing it until your hands become attuned to the changes in the dough. Then you are no longer someone who makes bread now and then; you become a baker.

Any recipe for bread has to be understood as a starting point. Flour can be dry or not, depending on its age, the environment it is stored in, the relative humidity, the type of flour it is ground from. All of this precludes absolute measurements: you add more or less flour and water as the dough needs it.

1 Tbsp.	yeast	15 ml
2 tsp.	sugar or melted honey	10 ml
1/4 cup	warm water	60 ml
4 cups	all-purpose flour	1 litre
2 tsp.	salt	10 ml
1 Tbsp.	canola or olive oil	15 ml
1–2 cups	warm water	250–500 ml

In a small bowl, mix together the yeast and sugar. Add the 1/4 cup (60 ml) warm water, which should be at body temperature to activate the yeast. Let the mixture stand until the yeast has bubbled up and the volume is about doubled.

In a mixing bowl, combine the flour and salt. Add the oil, the remaining warm water and the yeast mixture, and mix with a dough hook on your machine, or by hand. Mix well until the dough holds together and the gluten begins to develop, forming a smooth mass.

Turn the dough out onto the counter, dusted with flour, and begin to knead with both hands, pushing the dough away from you, turning it a quarter and pushing it again. Knead until the dough is as smooth and soft as baby's skin, at least 5 minutes. The dough will quite suddenly change texture, from flaccid to firm and alive. Lightly oil the mixing bowl and return the dough to the bowl, oiling the top surface of the dough as well. The best way to do that is to slide the ball around in the mixing bowl until the entire surface of the dough is lightly oiled. Drape a cloth over the top of the bowl and place it in a warm, quiet place to rise. (Some of the places I've used are the oven, turned on and off again almost immediately so that it is warm, but not hot; the top of the hot water heater; a table outside on a hot day; the top of the dryer, with several cloths under the bowl to keep it still while the dryer runs; the stovetop when the oven is running; a high shelf behind a wood-burning stove.)

Let the dough rise until it is doubled in bulk, about 1 to 1 1/2 hours, depending on the ambient temperature. Punch it down by briskly deflating the center of the dough with your fist. Turn the dough back onto the counter and divide it into 2 even pieces if you are making loaves. Knead them individually, then tidily shape into loaves and place in loaf pans that have been lightly oiled and sprinkled with cornmeal. Return the pans to your warm spot, let them rise a second time, and preheat the oven to 375°F (190°C).

Bake the bread in a single layer for 25 to 30 minutes, or until the loaves are brown and crusty. The loaf should sound hollow if you tip it out and tap on the bottom. Turn the finished bread onto a cooling rack to prevent it becoming soggy from steam as it cools.

There are many ways to vary the finished look and texture of your basic bread.
- Replace part of the all-purpose flour with different types of flour. Every flour has a different texture and varying amounts of gluten, so the results will differ with each flour.
- Develop a crisp crust by spraying the loaf with water just as you place it in the oven. Spraying twice more during baking will help develop the crust, but don't spray too near the end of the baking time or the crust will be soggy instead.
- Lightly brush the top of the bread with oil—sesame, olive, canola—during the baking.
- For a floury, rustic look, dust flour over the top of the raw dough just before baking.
- Different sheens can be achieved by brushing the raw dough with milk, well-beaten egg white, or whole egg mixed with a little milk or water.
- For a sticky top to please children, brush on a light glaze of honey or strained apricot jam near the end of baking.
- For a seedy, chunkier look to the top, brush the surface with well-mixed egg and water, then sprinkle on poppyseeds, sesame seeds, caraway seeds, mustard seeds, coarse salt crystals, hot chili flakes or cracked peppercorns, cracked wheat, oat or rye flakes, oat or wheat bran.
- If you like decorative slashes, glaze the loaf and sprinkle it, if you like, then use a very sharp knife to cut parallel slashes about 1/2" (1 cm) deep.

Pizza with Onion and Sausage Marmalade, Caramelized Pecans and Feta

Makes 2 13" (33-cm) pizzas

*O*nce you make bread now and then, you can begin to put the dough to other uses. The most acclaimed in our home is—what else?—pizza and flatbread. The toppings are limited only by your imagination and the contents of your fridge.

This makes a fine appetizer that you can make ahead, then reheat in the oven. Or you can add more vegetables—even meat leftovers—and call it dinner. Vary the cheese if you like, choosing well-flavored cheeses that melt well, like Asiago, Gorgonzola or Fontina. Use as little or as much cheese as you prefer.

1/2 recipe	Basic Bread Dough (page 188)	1/2 recipe
4 cups	Red Onion and Kielbasa Marmalade (page 16)	1 litre
2 cups	feta cheese, crumbled	500 ml
1 cup	Caramelized Pecans (page 24)	250 ml

Make the bread dough and let it rise once. After the first rising, divide it evenly into 2 pieces and flatten each with the heel of your hand onto a 13" (33-cm) round pizza pan that has been lightly oiled and sprinkled with cornmeal (or lined with a circle of parchment cut to fit). Be sure to create a small lip of dough to retain the sauce, and gently spread the dough out with the heel of your hand to thinly and evenly cover each pan. Cover and let rise for about 15 minutes. Set the oven to 450°F (230°C) while the dough rises.

Divide the onion marmalade in half and spread it evenly on each pizza. Sprinkle the feta evenly over the 2 pizzas and top with the pecans. Bake for 8 to 12 minutes, until well browned and crisp.

Slide each pizza onto a cutting board and slice into small wedges. Serve hot or at room temperature.

Variations

For **Pizza with Roasted Tomato Sauce, Grilled Vegetables, Olives and Asiago,** top each pizza crust with 1 cup (250 ml) Roasted Tomato Sauce (page 23), and evenly arrange slices of grilled eggplant, peppers, onions and mushrooms on top. Sprinkle each pizza with pitted and chopped olives and grated Asiago if desired and bake until crusty and brown.

For **Pizza with Black Bean Sauce and Barbecued Pork or Duck,** spread each pizza crust with 1 cup (250 ml) Black Bean Sauce (page 18). Top with 4–6 oz. (120–180 g) slivered barbecued pork or duck and 1 cup (250 ml) julienned red bell pepper. Brush the exposed crust with sesame oil for extra flavor. Top with minced cilantro and Pickled Red Onions (page 16) after the pizza is baked.

For **Focaccia with Garlic and Olive Oil**, dimple the dough with your fingertips to deflate it after it has risen on the baking sheets. Let rise a third and final time and dimple the dough again. Brush each round with 2 Tbsp. (30 ml) extra-virgin olive oil and 2 Tbsp. (30 ml) puréed garlic. Sprinkle the dough with coarse salt crystals and a pinch of dried oregano. Bake until crusty and golden. Serve warm.

Cornbread

Makes 1 11" x 17" (28 x 43 cm) pan

When I was growing up, one of my favorite after-school snacks was warm cornbread dripping with honey and butter. Hardly politically correct, but seven-year-olds shouldn't mess with politics anyhow. This version is far removed from that of my childhood; to restore it, all the cook needs to do is delete the corn, peppers, onions and hot chili flakes. Then the die is cast in favor of sweet childhood dreams. This makes a soft cornbread with a tender crumb. It is baked in a cookie sheet, which results in a thinner cornbread than usual.

1 1/2 cups	cornmeal	375 ml
2 1/2 cups	all-purpose flour	625 ml
3/4 cup	white sugar	185 ml
3 Tbsp.	baking powder	45 ml
1/2 tsp.	salt	2.5 ml
1 Tbsp.	hot chili flakes	15 ml
1 tsp.	ground allspice	5 ml
1 cup	corn kernels	250 ml
2	jalapeño peppers, minced	2
3	green onions, minced	3
2	eggs	2
2 cups	milk or buttermilk	500 ml
1/2 cup	vegetable oil	125 ml

Set the oven at 400°F (200°C). Line an 11" x 17" (28 x 43 cm) cookie sheet (with sides) with parchment paper, or lightly oil it.

Combine all the dry ingredients, then mix together the wet ingredients, including the corn, peppers and onions, in a separate bowl. Blend together, stirring only until no lumps are visible. Spread onto the baking sheet and bake on the center rack of the oven for about 20 minutes, until lightly browned on top.

Braided Bread with Squash, Prosciutto and Swiss Cheese

Makes 1 braid

Braided breads add a look of care and love to the bread basket. The directions I've included for 4-strand and 5-strand loaves require a little practice to get the flow and shape even, but the finished product is worth it. Even lumpy braids taste good, though, so don't despair over early efforts.

If you can't find prosciutto, substitute cooked bacon, ham or sausage.

1 Tbsp.	yeast	15 ml
2 tsp.	sugar or melted honey	10 ml
1/4 cup	warm water	60 ml
4 cups	all-purpose flour	1 litre
2 tsp.	salt	10 ml
1/4 cup	prosciutto, slivered	60 ml
1/2 cup	grated Swiss cheese	125 ml
1 Tbsp.	coarsely ground black pepper	15 ml
1 cup	cooked squash or pumpkin	250 ml
1 Tbsp.	olive oil	15 ml
1–2 cups	warm water	250–500 ml
	additional flour as needed	

In a small bowl, mix together the yeast and sugar or honey. Add the 1/4 cup (60 ml) warm water, which should be at body temperature to activate the yeast. Let the mixture stand until the yeast has bubbled up and the volume is about doubled.

In a mixing bowl, stir together the flour, salt, prosciutto, cheese and pepper. Add the remaining ingredients and the yeast mixture. Expect to use less water than usual because of the squash. Mix with a dough hook on your machine, or by hand, until the dough holds together and the gluten begins to develop, forming a smooth mass. Add more flour as needed.

Turn the dough out onto the counter and knead with both hands, pushing the dough away from you, turning it a quarter and pushing it again. Knead the dough until it is smooth and soft, at least 5 minutes. The dough will quite suddenly change texture, from flaccid to firm and alive. Lightly oil the mixing bowl and return the dough to the bowl, oiling the top surface of the dough by sliding the ball around in the mixing bowl until the dough's entire surface is lightly oiled. Drape a cloth over the top of the bowl and place it in a warm place to rise.

Braided bread looks like nothing so much as Celtic patterns. Trying to find a beginning, middle or end of the maze is nearly impossible, especially if you loop the bread around into a circle or oval. The challenge in braiding bread is in keeping the spacing even and the tension smooth. The strands should never be pulled, but lifted and allowed to gently drop down into place. For inspiration, walk down the aisle at a fall fair and admire the braided bread loaves on display.

Let the dough rise until doubled in bulk, about 1 to 1 1/2 hours, depending on the ambient temperature. Punch it down when it has doubled in bulk.

To braid bread, divide the dough into 4 or 5 equal pieces. Roll each piece out into a strand about 12–18" (30–45 cm) long and 1" (2.5 cm) thick. Make sure the strands are even in length and thickness, then gently pinch together the far ends, leaving the strands running toward you on the counter. Spread the strands as far apart as possible. Mentally number the strands from the left, 1 to 4 (or 5). The strands will change position as you braid. Just remember that whatever strand is on the far left is #1, and so on.

For 4-strand loaves, begin by moving strand #2 over #3. Then move #4 over the strand that is now #2. Next, lift #1 over #3. Repeat the sequence until you reach the end, then neatly tuck the tips under. Lift the braid onto a pan that has been lightly oiled and sprinkled with cornmeal and let rise until doubled in bulk. Bake at 375°F (190°C) until browned and crusty.

For 5-strand loaves, begin by moving #2 over #3, then lift #5 over #2; lift #1 over #3. Repeat the sequence until the braid is complete.

Let the loaf rise, covered with a cloth, until it is doubled in bulk. Bake for 30 to 40 minutes at 375°F (190°C), until crusty and golden. Remove the loaf to a rack for cooling.

Savory Tea Biscuits

Makes 10 2" (5-cm) biscuits

These biscuits freeze well after baking, so you can double or even quadruple this into a huge batch destined for freezing and serving at future meals. This is my favorite accompaniment for a pot of soup on a cold afternoon, and it's a quick piece of work to get them into the oven while your soup simmers. I'd like to nominate soup and biscuits for the Most Synergistic Food Award, but I don't know who to call.

1 1/2 cups	all-purpose flour	375 ml
1/2 cup	whole wheat flour	125 ml
1/2 tsp.	salt	2.5 ml
1 Tbsp.	baking powder	15 ml
1/2 cup	crumbled feta cheese	125 ml
1 bunch	minced green onions	1 bunch
1/2 tsp.	hot chili flakes	2.5 ml
1/4 cup	unsalted butter	60 ml
3/4 cup	buttermilk or milk	185 ml

Set oven at 375°F (190°C). Line a baking sheet with parchment paper or lightly oil it.

In a bowl, combine the dry ingredients, then stir in the cheese, green onions and hot chili flakes. Add the butter and work in with your fingers or a pastry cutter until mealy in texture. Add the buttermilk or milk, and blend by lightly tossing the dry ingredients up with stiffly extended fingers, using your hands like two large salad forks. The dough will begin to come together into blobs. Pack it all together into a ball, flatten it out with a minimum of handling, and form into a rectangle about 1" (2.5 cm) thick. Fold in half, pat out lightly with your palms and fold over three more times. This helps to create layers without developing unnecessary gluten. Pat or roll out with a floured rolling pin to a thickness of about 1" (2.5 cm).

Cut out rounds with a lightly floured 2" (5-cm) cutter, combining all the leftover scraps and cuttings to form more rounds. Arrange on the baking sheet, fairly closely together. These biscuits rise up, not out, so 1/2" (1 cm) clearance is fine.

Bake in a preheated oven for about 20 to 25 minutes, or until golden, turning the sheet end for end at the halfway point to ensure even baking. Serve warm or at room temperature.

Variations
For **Asian Accents Biscuits**, replace the feta with 2 Tbsp. (30 ml) grated ginger root, and add 2 Tbsp. (30 ml) sesame seeds, and 2 tsp. (10 ml) sesame oil.

For **Onion Biscuits,** leave out the cheese, and add 1/2 cup (125 ml) each of minced ham and cooked onion, and 1 Tbsp. (15 ml) mustard seed.

For **Italian Cheese Biscuits,** substitute grated Parmesan, Asiago or Fontina for the feta, and stir in 2 Tbsp. (30 ml) finely minced fresh basil.

Cheese Layered Quickbread

Makes 20 3" x 4" (7.5 x 10 cm) squares

This cheesy bread goes together in minutes, and is the ideal thing to throw together as an accompaniment to soup, chili, stew or any braised dish with juices that need to be mopped up. Use whatever fresh herbs you have on hand, and if it's only parsley, that works just fine.

3 cups	all-purpose flour	750 ml
1/2 tsp.	salt	2.5 ml
1/4 tsp.	hot chili flakes	1.2 ml
2 tsp.	baking powder	10 ml
3/4 tsp.	baking soda	4 ml
1/2 cup	minced fresh herbs	125 ml
3	green onions, minced	3
2	eggs	2
3 1/2 cups	buttermilk	875 ml
2 cups	grated cheeses, your choice	500 ml

Set the oven for 425°F (220°C), and line an 11" x 17" (28 x 43 cm) cookie sheet with parchment. Choose a sheet with sides to contain the batter.

Sift together the dry ingredients, then stir in the herbs and green onions. Combine the eggs and buttermilk and add to the dry ingredients, blending only until mixed. Spread two-thirds of the batter on the baking sheet. Sprinkle the cheese on top and spoon the remaining batter on, being sure to cover most of the cheese. This stage is usually quite messy, with batter sticking to everything but the place it's intended, so persevere.

Bake 20 to 25 minutes, until brown. Serve hot or at room temperature.

Cranberry Apple Tea Biscuits

Makes 10 2" (5-cm) biscuits

In this biscuit recipe, I've reduced the fat content by substituting grated apple for some of the butter. The dried cranberries are much less sweet than currants or raisins, and add a festive flourish of color. Serve these tender biscuits alone or split them open and heap with Very Berry Compote (page 210). Instead of serving with butter, serve with Sweet Yoghurt Cheese (page 50).

2 cups	all-purpose flour	500 ml
1/2 tsp.	salt	2.5 ml
3 Tbsp.	golden brown sugar	45 ml
1 Tbsp.	baking powder	15 ml
1	lime, zest only	1
2 Tbsp.	chopped dried cranberries	30 ml
1 Tbsp.	minced fresh rosemary	15 ml
1/4 cup	unsalted butter	60 ml
2/3 cup	grated tart apple	160 ml
1/2 cup	buttermilk	125 ml

Set oven at 375°F (190°C). Line a baking sheet with parchment paper.

On the counter or in a bowl, combine the dry ingredients, then stir in the zest, rosemary and cranberries. Add the butter and grated apple, and work in with your fingers until mealy in texture. Make a well and add the buttermilk. Blend by lightly tossing the dry ingredients up with stiffly extended fingers, using your hands like two large salad forks. The dough will begin to come together into blobs. Pack it all together into a ball, flatten it out with a minimum of handling, and form into a rectangle about 1" (2.5 cm) thick. Fold in half, pat out lightly with your palms and fold over three more times. This helps to create layers without developing unnecessary gluten. Pat or roll out with a floured rolling pin to a thickness of about 1" (2.5 cm).

Cut out with a lightly floured 2" (5-cm) round cutter, or cut into diamonds or triangles. Use the trimmings or scraps to make additional biscuits. Tuck in any protruding dried cranberries to prevent burning. Arrange on the baking sheet, fairly closely together. These biscuits rise up, not out, so 1/2" (1 cm) clearance is fine.

Bake in a preheated oven for about 20 minutes, rotating the baking sheet at the halfway point to ensure even baking. Serve warm or at room temperature.

Magic Muffins

Makes 12 large muffins

Books have been written, and careers launched, on muffins. Muffins have become a food group all their own, but many muffins are cupcakes in masquerade, loaded with sugar and oil. This basic formula, my favorite accompaniment to morning coffee, is easily adapted; in fact, I never make plain muffins but always find something to add in my baking cupboard or freezer. The main point about quick breads of all types is quickness; mix only until the lumps are gone and quickly get it into the oven.

2 1/2 cups	all-purpose flour	625 ml
1 Tbsp.	baking powder	15 ml
1/2 tsp.	baking soda	2.5 ml
	salt to taste	
2	eggs	2
1/2 cup	sugar, white or brown	125 ml
1/3 cup	vegetable oil	80 ml
2 cups	buttermilk	500 ml

Set the oven at 375°F (190°C). Brush muffin pans with oil, including the top flat surface, or line with muffin papers.

Stir together the flour, baking powder, baking soda and salt. In a separate bowl, combine the eggs, sugar, oil and buttermilk. Combine wet and dry, mixing only until blended. Spoon into muffin pans and bake 15 to 20 minutes, until set. Cool on a rack before removing from the pan. Serve warm.

Variations

Some favorite additions for muffins:

- 1/2 cup (125 ml) each chopped dates and chopped nuts
- 1/2 cup (125 ml) blueberries and 2 Tbsp. (30 ml) poppyseeds
- 1 tsp. (5 ml) cinnamon and 1/2 cup (125 ml) each raisins and chopped apple
- 1/2 cup (125 ml) chopped dried apricots and 1/2 tsp. (2.5 ml) powdered ginger
- 1/2 cup (125 ml) berries and 1 cup (250 ml) oatmeal
- 1/2 cup (125 ml) oat or wheat bran, 1/4 cup (60 ml) dried cranberries and 2 Tbsp. (30 ml) molasses
- the zest of 1 lemon and 4 Tbsp. (60 ml) puréed ginger root
- 1 cup (250 ml) berries and the zest of 1 orange
- 1 cup (250 ml) grated carrot, apple or zucchini, 1/4 cup (60 ml) chopped nuts and 1 tsp. (5 ml) each cinnamon and allspice

Sweets

Low-fat, lean sweets need not be a puzzle. In fact, most fruit-based desserts make it easy to enjoy a bit of something sweet. Crisp filo with small amounts of butter can provide crunch, and pastry really can be made with butter without sacrificing your monthly butter allotment. Cake and brownies are pushing it, and it's just as well to relegate them to high and holy days rather than eat them daily.

Many of the recipes here can be combined in a variety of ways to contrast textures and flavors. The central point in most is some form of fruit, so the end results tend to be light on the palate and easy on the digestive system.

Most of the other dishes in this book have wine suggestions; matching sweets and wine is to walk a fine line usually dominated by the sweets. The best solution is often to serve dessert separately from dessert wine, allowing each to shine without interference.

Pears Poached in Wine and Spices

Serves 6

Pears poached in white wine are sleek, simple and sophisticated. They make a stunning dessert on their own, or can form the backbone of more complex dishes. Pears poached in red wine are much more robustly flavored and dramatic in color, but both are equally elegant. The variety of wine you choose will affect the finished product, so choose wine of reasonable quality. For white, select a good Riesling, Pinot Blanc, Gewurztraminer, Semillon or Vouvray. For reds, pick a softer variety with lots of fruit like Zinfandel, Gamay, Pinot Noir or Merlot. Sauces that complement pears are Burnt Orange Caramel Sauce (page 205), Herb-Infused Crème Anglaise (page 206), Very Berry Compote, Coulis or Sorbet (page 210) and Pear Coulis (page 20).

Be sure to choose pears that are almost ripe, rather than completely ripe. Soft, ripe pears will become too mushy after poaching. Virtually any variety of pear will do, although I am partial to Packhams, Bartletts, Anjous, and red-skinned European pears.

1 bottle	wine	1 bottle
8	whole allspice berries	8
1	orange, zest only	1
2 whole	star anise	2 whole
6–8 whole	peppercorns	6–8 whole
2–3 sprigs	fresh thyme or rosemary	2–3 sprigs
1 stick	cinnamon	1 stick
4–6 whole	cloves	4–6 whole
4–5 slices	ginger root	4–5 slices
1/2	whole nutmeg, chopped coarsely	1/2
	lemon, juice and zest	1
4 cups	water	1 litre
	sugar to taste	
6	whole pears	6

Put all ingredients except the pears into a large pot, deep enough for the pears to stand upright. Taste and adjust the sugar content. Bring to a boil, reduce heat and simmer about 40 minutes, covered.

Peel the pears, leaving the stem attached, and trim off the base to allow them to sit level. Using a melon baller, core the pears from the bottom. Stand the pears upright in the simmering liquid, making sure it is deep enough to completely cover the fruit. Cover the contents with a circle of parchment paper, then with a snug lid. Cook until tender. Test them with the tip of a small sharp knife; the cooking time will vary with the degree of ripeness of the pears. Leave the pears in the poaching liquid and cool, covered, overnight.

Remove the pears from the poaching liquid; strain the liquid and return it to the stove. Reduce to glazing consistency, strain and serve with the pears.

Variations

To make **Pear Sorbet**, purée the poached pears, adding small amounts of poaching liquid until the purée is as smooth and sweet as you like. Stir in a little freshly ground nutmeg or 2 Tbsp. (30 ml) pear eau-de-vie, chill and freeze.

For **Stuffed Pears,** spoon a little jam or puréed poached fruit into the cavities of poached pear halves. Serve as is, or top each half with 1 Tbsp. (15 ml) Meringue (page 202) and bake on a parchment-lined baking sheet at 375°F (190°C) until the meringue is golden, about 15 minutes. Or purée one extra pear with a little pear eau-de-vie or brandy. Split the remaining pears lengthwise and place 1 Tbsp. (15 ml) puréed pear in the cavity. Add 1 Tbsp. (15 ml) biscotti/cookie/amaretti crumbs and top with Meringue. Bake at 375°F (190°C) until golden. (Alternatively, fold 1 cup (250 ml) cookie crumbs into the meringue before spooning the meringue onto the pear halves.)

Mocha Fudge Sauce or Sorbet

Makes about 1 1/2 cups (375 ml)

This fat-free sauce makes a great chocolate sorbet as well.

1 cup	hot espresso or strong coffee	250 ml
3/4 cup	sugar or honey	185 ml
1 cup	Dutch-process cocoa powder	250 ml
1 tsp.	vanilla	5 ml
1	orange, zest only	1
2 Tbsp.	Grand Marnier or brandy (optional)	30 ml

Combine the coffee and sugar or honey, bring to a boil and cook for 3 to 4 minutes to make a simple syrup. Slowly whisk in the cocoa powder, then remove from the heat, and add the vanilla, zest and liqueur, if desired. Cool before using. If you are making sorbet, chill completely before freezing.

Meringue

Makes 1 pie topping or 1 12" (30-cm) Pavlova

Meringue is often overlooked when dessert time arrives. It can be soft and tender as a topping for fruits and tarts; as Pavlova, it can be a fragile container for fruit and berries (the airy confection was named in honor of Anna Pavlova, the ballerina); it can even be a hard and crunchy cookie, a counterpoint to poached fruit. Don't make meringues on a humid day; they will stay sticky instead of becoming crisp.

If you are using a copper bowl and whisk, clean the bowl first with a solution of several tablespoons each white vinegar and kosher salt. Slosh this solution all over the inside of the bowl to remove the sulfur oxide layer that builds on any copper exposed to oxygen. Omit the cream of tartar when using copper bowls; it duplicates the effect of copper ions on egg white proteins.

3	egg whites	3
1/4 tsp.	cream of tartar	1.2 ml
1/3 cup	granulated sugar	80 ml
2 Tbsp.	cocoa (optional)	30 ml

In a mixing bowl, combine the egg whites and cream of tartar. Mix with a whisk attachment until frothy, then slowly add the sugar. Beat until thick and glossy. If you are using the cocoa, dissolve it in 2 Tbsp. (30 ml) hot water, stirring well to eliminate any lumps. Add 1/2 cup (125 ml) of the meringue to the cocoa paste and stir well, then fold into the rest of the meringue.

As topping for fruit or tarts, spoon or pipe the meringue on the top and bake at 375°F (190°C) until golden but still soft, about 15 minutes.

To make Pavlova, pipe or spoon the meringue onto parchment in a circle 12" (30 cm) in diameter, building up a wall on the outer edge. Place in a 450°F (230°C) oven, then promptly reduce the heat to 225°F (110°C) and bake for 2 hours. Because of its larger size, this meringue will remain a little soft. Cool, then heap with Very Berry Compote (page 210) and Sweet Yoghurt Cheese (page 50) or whipped cream. Serve in slices.

Copper bowls get a bad rap. I learned the hard way that non-cooks view them as elitist, hard to clean, heavy and a waste of space. In 1985 after classes with Madeleine Kamman, I bought a huge copper bowl. I ignored the fact that I was in France with a husband and a babe in arms until we began our journey home. My husband, burdened with baby, backpack and stroller, scowled at our luggage and urged me to leave my copper treasure. I crammed the bowl with souvenirs, stuffed it into a bag, and hauled it the width of France and across the Atlantic.

As well as being a first-rate heat conductor, copper ions interact positively with egg white proteins; beating egg whites in a copper bowl produces a sturdier, creamier foam that is more stable than one beaten in a glass, ceramic or stainless bowl. This may not be enough to send you off to France to haul home your own copper bowl, but it should dispel the myths and confusion surrounding this valuable metal.

For a hard meringue, double the sugar and bake at 225°F (110°C). Pipe or spoon the meringue into small rounds or lozenges on parchment paper. Bake for several hours, or leave it in the oven overnight after the oven is shut off. Store the crisp meringues at room temperature in a loosely covered box.

Peaches Broiled with Amaretti and Meringue

Serves 6

This is a variation of Stuffed Pears (page 201), but the advantage of peaches is that they don't require poaching—this tends to be a good dessert when you have no advance warning. Any kind of cookie crumbs will do. I'm partial to crumbled amaretti or biscotti, but use whatever you have on hand. Even finely crumbled sponge or pound cake will work, or in a pinch, baguette crumbs.

6	peaches	6
1 cup	cookie crumbs	250 ml
1 recipe	Meringue (see opposite page)	1 recipe
3 cups	Very Berry Compote or Coulis (page 210)	750 ml

Bring a large pot of water to a boil and slide in the ripe peaches for a few seconds. Remove the peaches from the liquid, immerse in cold water and slip the skins off. Split each peach and scoop out the pit. Make the meringue, stir in the cookie crumbs and fill each peach cavity with the meringue mixture.

Place the peach halves on a parchment-lined baking sheet. Preheat the broiler and broil the peaches until the meringue is golden-brown, just a minute or two. Ladle 1/2 cup (125 ml) compote or coulis onto each plate and center a peach half on the sauce. Serve warm.

Grilled Pineapple Spears with Burnt Orange Caramel Sauce

Serves 8

Many fruit desserts have the benefit of being quick and fuss-free, but not every one verges on the sublime. This one does. I know many avowed non-caramel fans who have licked their plates clean and begged for more, so be prepared.

I	ripe pineapple	I
I Tbsp.	canola oil	15 ml
I	lime, zest only	I
I cup	Burnt Orange Caramel Sauce (see opposite page)	250 ml

Peel and slice the pineapple into 8 wedges, cutting the core off each slice. Lightly brush the pineapple spears with oil, sprinkle them with lime zest, and grill until hot, juicy and well-marked. Serve with 2 Tbsp. (30 ml) caramel sauce per person.

Mango Sorbet or Coulis

Makes about 2 cups (500 ml)

There are many things you can do with this if you decide not to put it into your ice-cream maker. Use it as a fruit sauce with berries. Pour it over a hot cobbler stuffed with cherries. Spoon it over fruit in a tart. Eat it with Sweet Yoghurt Cheese (page 50). I like to freeze it until it reaches a soft, slurpy, not-quite-frozen state, and eat it with fresh blueberries and raspberries.

3	ripe mangoes	3
I cup	orange juice	250 ml
I tsp.	crystallized ginger	5 ml
1/2 tsp.	freshly grated nutmeg	2.5 ml
I Tbsp.	brandy, Scotch or Armagnac	15 ml

Peel the mangoes, then purée until entirely smooth. Add the orange juice to thin the mango pulp. Use a pair of kitchen scissors to finely sliver the crystallized ginger (a knife gets too sticky in a hurry). Stir in the crystallized ginger, nutmeg and liquor. Freeze according to your ice-cream machine's directions.

Burnt Orange Caramel Sauce

Makes 1 cup (250 ml)

This sauce combines some of my favorite flavors, and although the rosemary may be unexpected, it adds an elusive herbal quality. I like this on grilled or poached fruit, on anything chocolate, beside and on top of sorbets, in and around ice creams, and straight out of the bowl. Two tablespoons (30 ml) per person is plenty, but it keeps well, so make a large batch and dole it out, in exchange for promises of equal value, if you like to barter. Food this good deserves to be shared with those you love.

1 cup	white sugar	250 ml
1/4 cup	cold water	60 ml
2 twigs	fresh rosemary	2 twigs
2	oranges, juice and zest	2
1/4 cup	heavy cream	60 ml
2 tsp.	unsalted butter	10 ml

In a heavy-bottomed saucepan, combine the sugar, water, rosemary twigs and orange zest. Stir well, then bring to a boil. Using a pastry brush dipped in cold water, brush down any sugar crystals clinging to the inside wall of the pot. Don't stir the liquid once the sugar has melted, as this may cause the sugar to crystallize. (This is very interesting to junior and elder scientists, but immensely frustrating to cooks.) Cook the syrup over high heat until it begins to brown. Shake or swirl the pan or turn it if hot spots develop and cause uneven coloring, but be very careful: the heat is very high, well above boiling. Allow the caramel to cook until it is dark amber in color. A lighter color means less flavor, so be very brave and let the syrup color a little more deeply than you may be comfortable with.

Turn the heat down to low, stand well back and cautiously add the orange juice as soon as the caramel is dark enough. Wear protective gloves or long sleeves: IT WILL SPLATTER. Stir well with a long-handled wooden spoon to redissolve, then add the cream. Stir well, return to the heat and boil for 5 minutes, to reduce and thicken. Stir in the butter, then strain and store in the fridge. To use, reheat gently, stirring.

Making caramel can be intimidating at first. The trick is to protect yourself from splatters or spills: wear shoes, not sandals, to cover your feet, and wear pants to cover your legs. Then relax! It is an inexpensive treat, at least until the lily-gilding starts, and wasting a few cups of sugar while you learn is a small price to pay. You don't need to invest in expensive candy-making equipment, not even a candy thermometer, but a pastry brush (or clean, new paintbrush from the toolbox) is a useful tool.

Herb-Infused Crème Anglaise

Makes 2 1/2 cups (625 ml)

This stirred custard requires a little organization to prevent last-second panic. Be sure to assemble all your ingredients and tools, because the sauce cooks very quickly and will need immediate straining and cooling. On the counter next to your stove, lay out a whisk, a fine-mesh strainer with a bowl of suitable size to strain into, a wooden flat-edged stirring tool, a bowl of ice water large enough to cradle the first bowl, and a metal tablespoon. The herbs or spices you choose depend on how you will be using the Crème Anglaise.

4	egg yolks	4
1/3 cup	sugar, or to taste	80 ml
1	lemon, zest only	1
2–3 sprigs	fresh herbs	2–3 sprigs
2 cup	milk or cereal cream	500 ml
1 tsp.	fresh grated nutmeg (optional)	5 ml

Whisk together the yolks and sugar in a large bowl. In a heavy-bottomed pot, combine the lemon zest, herbs, milk or cream and nutmeg, if desired, and bring almost to a boil.

Pour some of the hot mixture over the yolks, whisking thoroughly all the while. Transfer the warmed yolk mixture to the pot and cook over medium-high heat, stirring constantly with a flat-edged wooden implement. Cook until thickened, about 5 minutes. DO NOT BOIL, but watch closely to notice a change in viscosity and thickness.

To check for doneness, dip a clean metal tablespoon into the custard and draw your fingertip across the back surface of the spoon. If the line you draw holds and the custard does not flow below the mark, the anglaise is done.

Strain into a clean bowl, cool over ice water and serve chilled.

Variations

For **Grilled Fruit with Crème Anglaise,** allow a few minutes in the kitchen beforehand to make and chill the custard. Lightly oil the cut surface of the fruit and quickly grill. Serve with cold Crème Anglaise, garnishing with a fresh sprig of whichever herb went into the anglaise. Fruits that grill well are sliced apples, pears, peaches, nectarines, Asian pears and firm bananas.

Wondering what else to do with this sauce? Quickly broil a shallow pan of Crème Anglaise and fresh berries for a surprising twin-textured warm dessert. Pour it over fresh fruit or berries, serve it with a simmered compote of winter fruits, ladle it alongside crisps, cobblers, crumbles, slide it onto the plate beside biscuits, cookies and cakes, or turn it into ice cream/ice milk in your freezer.

Homemade ice creams, ice milks and sorbets may not have the same rich, creamy texture we associate with store-bought brands, especially true if we lessen the cream or egg content of our own desserts, but the payback is knowing exactly what has gone into our own ice cream—no stabilizers, additives, coloring, or artificial flavors.

Anglaise can be as rich or light as you like, depending on your choice of milk or cream. In a pinch, I have made this sauce with skim milk, and in spite of a bluish tint to the finished sauce, it was refreshingly light. On the other hand, you can make it with cream for a sauce of intoxicating richness.

The flavor agents and enhancers you add to anglaise are nearly limitless. Try star anise, sliced ginger root, fresh mint, basil, rosemary, lemon balm, lemon thyme, citrus zest of any type, cinnamon, whole cloves—the list goes on and on. The idea, though, is an undertone of flavor, meant to accentuate rather than overwhelm, so use any herb or spice sparingly, and remember that its flavor will be more pronounced the longer the steeping time.

Melon in Mint and Marsala

Serves 2 to 6

This is light and refreshing, and could be served as a palate cleanser at a more formal dinner. In the lazy, warm days of summer, though, it makes a stellar way to end an evening. Choose sweet, fragrant melons at your farmers' market when they arrive in season. I particularly enjoy Crenshaw, Casaba and cantaloupe.

1	melon, sliced, diced or cut into balls	1
2 Tbsp.	shredded fresh mint	30 ml
1/2 cup	Marsala	125 ml

Peel and seed the melon. Dice or cut the melon into balls, or thinly slice if you want to serve on a plate rather than in a glass. Add the mint and the Marsala, toss well, and cover. Refrigerate for up to 8 hours before serving.

Cherries with Cassis and Sweetened Yoghurt

Serves 10 to 12

Cherries are my all-time favorite fruit—the only fruit I eat until I think I'll never eat again. Cherries this way is how cheesecake should be: all fruit and very little cheese! You can make this with other fruits as they come in season, but none have the visual or taste impact of dark Bing cherries.

2 lbs.	ripe Bing cherries	1 kg
	sugar to taste	
2 Tbsp.	cornstarch	30 ml
1/2 cup	black currant jam, syrup or liqueur	125 ml
3 cups	Sweet Yoghurt Cheese (page 50)	750 ml

Pit the cherries. Make sure to eat lots as you work—cherry season is fleeting.

Place the cherries in a heavy-bottomed pot and add a small amount of water just to start the juices flowing. Add sugar, and simmer the cherries over medium heat until they are loose and soft, about 30 minutes. Bring to a boil and stir in the cornstarch dissolved in a small amount of cold water. Taste and stir in the black currant jam, syrup or liqueur. Cool.

Turn the Sweet Yoghurt Cheese out onto a large platter with a lip. Spread the yoghurt around the outside to form a wall or dike, then pour the cherries into the middle. Serve with lots of napkins.

Summer Rhumtopf

*T*his is a market special, to be gathered throughout the summer months when fruit and berries are at their peak. It needs several months to stand, and is at its peak just in time for Christmas gift-giving. When we made and sold this at the restaurant, people would eye the huge glass jars in the cooler and ask, "When?" When the time came, we sold it all in one day. So make a lot . . . summer is briefer than you think, and this is a gorgeous reminder.

Use equal amounts of fruit and sugar by volume. Don't skimp on the sugar or the whole thing may ferment. Use only fresh fruit, as frozen fruit is too soft and mushy.

Layer fruits and berries in contrasting colors. Choose from:

blackberries
raspberries
strawberries
marionberries
black currants (in smaller amounts because of their strong flavor!)
red currants
blueberries
plums, split and pitted
apricots, split and pitted
cherries, pitted

Add an equal amount of sugar with each fruit, then cover with white or amber rum. Cover tightly and refrigerate. Do not stir. Ladle into small jars with the liquid for gift-giving. Serve with pound cake, chocolate cake, tarts, ice cream or yoghurt, shortcake, galettes . . .

Very Berry Compote, Coulis or Sorbet

Makes about 7 cups (1.75 litres)

I like mixing fresh berries with gently simmered ones for a juicy, fresh texture. Spike this compote with any herbal nuances or spicy tones you like: add whole cinnamon, sliced ginger, a few whole cloves, a star anise, a few allspice berries, a sprig of basil, mint, thyme or rosemary in any combination that takes your fancy. Try strawberries and fresh mint; raspberries and black currants; sour cherries and peaches; blueberries and lemon; blackberries and lime zest; peaches and fresh basil.

2 cups	Saskatoon berries or blueberries	500 ml
1 cup	blackberries or pitted plums	250 ml
1/3 cup	water or fruit juice	80 ml
1/4 cup	white sugar or honey	60 ml
3 Tbsp.	lemon juice	45 ml
1	lemon, zest only	1
2 tsp.	cornstarch	10 ml
4 cups	fresh berries	1 litre
2 Tbsp.	brandy, scotch or bourbon	30 ml

In a heavy-bottomed pot, combine the first 3 cups (750 ml) of fruit, water or juice, sugar or honey and lemon juice and zest. Bring to a boil and simmer until tender. Add the cornstarch dissolved in cold water and cook until clear. Cool, then add remaining ingredients. Chill. This keeps for several days, although the berries will soften.

For compote, serve as is, or purée part of the cooked berries and stir in with the whole berries. For a smooth-textured coulis, purée and strain the sauce. For sorbet, purée, strain and freeze.

Variation
Use red or white wine in place of the juice or water, and add a sprig of mint or fresh thyme while the fruit is simmering. Omit the spirits.

Sorbets can be made from any fruit purée, raw or cooked, depending on the fruit. Any sweetener should be in a liquid form, like melted honey, maple syrup or a cooled simple sugar syrup. Add flavor agents, like herbs, spices or citrus zest, to the sweet liquid and allow them to infuse their flavors for several hours or overnight before straining. All ingredients should be well chilled before you freeze the sorbet. If you wish, you can add fresh or frozen yoghurt to the puréed fruit before you freeze it, or stir in some heavy cream, whipped or unwhipped. Alcohol should be added sparingly; too much will impair freezing.

Slush of Ginger, Lemon and Pinot Blanc

Serves 10 to 12

This makes a superb palate cleanser or a tongue-tingling dessert. I never expect it to freeze entirely because of the high alcohol content, but it makes a great slush. If you have a mint patch, add a handful and let it steep with the other ingredients.

1/2 bottle	Pinot Blanc	1/2 bottle
3 Tbsp.	minced ginger root	45 ml
2	lemons, juice and zest	2
	sugar to taste	
2 cups	cold water	500 ml

Combine all the ingredients and boil just long enough to dissolve the sugar crystals, then chill thoroughly. Strain and freeze. Serve in chilled wine glasses, with a splash of Pinot Blanc on top.

Instead of wine and lemon, experiment with champagne and lime in this slush—an indulgent summery treat. Don't use an expensive classic bottle, but do choose a reasonable bottle that you would enjoy drinking.

Summer Cobbler with Buttermilk Crust

Serves 12 to 16 generously

This is what I take to potlucks, year in and year out. In the summer, I use fruit fresh from the market. In the winter, I use frozen fruits and berries, or good old apples and pears enlivened with simmered dried fruit.

8 cups	fresh or frozen fruit	2 litres
1	orange, zest only	1
	sugar or honey to taste	
1/2 tsp.	freshly ground nutmeg	2.5 ml
1/2 tsp.	ground ginger	2.5 ml
1/2	cinnamon stick	1/2
2 Tbsp.	cornstarch	30 ml
2 cups	water or juice	500 ml
1/3 cup	unsalted butter	80 ml
1/2 cup	sugar	125 ml
1 1/2 cups	all-purpose flour	375 ml
2 tsp.	baking soda	10 ml
1 tsp.	cream of tartar	5 ml
1/2 tsp.	salt	2.5 ml
3/4 cup	buttermilk	185 ml
1	egg	1

Set the oven at 375°F (190°C).

In a large pot, combine the fruit, zest, sugar or honey, spices, cornstarch and juice. Bring to a boil and cook until clear, then pour carefully into a large shallow baking dish with a diameter of 12" (30 cm). Place on a pizza pan with a lip to minimize spillage. Or use a 9" x 14" (22- x 35-cm) cake pan on a corresponding large cookie sheet.

To make the topping, cream together the butter and sugar in a large bowl. Combine the dry ingredients in a separate bowl. Combine the wet ingredients in a measuring cup. Beginning and ending with dry ingredients, alternately add the wet and dry ingredients to the creamed butter-sugar mixture. Mix only until blended, then immediately drop by spoonfuls onto the outside edges of the fruit filling. Do not cover the center—it takes too long to bake through. Bake in a preheated oven for 45 minutes or until done. Serve warm or cool.

Variations

Try the following fruit combinations. Add the dried fruits sparingly, as a flavor agent.

- raspberry and grape with rosemary and white wine
- apple, strawberry and rhubarb
- cherry and peach with cinnamon or nutmeg
- peach and blackberry with lime zest
- peach and blueberry with nutmeg
- cherry and black currant or blackberry
- raspberry, blackberry, blueberry and Saskatoon berry with lime zest
- three cherry (Montmorency, sour or Queen Anne, Bing)
- pear and apricot (fresh or dried)
- dried cranberry or cherry and apple with crystallized ginger
- plum and peach
- Damson plum and cherry
- plum and apple with cinnamon and cloves or cinnamon and basil

Tulips and Tiles

Makes about 3 dozen 2" (5-cm) cookies

These fragile flowers are worth the time and attention they require. They can be formed into tuiles, or tiles, draped into a flower shape to hold fruit, or rolled into tight cigarettes for dipping or stuffing. Whichever form you choose, you must do it while the cookies are still warm. The easiest solution is to leave the cookies to cool on the parchment without any shaping at all. Any cookies that become crumbs can be sprinkled on top of fruit compotes or sorbets. Store these cookies for as brief a time as possible—they quickly lose their appealing crunch. I usually keep them at room temperature, loosely packed in a box rather than in an airtight container. The orange flower water is usually available in European delis, but if you can't find it, substitute concentrated orange oil or leave it out. The cookies will still be orange-flavored without it.

2	egg whites	2
I cup	sliced almonds	250 ml
2/3 cup	white sugar	160 ml
3 Tbsp.	all-purpose flour	45 ml
I Tbsp.	cornstarch	15 ml
3 Tbsp.	melted butter	45 ml
1/2 tsp.	Armagnac or brandy	2.5 ml
1/2 tsp.	orange flower water (optional)	2.5 ml
I	orange, zest only	I
1/2 tsp.	ground ginger	2.5 ml
1/2 tsp.	almond extract	2.5 ml

Combine all ingredients, mix well and refrigerate overnight to allow the sugar to dissolve. Bring to room temperature before using. Set the oven at 375°F (190°C) and line baking sheets with parchment. Spoon about 1/2 tsp. (2.5 ml) of the batter onto the parchment and smooth it with the back of a spoon until it is very thin. Leave generous room for spreading.

Bake until golden. Remove from the oven, and quickly lift each cookie with a thin-edged metal spatula or palette knife. Drape over an inverted jar, bottle, ramekin or cup to achieve the tulip shape. For tiles, drape over a rolling pin or a horizontal wine bottle. For cigarettes, roll each cookie tightly around a chopstick. If the cookies cool too quickly and are no longer pliable enough to shape, return them briefly to the oven to soften. If desired, dip each cookie in melted semi-sweet chocolate or fill with fruit compote, whipped cream or Sweet Yoghurt Cheese (page 50) and serve immediately.

Variation
Substitute chopped hazelnuts for the almonds, replace the orange zest with lime zest, and use hazelnut liqueur in place of the almond extract.

Filo Cups

Serves 6

Many people think filo needs to be drowned in butter to work. Not so. Individual filo baskets, perfect receptacles for sweet or savory fillings, can be made with very little butter. I draw the line at spraying filo sheets with edible oil products; I think if you're going to have filo, enjoy it seldom, but eat it as it should be eaten, brushed lightly with butter.

This is simple and low-mess, with no burnt sugar and fruit to scrape out of the oven. The components are cooked separately and in advance, then combined just before you want to eat for the crispiest possible pastry.

4 sheets	filo pastry	4 sheets
1/4 cup	melted unsalted butter	60 ml
6 cups	Very Berry Compote (page 210)	1.5 litres

GARNISHES:
Sweet Yoghurt Cheese (page 50)
mint or lemon balm leaves (optional)

Set the oven to 375°F (190°C). Spread one sheet of filo on a surface that you can slice on. Using a pastry brush, lightly brush the filo with melted butter. Place the second sheet directly on top, and brush it with butter. Repeat with the remaining sheets. Slice the filo layers into six even squares. Gently pick up one square and tuck it into a muffin tin, being sure the bottom of the tin is covered with pastry. Carefully pleat or loosely fold the sides that stick up so that a large rough-edged cup is formed. Repeat with the remaining squares. Bake until the pastry is cooked through and lightly browned, about 10 minutes, then remove from the oven and cool in the muffin cups.

To serve, carefully remove one baked cup from the tin and place it on a plate. Ladle in fruit compote, spoon on a little sweetened yoghurt, and add a mint or lemon thyme leaf for garnish.

Variation

A baked filo cup adds a crunchy texture to the suave character of poached pears. Put the pear in the center of the pastry, drizzle a little top-quality melted chocolate over top for even greater pleasure, then stand back when you eat it—crispy bits of pastry will migrate to the farthest ends of your table.

You get what you pay for with chocolate, more so than with any other food. It makes sense to buy the very best you can find; I use Callebaut, a fine Belgian chocolate that is available throughout North America. Buy a little and do a side-by-side tasting with your current brand.

Fruit Galette

Makes 1 galette, enough to feed 8 to 12 people

A galette is a free-form tart, baked on a flat sheet without the use of a tart pan or pie plate for shape and support. It has a rustic, country look and it feeds more people with less work than regular tarts. The fruit that goes into a galette can be the same combinations that are used in cobblers, but the fillings should be drier so they stay within the loose boundaries of the pastry. Use fewer juicy berries and more structured fruits like apples and peaches. Fill the galette on the baking sheet; it is nearly inpossible to move a filled, raw galette without structural damage.

The pastry called for here is a brisée, which has a different structure from the flaky layered pastry many of us grew up with. The difference is in the method used to incorporate the butter in a brisée, a technique known as fraisage.

1 cup	all-purpose flour	250 ml
2 Tbsp.	white sugar	30 ml
	salt to taste	
6 Tbsp.	unsalted butter	90 ml
2–6 Tbsp.	cold water	30–90 ml
2 Tbsp.	unsalted butter	30 ml
6–8 cups	apple or pear slices, unpeeled	1.5–2 litres
	sugar to taste	
1 tsp.	cinnamon	5 ml
1/2 tsp.	ground star anise or nutmeg	2.5 ml
1/4 cup	dried cranberries or raisins	60 ml

Measure the flour, sugar and salt onto the counter. Blend the butter into the dry ingredients using two knives or a pastry cutter, until the mixture is the texture of meal. Make a well in the center of the ingredients and pour in the cold water, using the smaller amount. Err on the side of caution—you can add more, but you can never remove water. Blend by lightly tossing the dry ingredients up with stiffly extended fingers, using your hands like two large salad forks. The dough will begin to come together. When the pastry is almost holding together, smear, or *fraisage*, a quarter of it away from you across the countertop under the heel of your hand. Continue with the rest of the pastry, smearing it to incorporate the butter.

Gather all the groups of smeared pastry together into one round. Lightly dust the countertop with flour, then roll the pastry out with a lightly floured rolling pin. Aim for a circle, turning the round by 90 degrees after every pass with the rolling pin, and stop when you reach a

The amount of water needed to make pastry is subject to many variables. The type and age of flour, how and where it is stored, the humidity, the altitude, and even the weather all play parts in how much water is added to any pastry. How the fat is incorporated will also dictate the amount of additional liquid needed. The result is that no recipe can ever specify with any exactitude how much water to add. In brisée, the butter is smeared into the flour, reducing the amount of water needed.

Galettes work wonderfully well as savories. Mix together cooked leftover vegetables and onions with sliced or diced cooked meats for a total volume of 6–8 cups (1.5–2 litres). Spread the cool mixture over the rolled pastry and sprinkle with chopped green onion and herbs. Add grated or sliced cheeses, if you like, then fold the edges of the pastry up to encase the filling as in the fruit galette. Bake at 400°F (200°C) until brown and crisp, about 30 to 40 minutes. Serve hot with a salad for a light meal.

thickness of 1/8" (.25 cm). By then, the circle should be roughly 18" (45 cm) across. Don't worry if the outer edges are somewhat ragged—galettes cultivate a rustic look.

Carefully fold the pastry in half and place it on a round 13" (33-cm) pizza pan lined with parchment. Unfold it, centering the pastry on the pan. Loosely cover with plastic wrap and let it rest for 30 minutes. This allows the gluten to relax after being developed by mixing and the rolling pin. If you don't let the pastry rest, odds are better than good that it will shrink noticeably while being baked, so try to take the extra time for a rest. Drink a good cup of coffee and put your feet up, or make the filling and chill it. Cool filling works best— if it is still hot from cooking, the butter in the pastry may melt and cause leakage.

To make the filling, melt the butter in a nonstick pan and add the apple or pear slices, sugar, cinnamon, star anise or nutmeg and dried fruit. Cook until the apple slices are tender, 7 to 10 minutes. Cool.

After the pastry has rested, set the oven for 425°F (220°C). Spread the cooked and cooled filling onto the center of the pastry, leaving an uncovered border of 1/2"–6" (1–15 cm) around the outer edge, depending on the amount of filling you have. To contain the galette, fold the outer ring of pastry over the filling, partially encasing it. Pleat the outer edge of the pastry as you position it on the filling, ending with a tidy tart with a small, uncovered center of 3"–6" (7–15 cm) in diameter. The galette itself will end up with a total diameter of up to 13" (33 cm), just filling the pan.

Bake the galette for 30 to 40 minutes, until brown and crisp. To prevent fruit juices dripping onto the oven floor, make sure the baking sheet has a shallow lip.

Let the galette cool at least 10 minutes before slicing. Serve warm or at room temperature.

Cherry Berry Explosions with Raspberry Coulis

Makes about 20 firecrackers

In the summertime, make this with fresh berries or cherries. In the winter, use minced dried fruit or minced apple pieces sautéed in a little cinnamon, butter and sugar. Leftover mincemeat or poached fruit works as long as it isn't too moist, so that it soaks through the won ton wrapper. Serve these little firecrackers hot, garnished with raspberry coulis, frozen yoghurt or Sweet Yoghurt Cheese.

I cup	fresh raspberries or pitted cherries	250 ml
I cup	ricotta, mascarpone, quark, Sweet Yoghurt Cheese (page 50) or cream cheese	250 ml
I	lemon, zest only	I
	sugar to taste	
1/2 tsp.	freshly ground black pepper	2.5 ml
I package	square won ton wrappers	I package
	canola or vegetable oil	
2 cups	raspberries, fresh or frozen	500 ml
1–2 Tbsp.	black currant jam	15–30 ml
I	lemon, juice and zest	
	sugar or honey to taste	

In a bowl, gently toss together the fresh raspberries or cherries, cheese, lemon zest, sugar and pepper, being careful not to break the berries. Lay out several wrappers and spoon a little mixture on the diagonal for maximum length. Moisten the wrapper beside the filling, then roll up the wrapper into a log, gently twisting the ends in opposite directions to close.

To cook, roll the logs into a nonstick sauté pan with a little canola or vegetable oil. Sauté gently, rolling to turn the packages over, until at least one side is nicely brown. Add a small amount of water and a lid, and steam for several minutes until the wrappers are translucent.

To make the coulis, purée the berries, stir in the jam, lemon and sugar or honey. Strain for a smooth, mirrorlike sauce and serve under the fruit potstickers.

For an entirely different texture, layer 3 buttered filo sheets together. Cut them into 3" (7.5-cm) squares, and fill and roll them up as above. After twisting the ends shut, cut little nicks in the top of each firecracker to allow steam to escape. Bake at 375°F (190°C) until golden brown. Serve hot, with raspberry coulis.

Gram Doris's Gingerbread

Makes 1 9" x 14" (23- x 35-cm) cake

Grandmothers are supposed to be the world's best bakers, and mine are no exception. My Gram Doris Smith always had a treat on hand in at least two tins, including this quick and spicy gingerbread. Serve warm with sorbet, Sweet Yoghurt Cheese (page 50) or Burnt Orange Caramel Sauce (page 205).

1/4 cup	butter	60 ml
1/4 cup	brown sugar	60 ml
1/2 cup	unsulfured molasses	125 ml
1/2 tsp.	baking soda	2.5 ml
1	egg	1
3/4 cup	water	185 ml
2 Tbsp.	puréed ginger root	30 ml
1 tsp.	cinnamon	5 ml
	salt to taste	
1 tsp.	ground cloves	5 ml
1 tsp.	ground ginger	5 ml
1 1/4 cups	all-purpose flour	310 ml

Set the oven at 325°F (165°C). Butter and flour a 9" x 14" (23-cm x 35-cm) pan.

Cream together the butter and sugar in a large bowl. Add the molasses and baking soda. Stir together the egg and water. Combine the remaining ingredients in a separate bowl. Alternately add the liquid and dry ingredients to the creamed butter, starting and ending with dry. Turn into the prepared pan and bake for 20 minutes.

Classic Hot Fudge and Pecan Pudding

Serves 6

Straight out of my childhood, this is one of my favorite taste memories. It is an intensely chocolate, hot, self-saucing dessert that is best eaten the same day it is made. It does not double well, so bake it when there are 6 or fewer hungry chocoholics breathing down your neck.

1 cup	all-purpose flour	250 ml
2 tsp.	baking powder	10 ml
1/2 tsp.	salt	2.5 ml
3/4 cup	brown sugar	180 ml
2 Tbsp.	cocoa, preferably Dutch process	30 ml
1/4 cup	pecans, toasted and chopped (optional)	60 ml
1/2 cup	cold strong coffee or espresso	125 ml
1 tsp.	vanilla	5 ml
2 Tbsp.	melted butter	30 ml
3/4 cup	brown sugar	180 ml
1/4 cup	cocoa, preferably Dutch process	60 ml
1 3/4 cups	hot strong coffee or espresso	330 ml

Heat the oven to 350°F (175°C). Place an 8-cup (2-litre) baking pan on a baking sheet to catch drips and spillage.

In a mixing bowl, stir together the flour, baking powder, salt, sugar, 2 Tbsp. (30 ml) cocoa and pecans. Mix together the cold coffee, vanilla and melted butter, and combine with the dry ingredients, stirring only until blended. Spread evenly in the baking pan.

In the same mixing bowl, before washing it, mix together the remaining sugar, cocoa and hot coffee. Pour over the batter and immediately slide the pan into the oven. Bake for 45 minutes and serve hot.

Dutch processing refers to the addition of an alkaline powder to cocoa. This changes the pH level, darkens the color of the cocoa powder, gives it a milder flavor and reduces its tendency to clump. Many brands of cocoa commonly used in North America are Dutch process.

Index

About the Author

For eight years, dee Hobsbawn-Smith was the chef and owner of Foodsmith, a popular restaurant featuring avant-garde cuisine with a unique international twist. She trained with Madeleine Kamman in France and Darina Allen in Ireland, and has worked alongside many of North America's leading chefs.

Eager to share her passion for glorious, healthy food, dee now owns a catering company and teaches at the Cookbook Company. She is married to Don Hobsbawn. They live in Calgary, Alberta, with their two sons.

BLAINE ANDRUSEK